Children, Parents, and the Rise of the Novel

Children, Parents, and the Rise of the Novel

T. G. A. Nelson

DELAWARE

Newark: University of Delaware Press
London: Associated University Presses

Associated University Presses
440 Forsgate Drive
Cranbury, NJ 08512

Associated University Presses
25 Sicilian Avenue
London WC1A 2QH, England

Associated University Presses
P.O. Box 338, Port Credit
Mississauga, Ontario
Canada L5G 4L8

The paper used in this publication meets the requirements
of the American National Standard for Permanence of Paper
for Printed Library Materials Z39.48-1984.

Library of Congress Cataloging-in-Publication Data

Nelson, T. G. A.
    Children, parents, and the rise of the novel / T.G.A. Nelson.
    p.   cm.
    Includes bibliographical references and index.
    ISBN 0-87413-558-3 (alk. paper)
    1. English fiction—18th century—History and criticism.
2. Children in literature. 3. Literature and society—Great
Britain—History—18th century. 4. Domestic fiction, English—
History and criticism. 5. Parent and child in literature.
6. Family in literature. I. Title.
PR858.C5N45 1995
823'.809—dc20   94-47663
                                    CIP

For Helen, Vanessa,
Juliet, and Kit

Contents

Acknowledgments   9

Introduction   13
1. The Child in Restoration Comedy   36
2. Augustan Comedy and the Validation of Issue   51
3. Discourses of Concern   66
4. Education   85
5. Fathers   101
6. Mothers   129
7. Affection: Sentiment versus Comedy   160
8. The Child as Subject and Self   190
9. Issue and its Connotations   221

Bibliography   236
Index   247

Acknowledgments

I wish to express my gratitude to Martin Battestin, Robert Dingley, Ian Donaldson, Jocelyn Harris, A. J. Hassall, Arthur F. Kinney, Harold Love, C. J. H. O'Brien, Hermann Real, Peter Sabor, Paul Salzman, Alan Sandison, and Lawrence Stone. All these scholars have given advice or assistance which has contributed to the preparation of this book. While I do not expect them to endorse all my views, I willingly and gratefully acknowledge their help.

An earlier version of chapter 1 of this book appeared in *AUMLA*, volume 67, May 1987. An earlier version of chapter 2 was published in *The Eighteenth Century,* volume 30, number 1, copyright 1989 University of Texas Press. I am grateful to the editors of these two journals for their permission to use the material.

Finally I wish to extend my sincere thanks to the University of New England for granting me the study leave necessary for the completion of this book.

Children, Parents,
and the Rise
of the Novel

Introduction

"Until the last decades of the eighteenth century," wrote Peter Coveney in a pioneering book, "the child did not exist as an important and continuous theme in English literature. . . . In the major eighteenth-century novel, the child is absent, or the occasion of a passing reference" (1957, ix). More recently Tony Tanner, surveying the novel of adultery (which began to develop just after the period covered in this study), made an equally challenging comment:

> Although there invariably are children, or at least a child, often there is curiously little interest in them or it, even on the part of the mother. And the children themselves are seldom very notable presences; if anything they seem to incorporate some kind of negativity. . . . They become a pathetic kind of living evidence of the radical failure of marriage as a genuinely fruitful union or contract. (1979, 98)

Both Tanner and Coveney's views seem at odds with that of Mikhail Bakhtin:

> For the idyll, the association of *food* and *children* is characteristic. . . . This matrix is shot through with the beginnings of growth and the renewing of life. In the idyll, children often function as a sublimation of the sexual act and of conception. . . . Children first entered the novel from precisely this setting, still permeated with the atmosphere of the idyll. (Bakhtin 1981, 227)

Who is right? Are children in the early modern novel an absence or a presence? Do they carry connotations of fertility, festivity, and idyllic happiness, or do they suggest some kind of "negativity"? If children and childhood are more important to this body of fiction than Coveney would allow, what is their function? If they carry negative meanings, as in the slightly later novels considered by Tanner, why is this so? If children and childhood in the first great age of the modern novel carry less positive connotations, and assume a less important role,

13

than the ones Bakhtin found attached to them in earlier fiction, what are the reasons for the difference?

These questions deserve answers. As Leah Marcus writes, "Now that we are coming to recognize the historical relativity of the pervasive literary worship of childhood, it is necessary to explore its cultural meanings further" (1978, 246). My attempt to advance this exploration will center on the cultural meanings of children, childhood and to some extent issue in general within the discursive world of the early English novel.

A question which must be addressed at once is what is meant by "the novel." For Bakhtin the term evidently has a kind of global reference, embracing all longer prose fiction: he likes to contrast the novel with what he regards as the more elitist discourses of poetry, especially epic poetry. And when he writes of the movement of the child-figure from the idyll into the novel he apparently has post-classical Greek "novels" in mind. But there are dangers in accepting the idea of the novel as a global designation: few generalizations would apply equally well to *Daphnis and Chloe*, *Lazarillo de Tormes*, *Emma*, *Middlemarch*, and *The Brothers Karamazov*. In particular, the novel assumes very different social orientations at different historical periods. Yet it seems to me that Bakhtin's formulation about children can assist my investigation, even though it probably was not made with the eighteenth-century English novel specifically in mind; and for this reason I shall be referring back to it from time to time. The possibility of a warm, idyllic aura surrounding children in the novel is, after all, one which deserves to be kept in mind. Was the atmosphere of the eighteenth-century novel really as remote from this ideal as writers such as Tanner and Coveney seem to suggest?

It will already be evident that this book, unlike Bakhtin's, confines itself to a relatively narrow historical period and geographical location, namely England in the late seventeenth and eighteenth centuries, the period which Ian Watt identified as that of "the rise of the novel." Prose fiction was not, of course, born in England in the early eighteenth century, nor does Watt imply that it was. However, that place and time did see the emergence of a largely new genre of prose fiction, whose distinctive features were a strong interest in the development of the individual, an attempt to engage with what readers are invited to accept as features and problems of the "real" world, and a focus on characters who, though temporarily displaced, identify themselves with the gentry or prosperous trading classes.

While confining my attention mainly to English writing, I shall keep in mind the need to go beyond the recognized classics of prose fiction. Failure to pay sufficient attention to other discourses and to lesser-known novels is the main limitation of previous studies devoted to the child in the early novel (Gibson 1975; McGraw 1976): the result has sometimes been a literary version of that "monolithic and repressive 'history'" which, in the view of neohistoricist critics, works to suppress the heterogeneity of the past (Howard 1986, 23).

In order to keep in view the historical and cultural relativity of figurations of the child, I shall examine not only the world of the novel in the first part of the eighteenth century but also the contrasting, yet related, discourse of stage comedy in the half-century preceding the rise of the novel. I shall also give some attention to forms such as the periodical essay which profess to offer more direct and unmediated commentaries on, and representations of, real society. More controversially, perhaps, I shall invoke modern readings of early modern history. While I do not regard early novels, or indeed any novels, as straightforward social documentaries, I believe that early modern novelists— like modern historians—engage imaginatively with the society of their time and offer a distinctive vision of it.

Where the history of childhood is concerned, the last thirty years have thrown up a bewildering number of competing and diverging theories. That of Philippe Ariès, dating from 1962, is still, perhaps, the best known. Ariès argued that the concept of childhood as a separate state was unknown to the Middle Ages: it germinated during the fifteenth century and has been growing and spreading ever since. This new concern with childhood did not, according to Ariès, confer unmixed blessings on children: it took from them the easy integration into society which they had enjoyed in medieval times, shutting up "a childhood which had hitherto been free within an increasingly severe disciplinary system" (1973, 397). A very different case was presented by the neofreudian Lloyd deMause, who maintained, in a collection of essays by himself and others published in 1974, that ways of conceptualizing, treating, and responding to children had progressed steadily from ancient times to the present, with one of the biggest forward steps being taken during the eighteenth century (1976). The chief shortcomings of deMause's study are its simplistic notion of progress and its single-minded zeal for exposing and castigating all negative responses to children in the life and literature of earlier times. However, both deMause and Ariès accept that there was a profound change in attitudes to children in the early modern period, though their evaluations of the change are sharply opposed.

Among more recent commentators Shulamith Shahar, writing on the Middle Ages, and Linda Pollock, writing on the early modern period, have sought to stand the Ariès thesis on its head. Pollock challenges virtually all her predecessors, arguing not only that "there was a concept of childhood [as early as] the sixteenth century" but also that "there have been very few changes in parental care and child life from the sixteenth to the nineteenth century in the home, apart from social changes and technological improvements" (1983, 267–68). Pollock's brusque dismissal of social and technological change fails to inspire confidence, as does her excessive reliance on the minority of families which were in the habit of committing their thoughts to diaries and books of memoirs. Although this last body of evidence deserves attention, it is not a sound basis for generalizations about attitudes and responses to children across society.

Lloyd deMause's study offered a useful list of "modes of parent-child relations," from the "infanticidal mode" (antiquity) through the "intrusive mode" (eighteenth century) to the "helping mode" (mid-twentieth century onwards) (1976, 51–54). What virtually all commentators, including deMause himself, have failed to acknowledge is that, while any one mode of conceptualizing, or dealing with, children may be dominant at a given place and time, any one or more of the others may also be present as a minority response. To detect the presence of one mode in one group is not to establish that that mode was universal or even dominant in the wider culture.

Shahar, in her critique of Ariès, insists that a concept of childhood existed in the Middle Ages and cites many examples of fond and attentive behavior toward children by medieval people. The evidence she cites is plentiful enough to fill a substantial book, but to assemble it she has to range over a long historical period and a wide geographical area (neither of them defined very clearly). Besides, the author has to admit that, while preachers and didactic writers had a relatively sophisticated concept of the natures of children and of ways of behaving toward them, most other people "did not internalize" their teachings (Shahar 1990, 102). Both Shahar and Pollock deserve credit for calling attention to the overemphases of earlier writers, but neither succeeds in offering a convincing demolition of the rival thesis. Pollock, in the introduction to her recently published anthology of writings about children and childbirth, seems to recognize this. "We should beware," she writes, "of being blinkered by the concept of continuity: of allowing it to deaden our sensitivity to those slow and often subtle shifts in social, economic and cultural contexts which have modified the lived realities of parenthood and childhood through the centuries." And elsewhere: "If nothing has altered throughout the centuries then we have no history of childhood" (Pollock 1987, 12–13).

Leah Marcus's *Childhood and Cultural Despair* makes more allowance for differences between diverse social and cultural groups. Marcus's book predates Pollock's by some years, and anticipates Pollock's location of intense concern for children in pious and introspective families. But Marcus's more discriminating eye detects a contest during the seventeenth century between a "Puritan emphasis on original sin," leading to an attempted "transformation of individual children into agents of moral and social reform," and a "conservative Anglican emphasis on original innocence and idealization of childhood as a symbolic link with a past untroubled by Puritan agitation." After the Restoration of 1660, Marcus suggests, these two tended to unite in opposition to a frigid and intolerant attitude toward offspring among the aristocracy and upper gentry. In the eighteenth century, moreover, the more tolerant and caring approach increasingly prevailed: it "spread to the upper levels of society and became the preferred model" (Marcus 1978, 243–44). Thus far the account is essentially a refinement on that of Lawrence Stone, which we shall consider in a moment. But Marcus also has a powerful thesis of her own: namely that interest in, and identification with, children and the childhood state increases sharply in periods of cultural crisis, such as the English Civil War and the French Revolution.

In using and evaluating these varied representations of historical reality, I shall not ignore the difficulty highlighted by so many recent writers, namely the problematic nature of the concept of "historical reality" itself. In dealing with the history of childhood the difficulty becomes especially acute. Not only do different historians give contrasting analyses of attitudes to children at different historical periods: even first-hand accounts are beset by the condition known as "childhood amnesia" (Kuhn 1982, 10–11). "Childhood amnesia" results in a distortion in our memories of our own childhoods with the result that, while a written record of a childhood experience may appear innocent and truthful to the writer, it may in reality be deeply influenced by unconscious processes of selection, interpretation, and imaginative re-creation. Sometimes, but not always, the result is to make childhood seem in retrospect like a paradise. Gray's "Eton College" ode does so; Gibbon's *Autobiography* does not. There is no *prima facie* reason for concluding that one of these two creative (and therefore fictive) artefacts gives a more accurate impression of a "typical" eighteenth-century childhood than the other.

Among so many uncertainties one conclusion seems secure: relations between parents and children do differ greatly from one culture or century to another. Jean Howard, citing Nancy Chodorow, warns that "everything from maternal 'instinct' to conceptions of the self" may be seen as "the products of specific discourses and social processes" (Howard 1986, 20): literature, anthropology, and history all confirm that parental affection for children cannot be taken for granted. Claude Lévi-Strauss, for example, describes a group of South American Indians among whom there was "a strong dislike for procreation. Abortion and infanticide were almost the normal practice, so much so that perpetuation of the group was secured by adoption rather than by breeding" (Lévi-Strauss 1984, 233). Locke, in the eighteenth century, likewise remarked on the callousness with which some cultures treated their offspring. At first sight parental affection had appeared to Locke as one of the few exceptions to the rule that humans brought no innate ideas into the world: "If any [principle] can be thought to be naturally imprinted," he observed, "none can have a fairer pretence to be innate than this: *Parents, preserve and cherish your children.*" But Locke had to revise his view in the light of indications that there had been "whole nations, and those of the most civilized people," amongst whom "exposing their children, and leaving them in the fields to perish by want or wild beasts" had been common, and "as little condemned or scrupled as the begetting them" (1961, 1:30–33).

Anthropological evidence, like historical evidence, is often hard to interpret. Lloyd deMause records that when outside investigators began studying Apache society they were at first impressed by the "very tender and considerate" behavior of Apache mothers toward their babies. But the Apaches' approval rating fell when it was discovered that many of them were prepared to "abandon or give away children—babies they had been nursing lovingly only a week before" (1976, 15–16). Contrariwise, the early modern English practice of sending children

away for education or apprenticeship has sometimes been taken
as a sign of parental frigidity and lack of affection, but there are
other possible explanations: Peter Laslett, for example, suggests
plausibly that parents were simply unwilling to subject their
children to the discipline of work at home (Laslett 1983, 13).
Several other features of parental behavior in the early modern period, notably swaddling and wet-nursing, have become
equally controversial. Do they betray a lack of concern for children, or a wish to do what was best for them according to the
medical or educational theories of the time? In the late seventeenth and early eighteenth centuries mothers were discouraged from suckling in the first few days after birth because the
first milk (containing colostrum) was considered bad for the
baby. At around the same time, the experiment was begun of
dry-feeding young babies to protect them from possible infection
by contaminated milk from a wet-nurse. Both these practices
are now known to have been harmful, but there is no reason to
conclude that they were adopted as a result of unconscious hostility to the children: they seem to have been intended sincerely
as ways of improving babies' chances of survival, though their
actual effect was the opposite (Fildes 1988, 91–93, 136).

Again, Lawrence Stone may well be right to argue that parents in a time of high infant mortality try to avoid investing
too much emotional capital in their younger children (1977, 70).
But it is important to recall, with Linda Pollock, that many
eighteenth-century parents suffered acutely when their babies
died, even though such deaths were far more frequent, and so
less unexpected, than they are today. As Pollock notes, it is not
uncommon even in infanticidal societies for the older, surviving
children to be kindly and affectionately treated (1983, 124–28,
49). Even adult chimpanzees seem to feel spontaneous affection,
not only for their own offspring, but for those of other individuals, with young females achieving skill in nursing by fostering
young ones in the pubertal period before they have progeny of
their own. Gorillas, on the other hand, sometimes kill their
young (de Waal 1983; Schaller, 1991).

The hazards involved in interpreting historical and anthropological evidence, and the still greater risks of applying it to
literature, are well known to those writers who make up the
modern school of neohistorical criticism. Louis Montrose, for
instance, warns against the tendency to "read complex literary
works against a supposedly stable, coherent, and transparent
'historical background' that enshrine[s] the political and social

orthodoxies of [an] age" (1986, 304). Stability and coherence have certainly not characterized the representations of eighteenth-century life offered by social and literary historians in the period since the Second World War. Peter Coveney, for example, in the book already quoted, writes serenely of "the securities of the eighteenth-century peace" (1957, x); but this vision of a kind of secular idyll prevailing in Enlightenment Europe looks worse than simplistic in the wake of books like Dorothy Marshall's *The English Poor in the Eighteenth Century* (1969), Douglas Hay's *Albion's Fatal Tree* (1975), or E. P. Thompson's *Whigs and Hunters* (1975). A worthwhile historical critique must not only keep in mind the diversity of modern readings of eighteenth-century history but must also, as Montrose puts it,·

> resituate canonical literary texts among the multiple forms of writing, and in relation to the non-discursive practices and institutions, of the social formation in which those texts were initially produced—while, at the same time, recognizing that this project of historical resituation is necessarily the textual construction of critics who are themselves historical subjects. (304)

Perhaps the least misleading of historians is the one who makes no secret of biases or commitments. Prominent among these is Philippe Ariès, one of many twentieth-century thinkers to rebel against the representation of early modern and modern society as a fertile soil for the growth of individual freedom. "Where," Ariès scornfully demands,

> is the individualism in [those] modern lives, in which all the energy of the couple is directed to serving the interests of a deliberately restricted posterity? Was there not greater individualism in the gay indifference of the prolific fathers of the ancien régime? (393)

In Ariès's view the individualism based on the family, which set in so strongly from the beginning of the eighteenth century and reinforced itself in the twentieth, has become self-defeating: so, on the other hand, has the excessive supervision of the child practiced in Jesuit schools. Accordingly, Ariès situates his ideal of an open, life-encountering childhood in the Middle Ages, a period when birth control, the Jesuit order, and individualism in its modern manifestation were all, supposedly, unknown. Evidently his biases lead him to exaggerate the differences between medieval and modern concepts of, and behavior toward, children. Nevertheless, recognition of the influence of Ariès's particular complex of ideas on his conclusions does not oblige us to reject those conclusions outright. A writer's very prejudices may lead him to truths which others, lacking the stimulus of those prejudices, might ignore. In our scrutiny of eighteenth-century texts we shall find, side by side, traces of what Ariès would describe as the medieval approach to children and of what he would describe as the modern approach.

On the broader front of historical studies as such, there are signs that the flood of skepticism is beginning to abate. While most scholars would still "concede that true objectivity is impossible to achieve," most would probably now admit that "if objectivity is a myth it is a useful one—something worth aspiring to if only because the aspiration serves as a check on a scholar's subjective impulses" (Brinkley 1989). Where the debate about early modern parent-child relations is concerned, the nearest approach to objectivity is perhaps the following temperate statement by Lawrence Stone:

> Slowly, at a pace which varied from class to class and from individual family to individual family within each class, there took place ... between about 1660 and 1800 a remarkable change in accepted child-rearing theory, in standard child-rearing practices, and in affective relations between parents and children. . . . [It] was at first strictly confined to the middle ranks, . . . neither so high as to be too preoccupied with pleasure or politics to bother with children, nor so low as to be too preoccupied with sheer survival. (1977, 405)

Although I accept this as a substantially accurate representation, I shall eschew what Jean Howard slightingly refers to as the "cursory journey" (Howard 1986, 19) through the work of Stone or some other favored historian which characterizes some essays in literary history. And in giving general endorsement to Stone's view, I shall pay particular attention to his warning about variations between different families and different individuals (or, in the cases selected for closer study, different novelists and different fictional characters). Stone himself seems at times to forget his own warning, indulging in generalizations more sweeping than those of the temperate paragraph just quoted.

I shall likewise avoid what Howard disapprovingly calls "an unproblematic binarism between literature and history" (1986, 26): I shall refrain from treating fictional worlds as either wholly separate from, or wholly congruent with, the social

world. Finally, I shall take into account what has been judi-
ciously described as "the role of literature in changing human
consciousness and so, eventually, in affecting other material
practices instead of being affected by them" (1986, 28). Like
Lennard J. Davis's book on news and novels in the eighteenth
century (1983), the present study will postulate a complex and
shifting, but at the same time significant and unmistakable,
relationship between literature and historical reality.

Stone's vision of real society in the eighteenth century accords
fairly closely with the imaginative presentation of the world by
creative writers and artists, who likewise emphasize the slow-
ness of change toward an "affectionate and permissive" mode of
child-raising and a sympathetic, caring attitude to the child. In
Fielding's novels and in Hogarth's paintings, aristocrats—and
men (occasionally also women) with aristocratic tastes or lean-
ings—are especially likely to be represented as frigid, hostile,
or unsympathetic to the young. In Hogarth's *The Christening*
both parents are, as Ronald Paulson notes, "ignoring the ceremony, he admiring himself in the mirror, she slouched in a chair
and being courted by another man" (1971, 1:226). The same
writer observes, with equal justice, that in *The Conquest of Mexico,* another of Hogarth's paintings, the fathers in attendance
at a children's performance of Dryden's play seem to be paying
little attention to it, preferring to talk amongst themselves
(1982, 74ff).

We should, no doubt, beware of concluding from Hogarth's
satire that all those who moved in the upper reaches of society
lacked fondness for children. As Paulson remarks, the children's
production of *The Indian Emperor, or, The Conquest of Mexico*
was considered "a highlight of the social season" of 1732: the
Duke of Cumberland ordered a repeat before his own family at
St. James's Palace, while the rich householder who had arranged the original performance commissioned a painting of it.
These gestures cannot be dismissed as instances of hypocritical
social display: someone must have cared enough about children
to want to direct money and energy into those kinds of display
which would give scope for their acting talents and commemo-
rate their performances on canvas. However, Hogarth clearly
felt that there were elements in the audience, and in aristocratic
society in general, who were bored by or antipathetic to children, including their own children. Later we shall find a similar
message encoded in Fielding's novels, where influential and
moneyed men, reared in the aristocratic tradition, rejoice if they

are childless or behave frigidly toward any children they may have. We shall also cite independent expressions of the attitudes which the painter and the novelist repudiate, sufficient to prove that the frigidity toward children mocked by these highly individual satirists had a real existence in the society of their time.

If creative artists of the early eighteenth century agree with Stone in detecting frigidity toward children among titled and propertied people, they differ from the modern historian in locating warmer feelings among the poor. While Stone sees the typical poor parent of the seventeenth and eighteenth centuries as harsh and unloving (1977, 470–78), the early novelists often show parental feeling triumphing over poverty. There is no reason to regard this representation as implausible or remote from reality. The Protestant ideology referred to earlier, which clearly did foster caring attitudes to children, was not confined to the middle ranks of society (Hughes 1984), and it extended beyond a preoccupation with children's souls to a concern for their earthly happiness and material welfare. John Bunyan, a poor artisan, wrote touchingly, while he lay in Bedford gaol: "The parting from my wife and children hath oft been to me in this place as the pulling the flesh from my bones." Bunyan had, he confessed, been "somewhat too too fond of those great mercies," his wife and young ones. He was troubled by "the many hardships, miseries and wants" that his family might suffer if he was taken from them, and especially by the thought of his "poor blind child, who lay nearer my heart than all I had besides":

> O the thoughts of the hardship I thought my blind one might go under, would break my heart to pieces.
> Poor child, thought I, what sorrow art thou like to have for thy portion in this world? Thou must be beaten, must beg, suffer hunger, cold, nakedness, and a thousand calamities, though I cannot now endure the wind should blow upon thee. (Bunyan 1928, 97–98; cf. Laslett 1983, 120; Ariès 1973, 128)

As a great writer Bunyan may have been exceptional, but as a man of humble origins and firm beliefs who felt a strong commitment to his family he was one of thousands. Like Luther, he expressed the belief that even the needs of a beloved family must give way before duty to God; but his devotion to his wife and children is nevertheless unmistakable. In the minor novels which began to appear around the time of the publication of *Grace Abounding*, the religious frame of reference is less strong and sometimes disappears altogether; but what remains is a powerful sense of the affection of the poor for their children. Even a piece of picaresque fiction like Richard Head's *The English Rogue* shows the mother, who suffers an alarming descent to a state of poverty where she has to live on her wits, continuing to care for her son as best she can: her only betrayal of him is her death, which leaves him alone in the world. Here as elsewhere the love of the poor for their offspring renders them still more vulnerable to the cruelty and officiousness of local authorities.

It is, in fact, the last-named who are shown as embodying and implementing the harshest attitudes toward the young and those who care for them. Official harassment of pregnant women, of women who have recently given birth, and in general of poor families with no means of support who threaten to become a burden on the rate-payers of the parish in which they find themselves, is a recurrent theme, whether in the work of modern historians or in early novels.

Peter Laslett, in a now-famous passage, wrote that in the seventeenth century there were "children everywhere—playing in the village street and fields . . . hanging round . . . and getting in the way . . . The perpetual distraction of childish noise and talk must have affected everyone almost all the time." Yet these "crowds and crowds of little children" are, according to the early editions of Laslett's book,

> strangely absent from the written record. . . . There is something mysterious about the silence of all these multitudes of babes in arms, toddlers and adolescents in the statements men made at the time about their own experience. (1968, 104)

Laslett's evocation of the eloquent silence of seventeenth century children is striking, but like many striking ideas it has failed to survive closer scrutiny: in a later edition of *The World We Have Lost* (1983), it is silently dropped. Is it, perhaps, likewise time for students of literature to abandon the notion of the child as absence in the eighteenth-century novel?

It is certainly disappointing, when so much evidence to the contrary is available, to find Coveney's sweeping pronouncement about the insignificance of children in this body of literature remaining largely unchallenged after thirty years. While it is true that the child's role in the eighteenth-century English novel is limited, the limitations are far less severe than Coveney implies. Children and parenthood are part of the thematics of the early novel. A few critics have recognized this. Austin Flanders notes correctly that in the late seventeenth century "the life of the child and the adolescent comes to be of extreme interest" (1984, 31; cf. Spacks 1982). And Leah Marcus, in a veiled reference to Coveney, observes that "if we have tended not to find child subjects in earlier literature, it must be in large part because we have not been taught to look for them" (1978, 242). But Flanders accepts the misguided notion that an atmosphere of negativity surrounds family life in eighteenth-century fiction; meanwhile Marcus's more perceptive study seldom strays outside the author's favorite genres of lyric and meditative poetry or her chosen period of the seventeenth century. Even Reinhard Kuhn, who regards it as obvious that "the eighteenth century is the critical period in the total re-evaluation of the status of the child" (1982, 7), leaves his insight undeveloped, devoting most of his attention to novels of later times. A closer look at eighteenth-century novels shows both writers and readers forced, by a relentless narrative logic, to confront the problem of the child, and especially that of parent-child relations. As a first step toward discovering how this comes about we shall need to take a close look at the imaginative world of stage comedy, a genre which was dominant in the period immediately preceding the rise of the novel.

It is surprising that recent writers on the novel, apart from Laura Brown (1987), should have paid so little attention to its roots in Restoration and early Augustan comedy: Austin Flanders, for example, in a long list of formative influences, leaves out comedy completely (1984, 49). But there are times when the novel, which succeeded stage comedy as the dominant literary form, looks like Restoration comedy transposed to a new key: most early novels are full of plots, themes, characters, and devices inherited from the comic stage. In the case of Fielding, who was a successful comic dramatist before he became a novelist, this is predictable; in Defoe and Richardson, who distrusted stage comedy, it may come as a surprise. Defoe's allusions to the stage in the preface to *Moll Flanders* are unexpectedly temperate:

The Advocates for the Stage, have in all Ages made this the great Argument to persuade People that their Plays are useful, . . . Namely, that they are applied to vertuous Purposes, . . . and were it true that they did so, and that they constantly adhered to that Rule, ... much might be said in their Favour. (1976, 3)

Of his *Family Instructor,* a conduct-book with a strong narrative element, Defoe remarks that he originally intended "to have made it a dramatic poem," but refrained because the subject seemed "too solemn, and the text too copious" (1973, 1:9). Even specific references to comedy by Defoe are not uniformly hostile. Though he denounced not only Dryden's bawdy *Spanish Fryar* but also Farquhar's *Recruiting Officer*—a lively comedy, but hardly one of the most scabrous in the repertory—he could elsewhere bring himself to suggest that a novelist habitually "frames a story or intrigue full of events and incidents like the turns of a comedy" (Fletcher 1934; Novak 1964).

The tone of Richardson's allusions to drama in his fiction is similar to that in Defoe's. In the second part of *Pamela* the protagonist, visiting London for the first time after a sheltered upbringing in the country, is taken to see performances of a tragedy and a comedy. Her critiques of the two plays dwell mostly on their shortcomings, especially their treatment of the relations between the sexes (Richardson 1974, 44–72). Yet Richardson, like Defoe, clearly saw the novel as an application of dramatic techniques to narrative form. In the postscript to *Clarissa* he describes his masterpiece as a "history (or rather dramatic narrative)" (1932, 4:554), and in this and his other novels he deploys the traditional weaponry of stage comedy—masking, disguise, seduction, and trick- or mock-marriages—with great skill. Allusions, both veiled and open, to Restoration writers and their plays testify to the fascination that both held for Richardson: his critique of the drama of the previous age is based on detailed knowledge (Konigsberg 1968).

In stage comedy the child, whether it appears or is mentioned in passing, is nearly always a baby. Babies are treated and spoken of chiefly as burdens, the main question being who shall take on the irksome task of looking after them. In novels, too, babies abound; but here the narrators, and the sympathetic characters in the story, show more concern for their comfort and survival. Where writers of comedy often prefer not to lay stress on parenthood as a likely consequence of marriage, novelists seem to feel that no plot which leads to marriage can be complete without pointed, and sympathetic, references to children. The most likeable characters in novels (with the unexpected exception of Clarissa) not only respond favorably to other people's children but also want children of their own. Defoe's Moll Flanders and Roxana, for example, constantly relay thoughts about their children to their readers, and while some of these suggest hostility or indifference, many do not. Even Richardson's Lovelace broods with more than a touch of pride on the lusty children whom he has fathered or may father, though he invariably chooses to think of the responsibility for their nurture and education as incumbent on someone other than himself.

Childhood and parenthood are, then, important and continuous themes in the early novel, and increase in importance as the eighteenth century advances. In the 1720s Moll Flanders and Roxana agonize over the fates of their children; in the 1740s the second part of Richardson's *Pamela* dwells on Pamela's responsibilities as a mother; in 1751 Fielding's *Amelia* has Captain Booth babysitting (and enjoying it) while his wife fulfills engagements elsewhere (1983, 263). Even the formidable Squire Western in *Tom Jones* (1749) becomes so fond of his two grandchildren that "he spends much of his Time in the Nursery, where he declares the tattling of his little Grand-Daughter, who is above a Year and a half old, is sweeter Music than the finest Cry of Dogs in England" (Fielding 1974, 2:981). And by 1796 another hunting squire, Sir Hugh Tyrold in Frances Burney's *Camilla,* is shown living vicariously through his little nephews and nieces. His influence on the children is, as it happens, disastrous; but his fondness for them, of which he never seems ashamed, is not in doubt (Burney 1972, chap. 2; Doody 1988, 199–263).

If children force their way into the novel early, and soon consolidate their position there, that is largely because marriage and the family, predominantly negative in their connotations in Restoration comedy, appear in the early novel in a much more positive light. Fulfillment of the main characters' ambitions often requires an escape from repressive or rejecting parents, and the social world which they encounter once they leave home is full of unhappily married people; but in most cases this simply makes the central characters more determined to create, for themselves and their children, a family environment which will be free from want, oppression, lovelessness, and fear.

Yet in the novels of the first sixty years of the eighteenth century a strange hesitancy prevails. While children are no longer passed over in silence, and the positive connotations of childhood are thrown increasingly into relief, the challenge of

exploring the child's inner life, and of portraying it as a separate
being with an existence apart from that of its parents, is seldom
confidently met. The child figure appears more often as an object
than as a subject, and on those occasions when a first-person
narrator is made to tell the story of her or his childhood the
account is often tantalizingly brief. That is why this book seeks
to study not merely the child for its own sake, but the child as
part of a structure, and the responses of adults (especially parents) to individual children and to childhood as such.

The result is to uncover reasons for the relative failure on the
part of novelists and their characters to explore the mysterious
and elusive subjectivity of the child. One is a residual embarrassment on the part of the authors and of their imagined
readers about devoting too much time and attention to the supposedly trivial and sentimental details of childhood existence.
A more profound reason, as we shall see, is the mature person's
fear of a possible decentering of the adult (male or female) in
favor of the encroaching child, a fear which, of course, also lay
behind the dismissive treatment of children in earlier stage
comedy. The novelists seem willing at times to accept the challenge, thrown out by Locke and others, of treating children from
an early age as independent, reasonable creatures rather than
as appendages to their parents. But the strain involved in doing
so often proves too great. In the novel it manifests itself in a
tendency on the novelists' part to erase that part of the protagonist's life which lies between early childhood and late adolescence. This, of course, is the period which Ariès represents as
remaining, throughout the Middle Ages, without a conceptualization and without a name. The eighteenth century increasingly recognizes the need to conceptualize and thematize it, yet
the task is often shirked. The erasure of puberty in the fiction
of the period is far from complete, and this book will uncover
some of the traces. But those traces are not as clear or as numerous as we might expect.

There survives, indeed, in eighteenth-century fiction a noticeable reticence about children, one which sometimes seems about
to give way to the kind of open hostility found in the stage
comedies against which the novelists are supposedly reacting.
In Mary Manley's *The New Atalantis* (1709), a scandal-chronicle
which occupies a transitional place between stage comedy and
the novel, a treacherous lover explains to his mistress that a
marriage between them would bring "nothing but Fulness of
Cares, and Numbers of Children" (1971, 1:601). This, appar-

ently, is enough to make him rule out marriage. It is true that
the man in question is not treated sympathetically; but even
likeable characters and sensitive novelists often note that the
responsibility of children increases the vulnerability of the parents in a harsh and unpredictable world. It would be unaccept-
ably glib to suggest that in this the novelists are subverting
their own overt proposition, covertly rebelling against a positive
ideal of parenthood which they profess to uphold. But they do
find themselves broaching (without, of course, ever solving) a
difficult existential and theoretical problem. Which is the more
authentic: the wish to produce, love, and foster children or the
wish to avoid, reject, transfer, or erase them from one's life?

One of the most important questions in parent-child relations
was and is that of the moment at which the child ceases to be a
child and becomes emancipated from parental control. To many
seventeenth-century parents the answer appears to have been
"never." John Aubrey's recollection that in the early part of the
century "gentlemen of thirty and forty years old were to stand
like mutes and fools bareheaded before their parents; and the
daughters (grown women) were to stand at the cupboard side
during the whole time of their proud mother's visit" is often
quoted (Marcus 1978, 31–32; Stone 1965, 592). Among theorists,
Sir Robert Filmer held that death alone could loose the bond of
obedience (1949, 72); only gradually did Locke and others win
acceptance for the more liberal view that paternal authority
ceased once the child reached years of discretion and became
capable of living independently in the world (Locke 1968, 146;
1967, 322). Overtly, the novelists and other creative writers of
the eighteenth century mostly espouse Locke's view, in which
the ultimate aim of paternal authority, like that of state authority in Marxist theory, is to make itself unnecessary, with children progressing to the point where they become their parents'
friends rather than their subordinates or slaves. But the desired
break with authoritarian attitudes, and transition to a more
open and empathetic approach to children, prove hard to
achieve. The power and authority of a father continue (despite
some doubts on the part of Locke and others as to the validity
of the analogy) to be compared with those of a king: voluntary
abdication turns out to require a degree of resolution which
many parents, real and fictional, are unable to muster. Edward
Gibbon's father in the mid-eighteenth century, though his paternal feelings were kindly and his financial provisions generous,
shows himself even more disposed to prolong his authority over

his son than George Herbert's mother had been a century earlier (Gibbon 1971, 61–62; cf. Stone 1990, 52, 78; Walton 1906, 387). Some fictional parents, such as James Harlowe Senior in *Clarissa* or Squire Western in *Tom Jones,* are still more unreasonable.

Attitudes to other people's children were even harsher than the attitudes of the more reactionary members of the propertied classes toward their own, and in this instance the mood of severity lasted well into the eighteenth century. "Cultures, it sometimes seems," writes Wayland Young, "can be divided into two classes: those which, when they see a baby, say, 'Let's bring it up,' and those which say, 'Whose baby is that?'" (1969, 117). It would not be unfair to describe England in the seventeenth century as a "Whose baby is that?" culture, which moved very gradually toward a more humane and accepting attitude from the 1690s onwards. The contest to pin responsibility for a child on some other person, a favorite joke in stage comedy, appears in all seriousness in other forms of discourse and in social life. Swift's Lilliputians think "nothing can be more unjust, than that People, in Subservience to their own Appetites, should bring Children into the World, and leave the Burthen of supporting them on the Publick" (1965, 62–63). This does not seem to be one of those instances in which the Lilliputians are being held up to ridicule: their opinions about foundlings are echoed in one of Swift's own sermons, where irony would presumably be out of place. Of the vogue among his contemporaries for setting up charity schools, the preacher has this to say:

> In these Schools, children are, or ought to be, trained up to read and write, and cast Accompts; and these Children should, if possible, be of honest Parents, gone to Decay through Age, Sickness, or other unavoidable Calamity, by the Hand of God; not the Brood of wicked Strolers; for it is by no means reasonable, that the Charity of well-inclined People should be applied to encourage the Lewdness of those profligate, abandoned Women, who croud our Streets with their borrowed or spurious Issue. (Swift 1948, 202)

It is unnerving to see the views of the fictional inhabitants of Lilliput reproduced in a discourse which is apparently free of irony, and evidently intended to influence the social behavior and attitudes of its hearers. Swift continues:

> I do altogether disapprove the Custom of putting the Children 'Prentice, except to the very meanest Trades; otherwise the poor honest

Citizen who is just able to bring up his Child, and pay a small Sum
of Money with him to a good Master, is wholly defeated, and the
Bastard Issue, perhaps, of some Beggar, preferred before him.
(1948, 203)

What the child gets from charity is, it seems, to be determined
by the status and behavior of its parents: this amounts to treating the child, not as an individual in its own right, but as a
projection of other individuals, whose moral character will determine its fate. Swift's attitude here seems close to that over-
literal interpretation of the biblical formula "The sins of the
fathers are visited on the children" castigated by Mr. Allworthy
in Fielding's *Tom Jones* (1:79–80). Behind it lies a penny-
pinching concern lest honest citizens be asked to pay for the
fruits of other people's pleasures. Yet Swift, in his *Modest Proposal* (1729), showed anger and concern at the plight of Irish
children: the discrepancy between his utterances on the subject
exemplifies the uncertainty of response to the problem of child
poverty among intelligent people of his time.

The debate was a perennial one. In 1552 moves to provide for
foundlings through Christ's Hospital were scotched by the local
people, who feared that children taken in by the hospital might
ultimately become chargeable to parish rates. During the seventeenth century the beadles of the same parish were regularly
admonished "to prevent the laying down of children" in the hospital precincts, precisely the duty that we shall see the parish
officers performing in John Crowne's comedy *The Country Wit*
(1675). Once again the cry "Whose baby is that?" drowns out
"Let's bring it up." But "Let's bring it up" was to gain strength
as the eighteenth century advanced, until in 1741 it bore fruit
in Captain Thomas Coram's foundation of England's first endur-
ing foundling hospital. In most continental countries, institutions for the maintenance of orphans had already existed for
more than a century. However, foundling hospitals, whether in
England or abroad, did not necessarily afford a high chance of
survival even to those children whom they accepted, and there
were always more foundlings waiting to be taken than the institutions could afford to receive (Fildes 1988, chaps. 8, 10, 11;
McClure 1981, 3–15).

It is true that, even in England, parish authorities (as distinct
from special institutions) were obliged by law to provide for
children who had no other means of support. Most, however,
went to great lengths to avoid doing so. Different parishes com-

peted to ensure that vagrant women did not give birth within their boundaries, thus saddling the villagers with responsibility for some stranger's bastard child. As a result, pregnant women sometimes died after being driven from place to place in bad weather when on the point of giving birth. When a bastard was born to a parishioner, everything possible was done to pin responsibility on a man sufficiently prosperous to pay mainte- nance (Marshall 1969, 212; Stone 1977, 635–39). Midwives "took an oath that they would endeavor to extract the name of the father from any unmarried girl they assisted. Consequently, they often withdrew their assistance until the last minute in the hope that the pain of childbirth, and the possibility of death, would force the reluctant female to name the man concerned." Magistrates, when in doubt as to which of two men was respon- sible, did not scruple to charge both (Quaife 1979, 105, 211).

The obvious countermove was for the mother to name some substantial citizen, regardless of his guilt or innocence, as the woman is seen doing in Hogarth's painting *The Denunciation*. More imaginative, and just as reminiscent of the bold and even blasphemous pranks of characters in stage comedy, was an expe- dient reported by Mr. Wiseman in Bunyan's *The Life and Death of Mr. Badman:*

> I myself heard [a man] say, when he was tempting of a maid to commit uncleanness with him—it was in Oliver [Cromwell]'s days,—that if she did prove with child he would tell her how she might escape punishment—and that was then somewhat severe— "Say," saith he, "that you are with child by the Holy Ghost." (1984, 189)

It is hard to classify this last example. It occurs in a story which seems to be fictional; but the book has a didactic purpose and is supposed to be exemplary, and the anecdote is attributed to a character in whose truthfulness the reader is encouraged to believe. And there is no doubt that actual town- and country- dwellers, while they might stop short of blasphemy against the Holy Ghost, often schemed to lay the blame for illegitimate births on innocent men. "If Margaret Adams had been ruled by me," one seventeenth-century villager confessed, "she would have named William King or some gent. or farmer to have been the father of her child, that might have given her and her child maintenance." In another case a pregnant woman was counseled "to name the parson Hearn to be father of her child, for he is better able than [the real father] to pay for the keeping of her child" (Quaife 1979, 109). These are at the same time records of real cases and perfect comedy scenarios: examples quoted in the next two chapters will show how closely they resemble contemporary comic plots. The main difference between the comedies and the instances just quoted is that in the cases cited by historians the fathers of bastards are mostly men of humble station, whereas those in the plays involve the scapegrace sons of the gentry.

The more escapist comedies imply that assignment of responsibility for a foundling brings a happy ending for all concerned. The character charged with the child's upkeep may protest at first, but soon reconciles himself to his fate: the audience is left to infer that the child will grow and prosper. But when an actual bastard was put out to be suckled, the nurse was liable to spend as little as possible of the weekly maintenance payment on the baby, which would often die of neglect. An act of Parliament passed in 1767 sought to combat the problem by providing extra payment for nurses who succeeded in keeping their charges alive (Taylor 1979). Contemporaries (Lillie 1725) thought that "infanticidal nursing" was fairly frequent, and their view is confirmed by modern studies. The latter, however, indicate that allowing unwanted babies to die of neglect was probably commoner than actual murder (Malcolmson 1977; Stone 1977, 474–75; Wrightson 1975). These practices, detectable in English society from the early seventeenth to the mid-eighteenth century, are alluded to regularly in the more realistic stage comedies and even more often in novels.

To some extent, then, stage comedy and prose fiction do "reflect" reality. It is true that, especially in comedy, fantasy and dramatic exaggeration are of the essence: the witty characters are wittier, the fools more foolish, the brides younger, the dowries larger, the glamour more glittering, the fathers and other blocking characters more obstinate, the intrigues more complex, than their real-life counterparts. Most conspicuously of all, the likelihood of a disowned elder son or penniless younger son winning a rich and beautiful woman as his wife, slim in real society, is inflated in the comedies to something like an even chance. But fantasy always takes reality as its starting point, and the concerns and behavior of characters in Restoration and eighteenth-century comedy do impinge noticeably on those which can be discerned among real individuals and families of the time. Where the treatment of unwanted pregnancies and births is concerned, the negative connotations most often mentioned in Restoration and Augustan farce and comedy and in eighteenth-century English novels are precisely those best documented from nonliterary sources.

Some years ago Peter Laslett, one of the liveliest of modern historians, reached the opposite conclusion (1976). Challenging the traditional view that the goings-on in Restoration comedy bore direct relation to social facts, Laslett pointed out that there is no evidence of a rise in bastardy rates in the years immediately following the Restoration of the monarchy in 1660. But Laslett's analysis of the relation between stage comedy and social life is based on very few actual plays, and he also fails to take account of changes in the content and tone of the comedies between 1660 and 1700. In reality, the years immediately following 1660 were not the peak period for sex-comedy: this distinction belongs to the mid-1670s (Hume 1977 (1), 17). And even Laslett admits that in the years following 1675—when explicit sex-comedy was popular—a significant rise in the number of bastards born to noblemen did take place. Clearly the connection between life and comedy was closer than he allows. As for another claim of Laslett's, namely that bastardy is a topic seldom dealt with in Restoration comedy, the examples given in my next two chapters will show it to be unfounded.

Obviously there were some elements of seventeenth-century life which Laslett preferred not to see. Even in his more wide-ranging historical work his treatment of infanticide, whose prevalence is well documented by other historians, is almost willfully brusque (1983, 174–75); and he makes little allowance for the fact that, since bastardy, infanticide, and the marrying-off of pregnant women are all matters which people try to keep secret, their true incidence is unlikely to show up in surviving written records.

It may well be that writers like deMause and Stone have exaggerated the incidence of lovelessness in seventeenth-century families and the magnitude of the change which took place in parent-child relations during the eighteenth century. But while different historians may make differing assessments of the nature and magnitude of the change, most agree that some such change took place, and their conclusion is hard to dispute. The steady increase in the number and quality of toys, the emergence and growth of children's literature, and the shift of educational theory to more learner-oriented approaches are only a few of the indicators which reveal a new interest in children and an increased concern for their welfare. At first, however, the change was slow. A modern writer, William Sloane, assembles an impressive list of books for children published during the seventeenth century. Only a few display either the warmth and imaginative sympathy of Bunyan's *A Book for Boys and Girls, Or Country Rhymes for Children* (1686) or the "plain familiar style, . . . suitable to the age and understanding of youth" striven for in an anonymous book for apprentices published in 1698. The leading features of most of them prove to be "preachments, examples of divine judgement on sinners," and "stories of early piety and edifying deaths." In the mid-eighteenth century this situation was to change (Sloane 1955, 39, 55).

This book, then, will seek to bring children back from the margins of Enlightenment literature, while at the same time noting, and attempting to explain, the absences and missed opportunities which characterize writings about children at this time. The historical period on which I focus is the period from the acting of Congreve's *The Way of the World* in 1700 to the publication of the third edition of Richardson's *Clarissa* in 1751. For reasons already given I begin with a discussion of comedy in the last quarter of the seventeenth century, and in tracing the development of the novel I make some reference to books which post-date *Clarissa*. However, I shall not attempt a comprehensive coverage of the second half of the century: that would involve fuller discussion of Sterne and Rousseau, which would require another book.

1

The Child in Restoration Comedy

Comedy, it is often said, celebrates fertility. Why, then, is it so hard to find a comedy which unambiguously does so? In the century preceding the rise of the novel the most convincing example is probably Richard Brome's *The Antipodes* (1638), where a female character obtains blessed relief from barrenness after yearning for children all through the play. But in general childbirth and conception are rare in comedy, especially considering the amount of sexual congress that takes place. Copulation thrives in Wycherley's *The Country Wife* (1675) and Etherege's *The Man of Mode* (1676); but in these plays pregnancy and childbirth are rarely mentioned and never occur, and it is clear that if they did occur they would not be welcomed. Some years ago Virginia Birdsall represented Horner, the compulsive seducer in *The Country Wife*, as the "life force triumphant," and associated him with fertility (Birdsall 1970, 156). A reviewer, sensing a flaw in the argument, mused: "Imagine Horner surrounded by a pack of howling babies!" (Malekin & Crane 1972, 251).

It is perhaps right to say that when we think of comedy we think of the life force, and so of sex, and so of breeding. But at this point we find that the logic of association has led us astray. In most comedies babies and children do not appear and are mentioned only briefly; when they do appear or are mentioned, it is usually the fear and embarrassment, the responsibility and even danger involved in the bearing and rearing of offspring that are foremost in the characters' minds. If anyone welcomes the thought of posterity it is usually the grandparents, who will enjoy the pride and pleasure of offspring without the trouble. Thus Sir Paul Pliant in Congreve's *The Double Dealer* (1693) crows delightedly to his daughter Celia, who is getting married,

> And wilt thou bring a Grandson at nine Months end? . . . A brave chopping Boy.—I'll settle a thousand Pound a Year upon the Rogue as soon as ever he looks me in the Face, I will, Gad's-bud! I'm over-

joy'd to think I have any of my Family that will bring Children into the World. For I would fain have some Resemblance of my self in my Posterity. (1925, 176)

This speech is undeniably celebratory. But our reception of it is modified not only by awareness that Sir Paul will not have to bring up the children but also by the play's typing of him as a buffoon: a resemblance to him would be more of a handicap than a blessing for any child. His cries of pleasure at the prospect of offspring do not, then, impress us as strongly as they might otherwise do.

Children, according to a venerable proverb, are the poor man's riches. In the midseventeenth century the great preacher Jeremy Taylor elaborated charmingly, if naively, on the old saying:

We have a title to be provided for, as we are God's ... children, ... and every of our children hath the same title: and therefore it is a huge folly and infidelity to be troubled and full of care because we have many children. Every child we have to feed is a new revenue, a new title to God's care and providence; so that many children are a great wealth. (1875, 126)

But if the "huge folly and infidelity" reproved by Taylor had not been widespread there would have been no need for him to warn people against it. His utterance implicitly recognizes two antithetical attitudes to children. One is unworldly: it welcomes, or professes to welcome, offspring as a blessing, trusting in the Lord to provide for them. The other, more cynical and practical, deprecates breeding unless the growing family can be assured of subsistence by other than supernatural means.

A good example of the attitudes that upset Taylor is to be found in *The Ten Pleasures of Marriage,* a satirical squib from the mid-seventeenth century ([Behn] 1933). The book is full of grumbles about the expense associated with lyings-in, christenings, and the raising and education of children. Offspring are seen as a means by which the wife gains ascendancy over her husband, gradually leaving him less and less of his fortune to spend on himself and progressively decreasing the importance of his role within the family. The book is, then, an extended complaint, uttered not by a poor laborer or artisan but by a speaker who presents himself as a reasonably prosperous citizen. When poorer characters are in question, comic and satiric drama and fiction are even more inclined to harp on the sorrows of family life; this applies not only in seventeenth-century works

but also in those of a much later date. Voltaire's Candide notices
during a visit to Venice that the gondoliers are always singing,
but his wordly wise friend Martin reminds him, "You don't see
them at home, with their wives and squalling children" (1966,
61). Corporal Trim in Sterne's *Tristram Shandy* (1759–67) likewise seems to see misery as inseparable from family life. "I have
neither wife nor child," he reflects, "I can have no sorrows in
this world" (1967, 277).

Comedy, which traditionally celebrates the realization of selfhood by the central characters, is especially prone to query the
assumption that bairns are blessings: not only do the poor and
lowly characters question it but also, for different reasons, the
richer and better-bred. The worst nightmare for the man of substance was that of a child born in wedlock who was not the issue
of his own loins but the fruit of one of his wife's adulterous
affairs. Sir John Brute in Vanbrugh's *The Provoked Wife* (1697),
finding a false friend hidden in Lady Brute's closet, sees himself
condemned to raise a spurious heir to inherit all his wealth,
with the true father threatening revenge if the foster father
dares complain: "He comes to my House; Eats my Meat; Lies
with my Wife; Dishonours my family; Gets a Bastard to inherit
my Estate; and when I ask a Civil Account of all this—Sir,
says he, I wear a Sword" (Vanbrugh 1967, 1:168). Heartwell in
Congreve's *The Old Bachelor* (1693) is haunted by the same
specter:

> I would not be a Cuckold to e'er an illustrious Whore in *England*
> . . . to have a fleering Coxcomb scoff and cry, Mr. your Son's mighty
> like his Grace, has just his Smile and Air of's Face. . . . Then, I, to
> put it off as unconcern'd, chuck the Infant under the Chin, force a
> Smile, and cry, Ay, the Boy takes after his Mothers Relations—
> when the Devil and she knows, 'tis a little Compound of the whole
> Body of Nobility. (1925, 34–35)

In another version of the plot, a social inferior may trick a superior into fathering his child. Paul Salzman quotes several examples from early English comic and picaresque fiction, beginning
with one from Deloney in which Jack of Newbury manipulates
Sir George Rigley into marrying a servant who is pregnant by
Jack (1985, 104). Outside England Madame de La Fayette, in
her novel *La Princesse de Clèves* (1678), shows a malicious character trying to spite the queen of France by telling the king
that only his illegitimate children resemble him (1957, 35).

In Freud's Family Romance the child imagines a more illustrious ancestry for itself than society assigns to it (Freud 1959, 235–41). Comedy considers the same scenario from the foster parent's point of view: it then becomes transformed into the Family Nightmare, in which a man of modest origins finds himself saddled with a nobly born wife and a spurious heir, the by-blow of some aristocrat with whom the mother has been passionately involved. This scenario is especially prominent in Restoration comedy, but the same pattern of feeling survived until much later and can be discerned in serious works of social commentary as well as in frivolous plays. As late as 1782 William Alexander, in his *History of Women,* found himself explaining the double standard in these terms:

> The men generally have the care of providing for the offspring, and it would be hard that a man should be obliged to provide for and leave his estate to children, which he could never with certainty call his own, were the same indulgence given to the women as to the men.
> A shorter way of explaining the matter would have been to have said that men are generally the legislators. (Quoted in Smith 1978, 424)

The last sentence shows that Alexander was no unthinking apologist for men's privileges. But he recognizes the force of the apprehension which obsessed his male contemporaries.

For the children themselves, what would come to matter most as they grew to maturity was legitimacy in the eyes of the law. In this respect the cuckoo in the nest was more fortunate than the child born outside wedlock for, as Peter Laslett notes, children born in wedlock who were not the biological offspring of their legal fathers were "not illegitimate at all from the social point of view" (1977, 121n). For the unwilling foster fathers, however, this only made the situation more galling. We have already seen the elemental male fear of fathering other men's children tormenting Heartwell in *The Old Bachelor,* Congreve's first play. In the same dramatist's last comedy, *The Way of the World* (1700), the same scenario is seen from a different point of view, that of the frail woman and her accomplice, the seducer. A false alarm of pregnancy scares the rake Mirabell and his mistress Arabella Languish into ending their love affair precipitately and contriving a marriage for Arabella with a certain Mr. Fainall. "If" asks Mirabell with careful circumlocution, "the Familiarities of our Loves had produc'd that Consequence, of which you were apprehensive, where cou'd you have fix'd a father's Name with Credit, but on a Husband?" (Congreve 1925, 368). Fainall, then, was to have been tricked not only into marrying someone else's mistress but also into fathering the other's child if one had actually been born. In a case like this it was not only the deluded husband who was likely to find the birth of a child unwelcome: the fear of pregnancy could also inconvenience the lover and spoil the life of the putative mother. An event which frightened a woman into a hasty marriage with a man she did not love could hardly be said to be surrounded with a sense of festivity and celebration.

Later in the play, in the contract scene where Mirabell and Millamant assess one another's preparedness for marriage, Mirabell again brings up the subject of offspring, this time legitimate ones. Once again, however, childbirth is seen to carry some strangely negative connotations:

> *Mirabell:* . . . *Item,* when you shall be Breeding—
> *Millamant:* Ah! Name it not.
>
> . . . .
>
> *Mirabell:* I denounce against all strait Lacing, squeezing for a Shape, 'till you mould my Boy's Head like a Sugar-loaf; and instead of a Man-Child, make me Father to a Crooked-billet. (Congreve 1925, 408)

Mirabell, anxious for a healthy male heir, fears that Millamant's concern for her looks will make her lace herself too tightly: the baby may then be born malformed. Millamant, for her part, seems to feel some distaste for the whole subject. Though she does not go so far as to reject the conditions Mirabell imposes, she seems to regard motherhood with apprehension, as one of the unwelcome consequences of "dwindling into a wife."

Half a century later, in Richardson's *Clarissa,* the effect of marriage and motherhood on the sprightly, effervescent young woman is further explored. Colonel Morden is writing of the approaching marriage of the spirited Anna Howe to the rather tame Mr. Hickman:

> There is also another circumstance [sc. childbirth] which good-natured men who engage even with lively women, may look forward to with pleasure; a circumstance which generally lowers the spirits of the ladies, and *domesticates* them, as I may call it: and which, as it will bring those of Mr. Hickman and Miss Howe nearer to a par, that worthy gentleman will have *double* reason, when it happens, to congratulate himself upon it. (1932, 4:470)

According to this representation, the less mercurial man may hope that motherhood will tame his livelier wife, bringing her down to his temperamental level. Thus parenthood may signify, for either sex or both, an end to the comic phase of existence, the era of irrepressible high spirits and effervescent wit. *Clarissa,* of course, lies outside the comic mode. But this small instance of the negative presentation of motherhood exemplifies a tendency which we shall often encounter in the course of this study: an inclination on the part of novelists to appropriate, and use for their own purposes, motifs inherited from the comic drama of a former age.

In practice both Millamant in *The Way of the World* and Anna Howe in *Clarissa* will be shown accepting their destiny as wives and mothers. But there can be no doubt that, for them, childbirth carries some negative associations. Among those female characters who are credited with less good sense, good nature, and maturity, hostility to childbirth and parenthood is more marked. In *The Double Dealer* Sir Paul Pliant's second wife—a shrewd, if unlovable, figure—practices birth control by limiting her husband's access to her to one night a year (Congreve 1925, 163). In Steele's comedy *The Tender Husband* (1705) the romance-obsessed Biddy Tipkin admonishes an admirer, "To talk to me of Children—Did you ever hear of an Heroine with a Big-belly?" (1971, 240). In Mary Pix's *The Different Widows* (1703) the Frenchified, would-be fashionable Lady Gaylove does her best to conceal her almost-adult son and daughter from her acquaintances so as to prevent people from guessing her age. When a visiting aunt asks to see her nephew and niece, Gaylove protests: "Fy fy, is anything a greater Indecency, than to talk of ones Children? How can You raise such odd, Out of the Way Discourse?" (Pix 1967, 11). Swollen bellies and chatter about offspring are inimical to the aura of youth, romance, and sophistication that Tipkin and Gaylove are trying to cultivate.

There is, of course, an element of satire in these portrayals of women who want their own aging process magically arrested, and for this reason reject the maternal role. This satiric stereotype, like so many others, was to pass into the novel, as when a character in Henry Brooke's *The Fool of Quality* (1766–70) ridicules a widow of her acquaintance for keeping "three marriageable daughters in the nursery, for fear people should be so impertinent as to enquire who brought them into the world" (Brooke 1979, 2:240). A touch of pathos is added in the anonymous *Memoirs of a Coquet* (1765), where an unfashionable country gentlewoman laments, "I was counted handsome once, but a tribe of brats have spoilt my complexion, and made a bundle of my body" (Anon., 1974, 47–48). Both novels and comedies waver between ridicule and sympathy for woman's impulse to reject or deny parenthood so as to preserve her own liveliness and youth.

Comedy, indeed, habitually presents pregnancy and childbirth as jokes played by nature on unhappy victims, whose destiny of bearing or raising offspring condemns them to a premature loss of youthful high spirits and verve, sometimes even to a loss of social status and reputation. When these feelings are not expressed directly, they are often implicit in the characters' choice of imagery. In *The Way of the World* Lady Wishfort, eternally preoccupied with her appearance, looks in the mirror and exclaims in horror, "I'm as pale and as faint, I look like Mrs. *Qualmsick* the Curate's Wife, that's always breeding" (Congreve 1925, 378). In the same play Mrs. Marwood, casting about for an apt image for a secret which cannot be kept much longer, decides that it is "like Mrs. *Primly's* great Belly; she may lace it down before, but it burnishes on her Hips" (Congreve 1925, 387).

In tragic drama of the Restoration period children are, as Eric Rothstein notes, often introduced for pathetic effect, appearing as "archetypal innocents." In painting, as the same writer reminds us (quoting aptly from *Spectator* no. 44), numerous children "usually hang about the figure of Charity" (Rothstein 1967, 153–54): indeed this positive image of childhood is an iconographic commonplace from the Renaissance onwards (see, e.g., Spenser, *The Faerie Queene,* 1.10.16.29–31) and can be seen to resemble the figuration that Bakhtin finds in the idyll. Clearly, then, there was not a single, global attitude toward babies, children, and offspring which prevailed at this moment in cultural history to the exclusion of others. But while we should not ascribe to stage comedy a direct and accurate representation of "the" contemporary attitude toward children, we may legitimately give its figurations some extra weighting, in view of its status at this period of a dominant literary form. Its foregrounding of a particular set of responses to children clearly has some significance: it is surely worth asking what specific psychological needs were satisfied by, and what psychological or existential truths underlay, the negative figuration of offspring and of parenthood in comedy at this particular time.

In our own century, Freud has written:

Sexual love is a relationship between two individuals in which a third can only be superfluous or disturbing, whereas civilization depends on relationships between a considerable number of individuals. When a love-relationship is at its height there is no room left for an interest in the environment; a pair of lovers are sufficient to themselves, and do not even need the child they have in common to make them happy. (1961, 108)

"Do not even need" is an understatement: in the situation outlined by Freud the intrusion of a child is definitely unwelcome. Freud's disciple Norman O. Brown suggests plausibly that socialization and the founding of families require subordination of the pleasure principle, but that this self-denial is "rejected by the unconscious essence of the human being" (1970, 24). Outside the Freudian mainstream Simone de Beauvoir quotes Hegel's epigram, "the birth of children is the death of parents," and shows how the supposed obligation to reproduce—and especially the assumption that, for the female, motherhood alone should suffice for personal fulfillment—can work to restrict the individual to "immanence," that level of life which we share with the animals, at the expense of "transcendence," that which humans—and only humans—may experience through what they make of their lives (1972, 180). On the other hand eroticism, which exalts pleasure and ignores or subverts its possible biological consequences, represents a revolt of the instant against time, the individual against the universal. To this Georges Bataille adds that the pleasure of an embrace may be in inverse proportion to the lovers' consciousness that they may be engendering offspring (1979, 113), while Julia Kristeva notes that the reproducing female may come to be resented by her husband for introducing him into the repressive cycle of family responsibilities (1974, 143).

Northrop Frye, in his book *The Critical Path,* drew attention to an archetypal rivalry within the order of words that is literature between what he calls a "myth of freedom" and a "myth of concern" (1971). Comedy, and especially English Restoration comedy, privileges the myth of freedom: it is by no means fantastic to detect in the rakes of Restoration comedy, and to a lesser extent in the women they pursue and marry, the operation of principles similar to those just cited from modern philosophers and psychologists. The argument that Freudian notions are inapplicable to the literature of the early modern period fails to convince, for the very ideas which we have detected in the work of Freud, Brown, and Bataille also surface in some of the most influential writings of the Augustan age. "What father [in] a thousand, when he begets a child," asked Locke in his *First Treatise of Government* (1690), "thinks farther than the satisfying of his present appetite? . . . God in his infinite wisdom has put strong desires of copulation into the constitution of men, thereby to continue the race of mankind, which he doth most commonly without the consent and will of the begetter" (1967, 197). A quarter of a century later Locke's comment is echoed in Gulliver's account of the social customs of Lilliput:

> The Lilliputians will needs have it, that Men and Women are joined together . . . by . . . Concupiscence . . . for which Reason they will never allow, that a Child is under any Obligation to his Father for begetting him, or to his Mother for bringing him into the World; which . . . was neither a Benefit in itself, nor intended so by his Parents, whose Thoughts in their Love-encounters were otherwise employed. (Swift 1965, 60)

A shorter paraphrase of the same Lockean argument appears in *Tristram Shandy* (1760), where Parson Yorick declares: "The act, especially where it ends there, in my opinion lays as little obligation upon the child, as it conveys power to the father" (Sterne 1967, 383). Equally Lockean is the book's opening sentence: "I wish either my father or my mother, or indeed both of them, as they were in duty equally bound to it, had minded what they were about when they begot me." In passages like these we can see writers exploring the implications (especially the comic implications) of Locke's doctrines. If the sexual act is essentially selfish and irresponsible, there is no reason why children should be obliged in perpetuity to respect and obey their begetters: only if the father's care does not "end there"— with the gift of life—but is followed by careful fostering and rearing up, are the children under any obligation to him. Even then they may be under an equal or greater debt to their mothers. Parents have obligations to children as well as rights.

In comedy, prominence and a degree of sympathy are given to the proclivities of impulsive, irresponsible begetters and conceivers. Comedy is a celebration not so much of fertility as of pure sexual and mental energy: if the sexual energy results in the birth of children, the mental energy is often to get rid of them. In the comic world the child is not a true prize but a booby prize: renounced by its father the careless rake or its mother the artful slut, it is palmed off on a staid or foolish character who could not possibly be its true father, and who is flabbergasted when accused of an exploit which he would never have had the enterprise to commit. Thus in Crowne's play *The Country Wit* (1675) a country gentleman's servant, aptly called Booby, is left to guard his master's money bag in a London street: it is stolen by a beggar-woman who leaves another bag, containing a baby, in its place. When Booby grasps what has happened he makes as if to put the bag down. But before he can do so the neighbors and parish constable are upon him, determined to lay the child to his charge rather than have it left unclaimed in their parish: nobody wants another mouth to feed out of the rates. Booby protests that he is "but newly come to town" and has not had time to father a London bastard, but since he is the only available scapegoat he has to take the blame. Only after the contest for avoiding responsibility has been shown in all its starkness is the problem of the baby satisfactorily resolved: the foundling is adopted by a kindly porter's wife who actually wants a child (Crowne 1967, 3:117–20; cf. Middleton 1969, 44–47). We may note in passing that the stage device of the bundle which may contain either a baby or a more tempting item of goods goes back at least as far as Middleton, and reaches forward into the novel. (A recent writer [Erickson 1986, 57] notes its occurrence in *Moll Flanders,* though without apparent awareness of its intertextual dimension.) It epitomizes that marginal, deeply disturbing situation in which the child is reduced to an object, a commodity which the carrier or finder may covet, but may alternatively want to dispose of to whoever is gullible enough to receive it.

In *The Country Wit* the transfer of the baby is managed by its mother: the father is unidentified. Both mother and child are unconnected with the rest of the plot, introduced simply to provide a hilarious scene. But in other plays the contest to avoid responsibility for an infant is much more fully integrated into the favorite Restoration fable of the carefree rake who provides, by means of trickery, for his mistress and bastards before settling down to marriage. In Farquhar's *Love and a Bottle* (1698) Roebuck and Lyric, the rake and the poet, trick Squire Mockmode into marrying Mistress Trudge, who has a child by Roebuck. When Mockmode learns the truth about his wife's past he is horrified and wants his marriage annulled. Lyric demands five hundred pounds as a fee for procuring the annulment: having received the money he reveals that the marriage was not valid in the first place, since the wedding ceremony was a sham. Mockmode, seeing how he has been tricked, demands his five hundred pounds back; but Roebuck, with a gallant flourish, awards it to Trudge for the maintenance of herself and her infant. "It belongs to this Gentlewoman," he informs the angry squire, "you have divorc'd her, and must give her separate maintenance." Thus provision is made not only for Trudge but for the baby she has been carrying around since the beginning of the play (Farquhar 1988, 1:108).

The child and its mother, then, form a kind of package. As living proof of the hero's virility they are gratifying to his pride and have a share in his concern. But the privilege of taking financial or legal responsibility for them is one for which he would rather not compete. To be forced to take them on is the destiny of natural losers in the comic game. "Fools," as a character in an earlier play has it, "will serve to father wise men's children" (Middleton 1975, 42). Typically, then, the comic plot in which the child plays a passive role involves an illicit transaction, a trick or swindle, designed to transfer a baby, a cast mistress, or both from the rake to some other, less quick-witted, person. The sense of cruelty or callousness which might otherwise surround the disposal of the child is often mitigated by having it reach the arms of someone who undertakes to look after it; the task is usually accepted reluctantly, but in a few cases the recipient actually shows signs of affection for the infant which he or she has adopted. However, the main emphasis of the intrigue is on the skill and resourcefulness of the child's father or mother in getting rid of an encumbrance. The child is a kind of sediment left in the cup of pleasure. The last glass, with the dregs, is passed on to someone else.

An especially striking instance of this motif is James Howard's *All Mistaken* (first acted 1665—see Hume 1962), where for once a Restoration rake is actually seen surrounded by howling babies. Philidor is cornered by a gaggle of wet nurses with children of his, whose maintenance payments he can no longer afford. When he tries to sneak off and leave them, the nurses outmaneuver him and he is left to take care of the infants himself. The reluctant father goes off with his brood, lamenting that he has "run so much upon tick to the Parsons for christening of Children" that they now refuse to christen any baby of his without an immediate cash payment. "What shall I doe," he asks plaintively, "when these Infants begin to be hungry and youle for the Teat?" Earlier, one of the nurses ventured some remarks that suggested celebration of Philidor's procreative powers:

> Codge, Codge, does a laugh upon a dad, In conscience sir the child knows your Worship. . . . I cou'd not choose but smile to my self tother day, [as] I was making him clean about the Secret [parts], to see what God had sent him in a plentiful manner, it put me half in mind of your Worship.

But the nurse's chief motive in making the speech is to wheedle money out of the (hopefully) proud father: when she finds that he has none she flees, leaving him holding the child. Philidor's potency, which it seems he may have passed on to at least one of his offspring, is a thorough nuisance:

> I am at this time in Law with six or seaven Parishes about fathering of Bastards. . . . 'Tis a hard Case, that I should be sued for Multiplying the World. . . . Pox on't I cou'd never light of any but fruitful Whores. (Howard 1967, 7–12)

Children and swashbuckling sort ill together. The rake is by definition a freebooting, freewheeling figure: in comedies, and especially in those which tend toward farce, it is common for the scapegrace hero, burdened with children whom he cannot get rid of and can no longer afford to keep, to hint that they should have the decency to die. Rightwit in Elizabeth Polwhele's *The Frolics* (ca. 1670), chidden by his sister for squandering his money, reveals that it has been frittered away in maintenance payments. Resentfully he mutters: "There is a law that says . . . that children must not be knock'd i'th' head, and those that [be]get them must keep them" (1967, 62). Throughout the fourth act of the play different characters are duped by their rivals and find themselves with babies tied, symbolically, to their backs. When the trick is played on Rightwit, he growls: "So, this I pay for smock service. 'Twould never grieve me, if I were sure the burden I carry were my own. But who knows rightly who's the father of a whore's child?" (110).

Not that the play's approach to babies is uniformly hostile. Though several comments are made on their unwelcome crying, there is also some sympathetic recognition of their need for "cleanly pap" and for "dry clouts" to prevent them from becoming "pissburnt" (112). At one moment Rightwit even offers to "beget an excellent race of merry bastards" on Clarabell, the witty, chaste heroine: for once the play seems about to celebrate

the delights of offspring. But Rightwit's offer is met with a
blank refusal from Clarabell: "Never. I will hatch all I breed in
England" (100). For the most part the emphasis in *The Frolics*
is on the demands made by children and on the threat they pose
to the vital spirits of youth. To be left holding the baby is to be
menaced with care and responsibility: it is also to lose points in
the comic game.

Polwhele's handling of children was perhaps influenced by *All
Mistaken*. In that play, too, the hero is cheered by thoughts of
the high mortality rate prevailing amongst infants. "Death,"
he concludes with unconcealed satisfaction, "makes bold with
Bastards as well as other Children" (Howard 1967, 8). Such
remarks rapidly become standard for Restoration stage rakes.
Roebuck in Farquhar's *Love and a Bottle* admits that, having
refused to marry a girl he seduced in Ireland, he left the country
to avoid "the continual clamours of a furious Woman, and the
shrill bawling of an ill natur'd Bastard" (Farquhar 1988, 1:35).
Roebuck's mistress originally gave birth to twins; later, as Roebuck gratefully acknowledges, "Heaven was pleased to lessen
my affliction, by taking away the she Brat; but the 'tother is, I
hope, well, because a brave Boy" (1:35). The fondness expressed
for the male child (evidently identical with the "ill-natured Bastard" mentioned earlier) is little more than conventional; he is
valued, if at all, chiefly for the proof he offers of the manhood
of his father. (Elsewhere in the play a woman who feels drawn
to another of the male characters is reminded that fathering a
"lusty chopping boy" is living proof of a youth's "ability"—1:78.)
Later the happy-go-lucky lover, weighing the pros and cons of
marriage, lists "Children; squawling Children" on the debit
side; then, brightening up, he reminds himself that "there are
Rickets and Small-Pox, which perhaps may carry them all
away." In Susannah Centlivre's *A Bold Stroke for a Wife* a character callously announces, "I married, indeed, to please [my]
Father, and I [be]got a Girl to please my Wife; but she and the
Child (thank Heav'n) died together" (1872, 3:231). By this date
(1718), however, the myth of concern is already reasserting itself: this time the dismissive speech is made by a character who,
instead of being presented as a swashbuckling, outrageously
attractive rake, is made to appear ridiculous.

Comedy is vitalistic: it revels in the vigorous, barely control-
lable forces of life. But in celebrating the life-force the comic
writer periodically has to face the realization that organic life
is self-consuming, or rather that one organism survives at the

expense of another. The power of the life-force working in one generation brings a new generation into being; yet the new generation, with its own impulses and desires, poses by definition a threat to the old. Thus comedy often invites us to accept as the ideal comic compromise a situation where the rake or trickster begets a child and then successfully foists it on some other person. The assumption is that the lusty infant will win care and sympathy by the same means as its father won the affections of women: by its animal vitality and allure. But there is no serenity in this solution: it is fraught with anxiety and guilt. The elements of hostility and rejection in the rake's attitude to the child, inherent as they are in the dramatic situation—if not in the very relationship of parent and offspring—are never far from the surface. Life is a competition for scarce resources: the rake is always aware that if he cannot get the child brought up at someone else's expense it will have to be brought up at his own, or else left to die.

In the mideighteenth century, Rousseau wrote:

> If human beings were born big and strong, their size and strength would be useless to them until they had learned how to use them. Our size and strength would even be prejudicial to us, for they would prevent others from ever thinking of helping us; left to ourselves, we would die of want before knowing our needs. When we complain about the state of infancy, we fail to see that the human race would not have survived if each human being had not begun life as a helpless child. (1969, 246–47)

The argument here seems to depend on the existence of an impulse on the part of the older and more self-sufficient to foster the young and helpless—an impulse arising from the power of imagination or sympathetic identification. Restoration drama does at times acknowledge the existence of this impulse. But the typical comic hero seems to see it as something to be repressed. He sees himself rather as Shaw was later to see the Nietzschean superman: he belongs to the superior order of beings who must suppress any impulse that threatens their own self-realization. His abandonment of his children seems the less culpable because so many lesser beings—chiefly women and the poor—seem unable to resist the desire to foster an abandoned child. The job of rearing the rake's children will, with luck, be done, but he will not be the one to do it.

We may feel repelled by the irresponsibility or callousness of some comic characters in their attitudes to children; alternatively we may laugh, perhaps a little guiltily, at the confident self-centeredness of their rejection of whatever hinders their personal fulfillment. But at all costs we must, in dealing with these imaginative creations of an earlier age, avoid the moralistic orientation of such writers as the psychohistorian Lloyd deMause, cited in our last chapter. DeMause often seems intent on bringing before a jury of modern readers every retrievable instance of callousness or indifference toward children in past time; he makes little attempt to differentiate between examples from literature and those from life, let alone between one literary mode and another. The attitudes presented in Restoration comedy are often meant to be colored with jest and bravado: they are not to be taken as "typical" of the age. They do, nevertheless, appear to have had some correspondence with contemporary life. And, what is more, a distinct change can be seen occurring with the move from Restoration to Augustan comedy, and from there to the periodical essay and the novel. Hostile and rejecting attitudes toward children are still expressed in these literary modes, but they are increasingly attributed to characters who are clearly not offered for admiration. A profound change in the figuration of the child begins to take place, and it coincides with that which historians have detected in real society.

2

Augustan Comedy and the Validation of Issue

In the 1690s and in the early decades of the eighteenth century, comedy steadily becomes less ruthless and more humane. While the old comic types—madcap woman, freebooting man—persist, and indeed survive in much later drama and novels, their presentation undergoes a significant change. Audiences are still invited to enjoy the freedom and irreverence of swashbuckling characters, but there is an increasing awareness of the harmful consequences of such a way of life. This is unusual. Habitually, comedy projects a feeling of tolerance toward irresponsibility, especially sexual lapses and the abandoning or passing on of the offspring who result from them. But in Augustan comedy the representation both of childhood and parenthood changed: sympathy began to turn toward the child, and away from the impulsive begetter and conceiver.

A key transitional text is Congreve's *Love for Love,* first acted in 1695. At the beginning of the play the rake, Valentine, deeply in debt, is dunned for money by a woman who is nursing of one of his bastard children. Valentine flies into a rage:

> Pox on her, cou'd she find no other time to fling my Sins in my Face: Here, give her this [*Gives Mony*] and bid her trouble me no more; a thoughtless two handed Whore, She knows my Condition well enough, and might have overlaid the Child a Fortnight ago, if she had had any forecast in her. (1.4.225)

It would be hard for a seventeenth-century audience to avoid relating this speech to the facts of social life as they were then understood. "Overlaying" (the suffocating of a baby when the nurse or mother rolls over on it while sleeping) is today regarded as almost impossible unless the woman is drunk or drugged, but in the seventeenth and eighteenth centuries it was given as the cause of countless infant deaths. Some of these may have been what we now call cot deaths, for which nobody was to blame. Others, however, were probably caused by neglect. While wet nurses employed by rich families normally did everything they could for their charges, the parish nurses and those employed for a pittance to look after illegitimate children were not always so caring (Fildes 1986, 195ff; 1988, 94ff).

How, then, are we to take Valentine's speech about his child? Some critics see it as an instance of Congreve's callousness, others of Valentine's: the comment about "overlaying" the child is variously interpreted as a callous but sincere wish and as a "graceless joke." One writer even represents Valentine as showing "concern and affection" for his offspring (Birdsall 1970, 214; cf. Hume 1977 (1), 107 and note). And it is true that, when his friend Scandal offers money for the baby, Valentine protests, "*Scandal*, don't spoil my Boy's Milk": presumably he fears that if the nurse gets too much money all at once she will spend it on brandy, which will contaminate the milk drunk by the child. The best reading of the passage, then, is probably one which takes all possibilities into account. We need not see Valentine as an entirely uncaring parent. But he is a recognizable example of the traditional careless rake, for whom children do not stand especially high on the list of priorities. The rake is not gratuitously cruel, but in a contest for scarce resources he will put his own interests first. Since so many children die, it seems unjust to him that he should continue to be burdened with one whose upkeep he can ill afford.

It is unlikely to be coincidental that Valentine finds himself, a few scenes later, engaged in a conflict of interests with his own father, Sir Sampson Legend. Sir Sampson, angered by the debts his son has contracted, threatens to disinherit him and leave him to beggary. Valentine, in reply, puts his own case with dignity:

> *Sir Sampson:* ... Come, uncase, strip, and go naked out of the World, as you came into it.
> *Valentine:* My Cloaths are soon put off:—But you must also divest me of Reason, Thought, Passions, Inclinations, Affections, Appetites, Senses, and the huge Train of Attendants that you begot along with me.
> *Sir Sampson:* Body o'me, what a many-headed Monster have I propagated! ... 'Oons, what had I to do to get Children,—can't a private man be born without all these Followers?—Why nothing under an Emperor should be born with Appetites. (251)

Love for Love portrays, with a degree of tolerance but also a measure of satirical detachment, the devil-may-care attitude of the traditional rake. But it also puts this attitude into a broader, Lockean perspective. Though it does not acquit the young man of blame, it implicitly lays much of his insouciance toward family ties at the door of his father, whose treatment of his son is loveless, imperious, and dismissive. In the course of the play, Sir Sampson will even seek to have his own time over again at Valentine's expense: he will disinherit his heir and make a bid to marry Angelica, the woman Valentine loves. "Age," as Steele was to write a few years later "is so unwelcome to the generality of mankind, and growth toward manhood so desirable to all, that resignation to decay is too difficult a task for the father; and deference, amidst the impulse of gay desires, appears unreasonable to the son" (*Spectator* 263, 6 January 1712). He might well be paraphrasing the principal message encoded in Congreve's play.

Congreve, in *Love for Love,* deliberately links the struggle between father and son to the wider contemporary debate about patriarchy in family and state. Sir Sampson's defense of patriarchal authority echoes Locke's antagonist, Sir Robert Filmer: the old knight is obsessed with his own rights of "Authority," "Correction," and "Arbitrary Power" (246). He believes, too, that a son owes everything to his father for begetting him. It was these obsessions of Filmer's that called forth Locke's reminder that men during sexual congress think of their own pleasure, not of giving life to a child (Filmer 1949, 96, 231–32).

So hostile is Sir Sampson's treatment of his son in *Love for Love* that at times it seems likely to drive Valentine to despair or suicide. This adds plausibility to Valentine's dismissive comments on his own offspring. How can he be expected to care for his child's life when his own existence is so bitterly resented by his father? He has no money to save the baby from starvation; his father has plenty of money, but seems to relish rather than dread the prospect of seeing his own eldest son starve. A vista is opened up of a vicious cycle of lovelessness and rivalry between fathers and sons. However, the play is a comedy, and Congreve contrives an ending which implies that the cycle can be broken. The conflicts in *Love for Love* will, as the title suggests, be resolved at last by generosity, by altruism, and in general by what Lawrence Stone would call "affective behavior." However, it is Angelica, the woman Valentine loves, who will resolve them, not Sir Sampson, his father, who has resented his son and sought to erase him from his life.

One of the main targets in Locke's attack on traditional notions of patriarchy was the argument that a father had a right of dominion over his child through the mere act of begetting. "Can any Man say," Locke asked rhetorically, "[that] he formed the parts that are necessary to the Life of his Child?" (1967, 196; cf. Staves 1979, 142–44). To the argument that the act of begetting was neither willed, controlled, nor conscious, he added the further plea that the mother's part in bringing a child into the world was arguably more important than the father's, "For no body can deny but that the Woman hath an equal share, if not the greater, as nourishing the Child a long time in her own body out of her own Substance" (198). From this it was but a short step to arguing that the child owed a duty, not to those who were responsible for its existence in the crude biological sense, but to those who gave it sustenance and education once it came into the world:

> [Suppose that] a Father, unnaturally careless of his Child, sells or gives him to another Man; and he again exposes him: a third Man finding him, breeds up, cherishes and provides for him as his own. I think in this Case, no body will doubt but that the greatest part of filial Duty and Subjection was here owing, and to be paid to this Foster-Father (232).

Where Filmer stressed only the duties owed by the child to its parent, Locke insisted equally on those that parents owed to their children:

> Children being by the course of Nature, born weak, and unable to provide for themselves, they have ... a Right to be nourish'd and maintained by their Parents, nay a right not only to a bare Subsistance but to the conveniences and comforts of Life, as far as the conditions of their Parents can afford it. (225)

It may seem strange to cite such pronouncements in a chapter devoted to comedy. However, comedy is often darker, and political philosophy more ludic, than we might expect: in the *Treatises on Government* Filmer, Locke's opponent, the champion of the rights of paternity, is ridiculed in much the same way as heavy fathers had traditionally been in stage plays. It is no wonder, then, that the new comic writers, such as Congreve, found some of Locke's material readily adaptable to their purposes. But while mockery of the father was easy to incorporate in a stage comedy, calls for sympathy for helpless children— especially very young children—were not: the playwrights of the period always seem conscious that expressions of tenderness toward babies are apt to dampen comedy's traditional irreverence and wit. Nevertheless, from the mid-1690s there is a growing tendency among comic dramatists of both sexes, while admitting to the more irksome characteristics of children, to set against them the pleasure and duty of love and care, and to satirize characters who behave callously toward infants or speak slightingly of them.

In Durfey's *The Campaigners* (1698) Angelica, the lively heroine, can at times talk of children in a bluff, almost masculine way. She refers slightingly, for example, to an aunt who hopes that her niece will never marry, in which case (as the younger woman pungently puts it) the aunt's own "nasty Cubs, if ever she has any" will inherit Angelica's money. Elsewhere she expresses disgust at the fulsome baby talk lavished on her own illegitimate baby by the hired nurse: "Could one believe the Child would ever speak English, that hears her jabbering to't at this rate?" However, dislike of baby talk is not synonymous with dislike of babies: Angelica's comment is in fact a sign of concern for her child, as the context shows. Though Durfey is careful not to let her bill or coo too extravagantly over the baby, he occasionally lets her refer to it as a "dear little Angel" and express a longing to see it. He also aims some unmistakably satiric shafts at the rake who begot the child, by means of what almost amounted to a rape, but who hesitates to marry Angelica and legitimize her baby on the dubious grounds that he cannot be sure it is his own (1967, 12, 17, 19).

A more radical revision of Restoration values takes place in the farce *Three Hours After Marriage* (1717), written by John Gay in collaboration with Pope and Arbuthnot. The play centers on the physician and virtuoso Doctor Fossile, who finds within hours of his wedding that he has married an unchaste and unsuitable wife. He is rescued in the end by the discovery that the first husband of his supposed wife is still alive, but in the meantime a sailor has called at his house and deposited a baby which the sailor's wife, recently dead, was wet-nursing. Fossile has "never had Carnal Knowledge of any Woman," and so knows the baby is not his (1983, 1:260). But the local magistrate, Justice Possum, anxious to avoid charging the baby to the parish, follows the practice of real-life magistrates in similar circumstances (Marshall 1969, 212): he ascribes it to Fossile, the nearest solvent male.

Possum's decision is backed by a delightful mock-logic. Fossile, in Possum's presence, is indiscreet enough to order a servant to get the crying child some water-pap. The doctor's own explanation of this is that he is too humane to starve a member of his own species, but the justice takes his gesture as evidence of "paternal piety," as if no man would bother about protecting a baby from starvation unless it was his own. Another suspicious circumstance, according to Possum, is that Fossile has not issued an injunction against having the child registered in his (Fossile's) name. A third supposedly incriminating detail is that the doctor admits to cohabiting (since seven A.M. that morning) with the baby's mother. "Let any Man in the least acquainted with the Powers of Nature, judge whether that Human Creature could be conceived and brought to Maturity in one Forenoon," Fossile vainly protests (257). Even when the news arrives that the mother's real husband has returned from the colonies and has issued a warrant to get his wife back, Possum refuses to abandon his original line of argument: "By your favour, Doctor, I never reverse my Judgment. The Child is yours: for it cannot belong to a Man who has been three Years absent in the East-Indies" (260). Fossile, borne down by Possum's crazy reasoning, reluctantly accepts the infant. But as the other characters leave the stage, his attitude toward the foundling begins to change:

> What must be, must be. [*Takes up the child*] *Fossile* thou didst want Posterity: Here behold thou hast it. A Wife thou didst not want; Thou hast none. But thou art caressing a Child that is not thy own. What then? A Thousand, and a Thousand Husbands are doing the same Thing this very Instant ... What signifies whether a Man beget his Child or not? How ridiculous is the Act it self, said the great emperor Antoninus! I now look upon myself as a Roman citizen; it is better that the Father should adopt the Child than that the Wife should adopt the Father. (261)

The action of the play, up to the discovery that Fossile's marriage is invalid, has consisted chiefly of the doctor's hair's-breadth escapes from becoming a cuckold. The last thing the audience has anticipated is that he will accept the most dreaded consequence of cuckoldom, that of bringing up another man's child. But there is a zany plausibility in Fossile's growing conviction that he has won, not lost. The experience of being married (supposedly) has convinced Fossile that to acquire a son without the inconvenience of a wife is a rare privilege. (Gay may be indebted here to the *Poenulus* of Plautus, where an old man adopts a child because he wants an heir but hates women.) The living creature which he takes into his home contrasts pleasingly with the stuffed alligators and other dead things that crowd his study and have hitherto filled his life. Gay in his way, like Locke in his, has offered a striking refutation of assumptions about the supreme importance of begetting.

In Augustan comic literature some of the old comic connotations of childhood and paternity do, however, persist. For example, it is still chiefly the older and more simple-minded characters who prize children: their tenderness toward infants marks them as lovable, but also as somewhat soft in the head. There is a certain vulnerable simplicity not only about Fossile in *Three Hours After Marriage* but even about Squire Allworthy in *Tom Jones* (1749), with his unjustified confidence that the village community will not identify him as father of the foundling discovered in his bed (Fielding 1974, 1:58). Perhaps the ultimate in amiable folly is the protagonist of Goldsmith's *Vicar of Wakefield* (1766), who takes literally Jeremy Taylor's injunction to regard offspring as a form of wealth:

> When I stood in the midst of the little circle, which promised to be the supports of my declining age, I could not avoid repeating the famous story of Count Abensberg, who, in Henry II's progress through Germany, while other courtiers came with their treasures, brought his thirty-two children, and presented them to his sovereign as the most valuable offering he had to bestow. In this manner, though I had but six, I considered them as a very valuable present to my country. (1966, 4.19–20)

The Vicar's optimism about his children is not justified in terms of the developing action of the book: his daughters will prove hard to marry and his sons hard to employ. In this respect *The Vicar of Wakefield* is typical. The eighteenth-century novel inherits from comic drama a consciousness that children may be a liability rather than an asset, but at the same time it becomes steadily more hospitable toward parental fondness. It also extends increasing tolerance and affection toward the lovable, unworldly, fostering simpleton.

But this is to anticipate. For the moment we must turn back to the beginning of the eighteenth century to consider two historical tendencies which emerge at this time and which are clearly echoed in contemporary comedy: a rise in the population of England after a period of decline—including a rise in the *rate* of bastardy, beyond the rise in the general birthrate—and the nation's entry into a European war which required large-scale recruitment for the army and navy (Stone 1977, 629–30, 637–38; Wrigley 1966, 83). In *All Mistaken,* which appeared as early as 1665, the rake Philidor is already to be found jokingly remarking that the chatter of women and the yowling of children daunt him more than the tumult of battle (Howard 1967, 12). This semic move gives war and death a new connotation: they come to be seen as the roisterer's ultimate refuge from the cares of family life. To enlist in the armed forces, or take to the road as a highwayman, is to embrace an exhilarating, though probably brief existence, free from the responsibilities of the conventional father and husband. (For enlistment as a common form of desertion in real life, see Stone 1990, 142.) It is the logical conclusion of the rake's vital, swashbuckling, but ultimately immature approach to existence.

Howard's activation of this motif in *All Mistaken* was premature: it enjoyed no great vogue in the 1660s because the idea it enshrined was insufficiently topical. But in the years following the Battle of Blenheim it entered comic drama once more, holding the stage until at least the time of *The Beggar's Opera* (1728). There the highwayman Macheath, confronted in the last scene with a choice between death by hanging and the demands of a rabble of wives and children, unhesitatingly opts for execution. Only in the sentimental ending imposed by the audience is the swaggering fellow reprieved; even then he escapes his unwanted obligations by casually distributing wives and babies to the other men on stage. ("I hope," he cries gallantly to the women, "you will give me leave to present a Partner to each of you"—Gay 1983, 2:63–64.) As usual the energy and freebooterism of the comic hero are aligned not only with the ability to beget children but with the impulse to escape from responsibility for them once they have been begotten. In the last resort, the swaggerer prefers death to parenthood and marriage.

It is in Farquhar's *Recruiting Officer* (1706) that this theme, with its many resonances and implications, is first thoroughly explored. In the second act Sergeant Kite, in an attempt to encourage more men to enlist, leads a chorus in praise of army service as a means of escape from family life:

> We all shall lead more happy Lives,
> By getting rid of Brats and Wives,

> That scold and brawl both Night and Day,
> Over the Hills and far away.
>
> (1988, 2:59)

What is, perhaps, most sinister about this is its suggestion of a direct causal relationship between recruiting and careless procreation: the army finds its task of recruiting easier because the procreators wish to escape from their children and wives. Later it will be noted that procreation contributes to recruiting in another way. Justice Balance, hearing that Captain Plume has begotten an illegitimate child, comments half-admiringly on the young man's fertility and its possible consequences in swelling the ranks of the army: "If all Officers took the same Method of Recruiting with this Gentleman, they might come in time to be Fathers as well as Captains of their companies" (73n). Procreators will often join the army to escape the tedium of family life; their sons, when they grow to manhood, may do so because they have nowhere else to go.

These disturbing associations between love and procreation on the one hand and war and killing on the other are not casual or accidental: they pervade Farquhar's play. Even in the closing lines, when Plume is settling down to marriage with the heiress Silvia Balance, he is permitted by the dramatist to utter words like these:

> With some Regret I quit the active Field,
> Where Glory full reward for Life does yield;
> But the Recruiting Trade with all its train,
> Of lasting Plague, Fatigue, and endless Pain,
> I gladly quit, with my fair Spouse to stay,
> And raise Recruits the Matrimonial way.
>
> (122)

If any of this is festive, celebratory, it is so in an uneasy and paradoxical way. The rogue male's comic qualities—vigor, sexual energy, freebooterism—fuel the fires of war. On the one hand, the rambunctious comic character may get tired of the family he has spawned and decide to desert it for a life of campaigning. On the other hand, he who decides to stay at home will in practice be "raising recruits the matrimonial way." (For the wide currency in the social world of the notion of children as cannon-fodder, see Stone 1990, 126.) Some of Plume and Silvia's sons will presumably enter the army and risk death as their father did, or at best be subjected to the "lasting Plague,

Fatigue, and endless Pain" of drumming up recruits. Such a conclusion problematizes the celebratory comic ending. It forces the audience to look—almost in spite of itself—beyond the fifth-act marriage to its likely consequences in the next generation.

If Plume partly exemplifies the old dismissive attitude toward children, the positive approach to them is manifested in Silvia, the woman he loves and eventually marries. When he returns to Shrewsbury, Plume learns that his "old Friend Molly at the Castle," a woman of low degree, has recently borne him a child (43). He sends Sergeant Kite to look after Molly, but Kite finds she has been "better comforted before": Silvia has sent her ten guineas to buy baby clothes (47). Silvia knows the baby is Plume's, and twits him on it (54). But Farquhar endows this well-born young woman with the generosity of mind to pity the poor mother and her child: Molly is, after all, a kind of surrogate or scapegoat for Silvia herself. The chaste and clever heroine's concern for the mistress and/or child of the rake becomes, indeed, almost as much of a stock motif as the rake's own cavalier attitude toward them. In Polwhele's *The Frolics*, Clarabell offers to "carry, for the father's sake" one of the bastard children Rightwit has begotten (Polwhele 1967, 115); in *Tom Jones* Sophia Western will take a compassionate interest in Tom's mistress Molly Seagrim (Fielding 1974, 1:177).

In Farquhar's play, Plume's attitude toward the child is not entirely uncaring. When Silvia accuses him of paternity he tells the expected lie: "'Twas none of mine ... The poor Creature [Molly] gave out that I was Father, in hopes that my Friends might support her in case of Necessity" (54). But the scapegrace does take steps—skimpy and improvised, it is true, but the best he can manage—to provide for the child. "Set the Mother down in your List [of wives]," he tells the sergeant, "and the Boy in mine [of recruits]; enter him a Granadeer by the name of Francis Kite, absent upon Furlow—I'll allow you a Man's Pay for his Subsistence" (43). The play establishes that Plume's income as a junior officer is meager: he cannot afford to be lavish, but he does have the grace to cheat the government on the baby's behalf.

A further dimension to the play's theme of procreation as a source of warriors is added by the scene where Plume's recruits are reviewed by the Shrewsbury magistrates to decide whether they have been legally conscripted. The magistrates bend the rules so as to get men they consider undesirable into the army and out of the district: the victims include a notorious poacher who destroys the landowners' game and fills the parish with children. One magistrate protests against the harsh decision, while the poacher's wife boldly questions the magistrates' motives for wanting her husband sent away:

> *Justice Scruple:* But his Wife and Children, Mr. *Ballance!*
> *Wife:* Ay, ay, that's the Reason you wou'd send him away—You know I have a Child every Year, and you're afraid they should come upon the Parish at last. (112)

It is sobering to note that at this point Plume—himself an impulsive populator and marksman who has unwillingly ended up in the army—does not support the victims, but simply eggs the severer magistrates on:

> *Captain Plume:* Look'e there, Gentlemen, the honest Woman has spoke it at once, the Parish had better maintain five Children this Year than six or seven the next; that Fellow upon his high Feeding [i.e. the game he poaches on gentlemen's estates] may get you two or three Beggars at a Birth.
> *Wife:* Look'e, Mr. Captain, the Parish shall get nothing by sending him away, for I won't lose my Teeming Time if there be a Man left in the Parish.
> *Justice Balance:* Send that Woman to the House of Correction. (112)

It is impossible not to admire the wife's retort: for a moment anarchic fertility seems to be getting the better of the argument against the representatives of established order. So when Plume and Balance show an uncharacteristic lack of humor and compassion, taking sides against the woman, it is hard not to see the magistrates and the recruiting system as enemies of exuberant fertility. The solitary protest of Scruple against the injustice to the conscripted man's wife and children is simply ignored.

In 1715, nine years after *The Recruiting Officer,* came Gay's tragi-comi-pastoral farce *The What D'Ye Call It,* which was deeply influenced by Farquhar's play. But where Farquhar had sought a balance between careless and compassionate attitudes Gay, under the guise of farce, launches an outright social criticism. The play's most outrageously fantastic, yet most chillingly topical, scene is one in which callous country magistrates are visited by the ghosts of local people whose deaths they have brought about, including those of an unborn child and its mother. Prominent among the causes of death are disciplinary whippings of pregnant single girls:

A Ghost of an Embryo rises

Fourth Ghost: [To the Justices] I was begot before my Mother married,
Who whipt by you, of me poor Child miscarried.

A Woman's Ghost rises

Fifth Ghost: Its Mother I, whom you whipt black and blue;
Both owe our Deaths to you, to you, to you. (1984, 1:189)

In his preface, Gay engages in a mock-serious discussion about the propriety of bringing an embryo's ghost onto the stage. But this affectation of frivolity is part of a conscious strategy, used not only in the critical apparatus but in the script, to generate uncertainty of response in the audience or reader: the farcical tone of the piece and the mock-solemn discussion of aesthetic issues like *vraisemblance* in the preface tend to distract us momentarily from the horror of the social facts.

For social facts they were: the whippings, miscarriages, and deaths in childbirth alluded to by the ghosts are inscribed in the court and parish records cited by Dorothy Marshall and Lawrence Stone. "In the Hertford quarter sessions books," writes Marshall, "are many cases of women being moved from one parish to another when they were so near their confinement that the removal caused their death" (1969, 212). Richer urban parishes were only slightly more humane than their poorer counterparts in the country. "The rate books of Chelsea," Ruth Perry records, "are filled with records of disbursements to pay for one night's firing for some poor woman or another, just delivered of a child or just about to be, and the coach fare to ship her off to some other parish in the morning" (1986, 144; cf. Hill 1989, 136–38).

Gay's little farce disturbs its reader with the suggestion that the lusty poor cannot win. A poor woman who bears illegitimate children is treated as a criminal; but love and care lavished on legitimate ones becomes a mockery when the offspring are pressed into the army as soon as they grow old enough to fight:

Grandmother: Must Grandson Filbert to the Wars be pressed?
Alack! I knew him when he suck'd the Breast,
Taught him his Catechism, the Fescue held,
And join'd his Letters, when the Bantling Spell'd.

His loving Mother left him to my Care.
Fine Child, as like his Dad as he could stare!

(184)

Throughout *The What D'Ye Call It,* associative links are built up between poverty, love, incontinence, prolific breeding, and being sent to the wars. One peasant, Peascod, who is about to be shot for desertion, has his illegitimate daughter Joyce brought before him; on seeing her, he exclaims:

> Oh! My Sins of Youth!
> Why on the Haycock didst thou tempt me, Ruth?

(194)

We don't discover whether Peascod was originally pressed into the army because of his propensity for begetting bastards (though he seems to see some causal connection between being shot as a deserter and giving way to lust). But this is shown to be the case with the other victim of authority, Filbert, who has been falsely accused of getting Dorcas with child. The justices give Filbert the choice of marrying her or serving in the army abroad. The sergeant chips in with the old cliché that marriage is the real servitude, compared to which soldiering is freedom:

> Zooks! never wed, 'tis safer much to roam;
> For what is War abroad to War at home?
> Who wou'd not sooner bravely risque his Life,
> For what's a Cannon to a scolding Wife?

(183)

But this swaggering, cynical pose, which would sound just right in a Restoration comedy or even in *The Beggar's Opera,* fails to command assent in the world of *The What D'Ye Call It.* The play's pastoral setting of village, family, neighbors, and country pursuits is in some ways a little Eden: the punishment for sin is to be sent away to the army, to the fallen world of rootlessness, lovelessness, and death. And those most likely to be punished in this way are those with the greatest propensity for breeding illegitimate children, or more legitimate ones than they can well support.

Many, perhaps most, social laws and sanctions are aimed at protecting and fostering family life. But in the world of *The What D'Ye Call It,* as in the real world of eighteenth-century England, charges are fabricated and rules bent in order to expel compulsive breeders from the community. Likewise the law relating to orphans is administered in such a way as to discourage the poor from thinking that the infants they spawn will be brought up in comfort at the public expense. When Peascod, one of the rural laborers, tells his daughter that the parish will be bound to maintain her after his death, she reminds him that parish children work long hours, and even Peascod himself admits that they are better taught than fed. Most of what the children earn by their labors goes to maintain the churchwardens, as well as the schoolmistress and her idle husband, in relative luxury (195). Here again there is a clear reference to actual social conditions. According to a modern historian, the organizers of charity schools "soon saw that it paid them to farm out the work of the children to the master and mistress, allowing them to pocket all the profit they could make after paying expenses. This tempted the masters and mistresses to press the children to work more than was good for them" (Rodgers 1949, 5). In content the criticism is identical to the one which is advanced, under cover of farce and ludicrous comedy, in *The What D'Ye Call It.*

In Restoration comedy, a character who showed carelessness or even callousness toward offspring would not necessarily lose the sympathy of the audience. In the new cultural climate of the early eighteenth century that is no longer the case. Dislike of children, or even childlessness, come to be seen as marks of frigidity. In Durfey's *The Campaigners*, it is the ugly and mulish characters who have no children; temperamental reluctance to take on parental responsibilities is associated, not with liveliness, potency, and youth but with sluggishness, barrenness, impotence, and coldness. A character who has married an unattractive woman for her money arouses the audience's derision by admitting in soliloquy that he is "not so capable" of begetting children to inherit a relative's fortune as his wife's "inclinations would prompt"; and the ridicule extends to his wife when he describes her as "so fat, and so incapable of Childing, that an Irishman may as soon [be]get a Bantling out of a Bog." The same man's scheme to acquire a fortune by marrying his niece to a rich husband, instead of by the more natural way of raising a family of children of his own, is typed as "baseness . . . meer frigidity" (1967, 13–14). Suddenly stage comedy, instead of contributing to a revulsion against parenthood in the wider culture, can be seen succumbing to a new cultural pressure, placing a positive valuation on the breeding and raising of children. Nor is this merely a thematic concern. It affects language, tone, connotation, in short the whole semiotic system of the comedies.

In the mainstream eighteenth-century English novel, which retained so many of the themes and patterns of Restoration and Augustan comedy, these tendencies were to become steadily more marked. Yet the old comic, dismissive attitudes still surfaced from time to time. Authors and narrators, though they usually took care to express disapproval of characters who derided or disparaged children and childbearing, still understood and even, at moments, shared the old attitudes. At times even Richardson can laugh in the old comic manner at a woman embarrassed by an inopportune pregnancy. In that most exemplary of novels *Sir Charles Grandison*, we stumble on a passage which, for its comic put-down of the pregnant mother, might have come from a comedy of the 1670s:

> Sir Thomas was grateful to [his daughters' governess] in a way that cost her her reputation. She was obliged, in short, in a little more than a twelvemonth, to quit the country, and to come up to town. She had an indisposition, which kept her from going abroad for a month or two. (1986, 319–20)

It is in the context of a partly outmoded, but still at times irrepressible, comic tradition that such passages in eighteenth-century novels are to be understood.

3

Discourses of Concern

Comedy, though it never quite ignores the positive associations that may attach to children, habitually privileges the freedom and selfhood of the young adult, which the birth and continued existence of children endangers. Yet even comedy moved in the early eighteenth century to explore ways in which the interests of the impulsive seducer might be reconciled with those of his vigorous offspring and to signal to the audience its latent concern for the forces of new life. Polemical prose of the same period and even earlier expresses sympathy for children, and disapproval of promiscuous begetters and conceivers, more strongly. Mr. Wiseman in Bunyan's *The Life and Death of Mr. Badman* (1680) is made to note "how common it is for the bastard-getter and bastard-bearer to consent together to murder their children" (1928, 187). Addison devotes an angry essay to the problem of the orphan in the *Spectator* (23 October 1711): here the figures who appear in comedy as lively, impulsive, charming rakes are transformed into "abandoned Profligates" who "raise up Issue in every Quarter of the Town, and very often for a valuable Consideration father it upon the Church-warden."

Addison's tone, however, is less relentlessly moral than Bunyan's. While transforming the comic scenario, he still avails himself of some of the favorite topoi of wit and metaphor that had pervaded the comedies:

> When a Man once gives himself this Liberty of preying at large, and living upon the Common, he finds so much Game in a populous City, that it is surprising to consider the Numbers which he sometimes Propagates. . . . I have heard of a Rake who was not quite Five and Twenty declare himself the Father of a Seventh Son, and very prudently determine to breed him up a Physician. (1965, 2:203, 295)

The metaphor by which the rake is seen as stalking the common land—the ground lying outside the enclosed park, symbolic of

66

order and civilization—is a commonplace of Restoration comedy; the idea of breeding up a bastard child to a useful profession is anticipated in *All Mistaken* (1.12), where Philidor thinks of making one of his illegitimate children a parson so that he can christen his siblings. But behind Addison's essay lie darker hints. Where *All Mistaken* plays cheerfully with the idea of breeding one child as a parson to save christening fees for the rest, Addison's essay has the rake breeding one son as a physician, presumably to treat the ailments his father may have contracted during his debauched youth.

A letter intended for the *Tatler* paints the same scene in even murkier colors, evoking the complex transactions between pregnant or recently delivered women, informers, parish authorities, and the fathers of bastard children. At this time parishioners were rewarded for betraying the presence in a parish of any pregnant, unmarried woman:

> No sooner does any woman of almost any condition whatever, come to lodge any where about this town, that is but suspected to be with child, but notice is carried, for the sake of five shillings (which is the usual price of such information) to the overseers of the poor, who thereupon immediately come in a body to make an enquiry of, who begot it? when? how? where? mixing such odious lewdnesses with their pretended authority, while the affrighted, fainting, poor creature, half dead with shame, fear, and anger, is at once become their pastime and their prisoner.

The father of a bastard, once his name had been extorted from the woman at a hearing before a "wise unjust justice of the peace," was likely to be subjected to blackmail, a process which usually ended in an unholy bargain. The custom, the writer of the letter alleged, was to

> give in sale with the wretched mother and unborn vagabond, a sum of mony, and to saddle the spitt, (the main foundation of this wicked babel), their dirty phrase for dirtily devouring and guzzling two or three pieces for a supper. This ended, the man goes off clear.... Nothing is more common amongst [the rakes], than brags and boasts, that they have sold a chopping boy or wench, or have been (in human form) at the eating up of their friend Jack's or Dick's child.

The baby itself was subsequently put out to nurse. But this, in the opinion of the writer, almost amounted to a sentence of death:

I think [it] is a kind of negative murder . . . For as the sum usually taken in this affair is seldom more than ten pounds, more wages than is above-mentioned cannot be afforded to be given, for by every child that lives above two years, the parish at their present rate is out of pocket. (Lillie 1725, 46–54)

It will be noticed that this letter, like the Addison essay quoted earlier, shares important features with comedy and prose fiction. The plot involving the rake, his women-folk, and his bastards is itself a staple of comedy. An important innovation in the prose texts is that of foregrounding a first-person narrator, often a woman, who is posited as being directly involved in the events, and who presents them in an unusually vivid and direct way. The letter intended for the *Tatler* purports to be written by "Mary K———," a woman who has personally experienced the "flagrant and mischievous misfortunes" to which pregnant spinsters and single mothers are subjected. There are close parallels in structure and content between this piece and (for example) Aphra Behn's novella "The Black Lady," where parish officers molest a seduced woman who has fled from her country home, seeking the anonymity of London during the last months of her pregnancy (1967, 5:3–10).

In comedy the more threatening possibilities latent in the scenario are distanced by wit and fantasy. The transaction involving the child is typically achieved by an ingenious stratagem rather than by payment, and the plot is handled so as to give the impression that nobody will be permanently hurt. But the letter to the *Tatler* transforms the comic mythos of the rake scheming to rid himself of unwanted children, deliberately exploring its noncomic possibilities. Specifically, the letter hints at the latent hostility of the father toward the child, whose needs he regards as an unfair tax on his own pleasures; it stresses the want, misery, and hardship that await the baby and its mother and the neglect, sometimes giving way to active "furtherance towards death," that they can expect from the parish officers and from the hired nurses, beggar-women, or bawds into whose hands they are delivered. The characters and setting are painted very much as they will be later in Hogarth's prints and paintings, or in realistic novels like *Moll Flanders* and *Roderick Random*.

One consequence of the intertwining of news, novels, and social commentary at this time is that the modern reader must be cautious about accepting any of them as reliable accounts of social praxis, which in any case was itself very diverse (Davis 1983). In any era there will be people who think of themselves as caring and responsible in their treatment of children, and others who profess a cheery insouciance about them. The latter are never wholly exempt from the temptation to shock their respectable critics by telling them horror stories or striking extravagantly misoprogenitive poses; while the former, predisposed as they often are to believe their swashbuckling rivals capable of unspeakable crimes, may accept horror stories too literally. The following story from Bunyan's *The Life and Death of Mr. Badman* is a case in point:

> An ancient man . . . of good credit in our country, had a mother that was a midwife. . . . To this woman's house . . . comes a brave [sc. well-dressed] young gallant, . . . to fetch her to lay [sc. assist in childbirth] a young lady. . . . Away they went till they came at a stately house. . . . [The] old midwife laid the young lady, and a fine sweet babe she had. Now there was made in a room hard by a very great fire; so the gentleman took up the babe, went and drew the coals from the stock, cast the child in . . . and there was an end of that. . . . This story the midwife's son, who was a minister, told me, and also protested that his mother told it him for a truth. (187–88)

This anecdote, for all its strenuous protestations of authenticity, has the mark of a fiction, a contribution to the archetype of the sexually promiscuous rake, devoid of all feeling for the children born of his amors. However, the letter to the *Tatler* seems to belong to a different category. Although strongly colored by indignation and perhaps rhetorical exaggeration, it corresponds reasonably closely with what we know of contemporary procedures from other sources (cf. Gibson 1975, 33–34; McClure 1981, 13–14). The whole question of the relation between discourse and social reality is, of course, a complex one. But it is not one which should be shirked: the perception that the relation between the two is not direct or simple should not be allowed to obscure the fact that a relation exists. Especially important is the consideration that there may be a two-way relation, with discourse and praxis influencing one another. The letter intended for the *Tatler* is clearly intended to influence opinion: so, for that matter, is the "realistic" novel. Both are imaginative constructs, but both are responses to real problems of contemporary life.

The most emotive idea in the texts just examined is that of infanticide. Only a little less threatening is that of the theft of children, which also enters prose fiction at this time. Defoe's *Colonel Jack* alludes in passing to a gang of street boys, orphans themselves, who steal children from settled families and sell them as slaves for the American colonies. One of Colonel Jack's brothers belonged to the gang. He

> us'd to Spirit Peoples Children away, that is snatch them up in the Dark, and stopping their Mouths, carry them to such Houses where they had Rogues, ready to receive them, and so carry them on Board Ships bound to *Virginia,* and sell them. . . . If a little Child got into his Clutches he would stop the Breath of it, instead of stopping its Mouth, and never Trouble his Head with the Childs being almost strangl'd, so he did but keep it from making a Noise. (1965, 11)

Once again, as in the passage from Bunyan, there is an implied invitation to take the tale as documentary, whereas it may in reality partake more of legend or nightmare. It seems a little unlikely that shippers would risk receiving children stolen from rich and influential families when there were plenty of orphans and street children available, especially considering that the latter, accustomed to hard conditions, would be more likely to survive the voyage to the New World. Nevertheless, tales of the theft of children from prosperous families are quite numerous in the first half of the eighteenth century. An impressive example, which I shall not discuss because it involves the kidnapping of a boy in his mid-teens, not of a young child, is the anonymous *Adventures of a Kidnapped Orphan* (1747).

More important for our purposes, however, than the documentary plausibility of the story is the further indication it gives of the emergence of a discourse of concern, informed by outrage at the real or alleged maltreatment of children in contemporary society. The safety of one's children has clearly come, for a certain class of reader at least, to signify the good, secure life in general: the kidnapping of children has become a representative nightmare, a dark threat to the happiness, serenity, and stability of middle-class existence. The two states are strikingly evoked and contrasted in another child kidnapping episode in the first few pages of Defoe's *Captain Singleton* (1720). The young Singleton represents himself as having been at one moment swathed in the luxury and protectiveness of a middle-class household—

> I was a little Boy, of about two Years old, very well dress'd, had a Nursery Maid to tend me, who took me out on a fine Summer's Evening into the Fields towards *Islington*

—and at the next a helpless victim of "one of those sort of People, who, it seems, made it their Business to Spirit away little Children." He is soon "disposed of to a Beggar-Woman that wanted a pretty little Child to set out her Case, and after that to a Gypsey, under whose Government I . . . was continually dragged about . . . from one Part of the Country to another, yet [she] never let me want for any thing" (1972, 1–3).

Another emotive idea which enters polemical prose at this time, still more provocative than kidnapping or even simple infanticide, is cannibalism. In the *Tatler* letter the idea of adults having an interest in a baby's death is reinforced by locutions which evoke this ultimate horror: instead of being thought of as a participant in the banquet, as in Bakhtin's idyllic picture, the child comes to be considered metaphorically as part of the meal. The rakes and parish officers are shown sharing a feast; the feast seals a bargain, one of whose implied conditions is the baby's premature death. The diners even refer jocularly to the dinner as the eating of the child, the implication being that they might as well be eating a baby in reality: as the participants know, it is in all their interests that the child be allowed to die.

The same associative logic is deployed on a larger scale in Swift's *Modest Proposal* (1729), which pretends to offer a solution to the economic problems of Ireland through a project for breeding and selling Irish children for food. The informing idea is the familiar notion of rich people feasting at the expense of the poor, in this case destitute Irish families. Prohibitions against the importation of Irish goods into England help to keep certain Englishmen wealthy, but these same prohibitions virtually condemn Irish children to starvation. The hyperbolical proposition which climaxes the pamphlet is that it would have been no worse, from the children's own point of view, to have served them up for rich men's tables when they were babies than to let them grow up to a life of misery and want:

I desire those Politicians, who dislike my Overture, and may perhaps be so bold to attempt an Answer, that they will first ask the Parents of these Mortals, Whether they would not, at this Day, think it a great Happiness to have been sold for Food at a Year old, in the Manner I prescribe; and thereby have avoided such a perpetual Scene of Misfortunes, as they have since gone through, by . . . the Want of common Sustenance . . . and the most inevitable Prospect of intailing the like, or greater Miseries upon their Breed for ever. (Swift 1955, 117–18)

The grisly notion of cannibalism is used, then, in the *Modest Proposal,* to shame or discredit a governing class which allegedly is almost callous enough to eat babies. It is worth noting that Swift in the *Proposal* was not the first eminent writer to adopt this strategy: Locke likewise had used it in the *First Treatise of Government,* directing his irony not merely at the Tory gentry of his time but at the whole ideology of patriarchy. In ridiculing certain claims of Sir Robert Filmer, which reduced children to items of property to be disposed of by the father, Locke artfully sets up an association between Filmer and a whole series of unnatural crimes:

> Be it then as *Sir Robert* says, that *Anciently,* it was *usual for Men to sell and Castrate their Children.* . . . Let it be, that they exposed them; Add to it, if you please, for this is still greater Power, that they begat them for their Tables to fat and eat them: If this proves a right to do so, we may, by the same Argument, justify Adultery, Incest, and Sodomy. (1967, 6.59.201)

Here Locke does his best to associate arbitrary paternal power with arbitrary political power, linking both with unnatural, oppressive, and inhuman behavior. This coupling was reinforced by succeeding writers throughout the eighteenth century (Fliegelman 1982).

It is perhaps needless to point out that cannibalism, as it appears in Locke, in Swift, and in the *Tatler* letter, is not represented as a real social practice: it is used as an evocative image, a hyperbole, a propaganda device. Locke, for example, is well aware that Filmer has not claimed for parents the right to eat their children; he simply slips cannibalism in mischievously among the suggestions that Filmer has actually made:

> History would have furnish'd our A[uthor] with Instances of this *Absolute Fatherly Power* in its heighth and perfection, and he might have shew'd us in *Peru,* People that begot Children on Purpose to Fatten and Eat them. . . . They spared not their own Children which they had begot on Strangers taken in War: For they made their Captives their Mistresses and choisly nourished the Children they had by them, till about thirteen Years Old they Butcher'd and Eat them. (1967, 200)

The story about the Peruvian warriors and their slave children is one of Locke's own choosing, cited from Garcilaso de la Vega. But a careless reader might come away with the impression that Locke's adversary Filmer ("Our Author") had himself recorded and approved the practice of raising and fattening children for meat. Filmer had indeed referred, without any sign of disapproval, to the practices, "much in use in old times," of "castrating, and making eunuchs" of children and of selling them out of the family (1949, 231). But Locke, it seems, was not satisfied with pointing out this enormity: evidently he felt the need to associate his opponent, not only with the practices of castrating and selling children, but with the ultimate barbarity of eating them. It is this strategy, on a larger scale, that Swift uses in *A Modest Proposal:* indeed, the strategy adopted in the pamphlet may have been suggested to Swift by the passage cited here from Locke. Incidentally, it is clear that Locke, Swift, and the *Tatler* writer all feel they can rely on their readers to dissociate themselves from mistreatment and neglect of children. In a paragraph of the *First Treatise* that stands close to those which we have just quoted, Locke describes the exposure of infant children as "the most shameful Action, and most unnatural Murder, humane Nature is capable of": he seems entirely confident of his readers' assent (6.56.199).

That some groups and individuals in early modern England were marked by real frigidity, and by overt or covert feelings of aggression toward children, is likely enough. But at the same time it is clear that much of the energy behind the polemical writing of the early eighteenth century went toward discrediting these callous and rejecting attitudes. Hostility is directed not only at those who reject or mistreat children but also at those who seek to preserve their own youth and freedom by limiting their own fertility. We have already seen Addison, in an essay dating from 1711, attack abortion and contraception: he was anticipated by the anonymous author of *Marriage Promoted* (1690), who attacks not only these procedures for restricting births but also the tendency he detected among contemporary youth to postpone or avoid marriage.

While the chief concern of this writer was the probable consequence of a decline in Britain's population, which he mistakenly predicted, he also expresses some fondness for children for their own sakes, commending "the Indians of America" as the "fondest People (perhaps in the World) of Children." Those whom he sees as his chief adversaries are "the Men of Quality and the Rich" in his own country, "who partly out of Debauch'd Principle; and partly out of a Covetous Humour forbear to marry" (*Marriage Promoted* 1984, 19, 28). Defoe, in his tract *Conjugal*

Lewdness (1727), likewise attacked fashionable married couples who announced their intention of remaining childless, and of using "means physical or diabolical" to prevent conception. In the chapter where these words appear as part of the heading, we encounter a young wife who professes "an Aversion to the very Thoughts of Children" and a man who affects to feel "such an Aversion to Children in the House" on account of their "Noise and Impertinencies" that he cannot "bear the Thoughts of them" (1967, 137, 129).

Like the diatribe against baby-traders in the letter intended for the *Tatler,* Defoe's polemic against refusers of issue clearly had some basis in social reality. A recent survey of early modern writings on fertility reveals much advice on means of preventing or aborting pregnancies, though it also shows an equally large body of work giving counsel on how to induce conception (McLaren 1984). There are moments when early modern writing on children and childbirth tempts us to see Britain as divided at that period into two nations, the child-lovers and the child-haters. (In mundane demographic terms, of course, the populators were winning: whatever the case may have been in a few wealthy families, the figures recovered by historians [e.g., Wrigley 1966] strongly suggest a rise, rather than fall, in the overall birth rate at the time.)

Parallel to characterizations of the child-hater as mean and frigid runs a series of rhapsodies on parenthood and fostering as marks of humanity and goodness. Tom Brown, in the preface to his translation of Gaya's *Marriage Ceremonies,* writes lyrically:

> I dare appeal to any good Man that ever was in [the married] State, if he thought it not a sweetning of his daily Labour to bring home a Loaf to his poor Family, and share it amongst 'em. The very Reflection that it was to maintain his Wife and little Babes, made him think the Sun and the Rain less intollerable; . . . and no Fatigues of the Day can so much dispirit him, but he will play with his Children when he comes home at Night.

"The secret Joys that Parents have in the Health and Well-doing of their Children," Brown further opines, "are impossible to be exprest, and can be comprehended only by them that have Children." He goes on to reprove those whose "Pride . . . tramples upon natural Affection" and who "show little or no concern" for their offspring (1704, A2v–3r).

It is notable that several of the writers mentioned in the preceding paragraphs single out for praise the poor, who care for their children despite the extra burden imposed by a family, at the expense of the rich, who avoid parenthood though they are better able to afford it. Occasionally this impression is confirmed by pronouncements from actual members of the stigmatized group, as in the following passage from the *Gentleman's Magazine* for 1732:

> The Common people generally express more Fondness for their Children than persons of Rank and Distinction; the good Sense of the latter prevents their Affection from being troublesome, whereas the other, thro' want of Consideration, are continually plaguing Company with a Detail of the Beauty, Wit, and Spirit of the Child, and are affronted, if you are not as much delighted with its Impertinencies as they are. In Consequence of this Fondness they indulge their Children in all their Follies and Extravagant Humours. (Quoted in Marcus 1978, 33)

A writer can hardly be blamed for criticizing the antics of spoiled children. But there is also a less attractive impulse behind the paragraph, one that seeks to engage the reader on the side of frigidity rather than warmth. The passage is reminiscent of those moments in Restoration comedy when citizens are laughed at for their supposedly excessive and public demonstrations of affection for their wives: it ridicules excessive warmth between family members as ill-bred. More specifically, it represents indulgence to children and the practice of letting them intrude on visiting adults from outside the family as characteristic of an inferior social group. A passage like this, which actually sets up aristocratic frigidity toward children as exemplary, should warn us not to place too low an estimate on the incidence of such attitudes in real society. The child-haters really existed, and sometimes gave public expression to their views.

Steele's *Guardian* essay of 2 September 1713 (no. 150) takes the opposite approach. The paper is a piece of propaganda in favor of children; but this time, instead of chiding the more prosperous classes for their indifference or hostility toward the very young, the writer seeks to offer them an alluring picture of family life to help overcome their hostility. The essay describes a visit paid by the Guardian, Nestor Ironside, to Eliza, a well-off, middle-class, married woman who has several children but is still "in the perfect Bloom of Beauty." (Point number one: a woman can be beautiful and fashionable even though she is a wife and a caring mother.) As the Guardian enters, Eliza says with a blush, "Mr. IRONSIDE, though you are an old Batchelor, you must not laugh at my Tenderness to my Children." (Point number two: people who congratulate themselves on avoiding the snare of marriage are wrong to jeer at fond scenes involving toddlers.) The Guardian protests that, on the contrary, Eliza's "Matronlike Behaviour" gives him "infinite Satisfaction": he himself takes pleasure in playing with children and is "seldom uprovided of Plumms or Marbles, to make [his] Court to such entertaining Companions." (Point number three: a parent, or even an old bachelor, can be proud of a fondness for young children, and need not be ashamed to be seen playing with them.) Inevitably, perhaps, the essay sentimentalizes children: it is full of expressions like "pretty Trifler," "pretty Prattlers," and "smiling Boy." But on the positive side it resolutely rejects the comic put-down: it moves closer to what Bakhtin sees as the atmosphere of the idyll, though of course Steele's idyll is of a distinctly bourgeois kind. In this *Guardian* essay children have become a source of joy and celebration, not of worry or despair (Steele et al. 1982, 490–93).

The interpenetration of social comment and documentary with imaginative and polemical responses takes a different form in another of Steele's pieces, the *Spectator* essay for 12 December 1711 (no. 246). This paper is devoted to breast-feeding, a controversial subject throughout the century. Steele inveighs against putting babies out to wet-nurses and pleads for suckling by the natural mothers. Part of his argument is rational and practical: the babies will suffer in their moral or physical health if they are suckled by disreputable or badly dieted nurses. But Steele also relies heavily on the plea that breast-feeding strengthens the bonds of affection between mother and baby, and as his argument proceeds he resorts to ever more emotive terms. "It seems to me very unnatural," he complains, "that a Woman that has fed a Child as part of her self for nine Months, should have no Desire to nurse it farther, when brought to Light and before her Eyes, and when by its Cry it implores her Assistance and the Office of a Mother." It seems to me that Ruth Perry, in her important article "Colonizing the Breast," underestimates Steele's sensitivity to "the naturalness of tender maternal feelings, the advantages of establishing a deep and primal bond between mother and child" (1991, 220–21). Indeed in the essay by Steele from which I have just quoted, the high value Steele places on the sensual and bodily aspect of maternal love is undeniable.

The eighteenth century is often represented today as having inherited, and suffered from, the Cartesian division between mind and body. Thus Dorothy Van Ghent, in her seminal book on the English novel, detects in Defoe's Moll Flanders the sad irony of a female protagonist who in many ways is a "lusty, full-bodied, lively sensed creature," yet has had to assign a drastically diminished importance to her sensual life (1959, 35). It was, of course, writers like Defoe, Steele, and Richardson—liberal, bourgeois writers—who perceived this danger most clearly at the time and who campaigned most strongly for the reintegration of the sensual life into the value system of their culture. One problem which they did not solve, of course, was that of the woman who wanted to find some other use for her life besides that of raising children: this figure, generally shown as a "learned lady," was treated with suspicion (Harris 1979). But the claims of those women who did feel a strong need for sensual fulfillment through motherhood were voiced powerfully in both the periodical essay and the novel.

In exhorting mothers to suckle their own children, Steele may have been influenced not only by Locke, who stressed the physical bond between mother and child and used it to prove that mothers had as much right and interest in their children as fathers (1967, 198), but also by the failure of his own baby son to thrive in the care of a wet-nurse. The boy was never healthy—Steele described him in one letter as a "peevish chit"—and finally died at the age of six in 1716 (Connely 1937, 202–3, 302). At the same time as he asserts that women should feel a natural urge to suckle their children, Steele shows his awareness that many feel no such impulse: following Locke, he notes that "the Generation of the Infant is the Effect of Desire," whereas "the Care of it argues Virtue and Choice." Just as a male rake may wish to dispose of his bastard child at the smallest possible expense, without worrying too much about its prospects of survival, so a mother may in practice prefer to

> turn off her innocent, tender, and helpless Infant, and give it up to a Woman that is (ten thousand to one) . . . neither sound in Mind nor Body, that has neither Honour nor Reputation, neither Love nor Pity for the poor Babe, but more Regard for the Money than for the whole Child. (*Spectator*, 12 December 1711)

We may doubt, of course, whether wet-or dry-nurses were generally as physically unhealthy and morally depraved as Steele

and others make out: certainly they were not always so represented in contemporary texts. As we have seen, in Durfey's *The
Campaigners* the wet-nurse behaves with almost ridiculous
fondness toward the child; while at the beginning of Defoe's
Family Instructor, that strange conduct book which its author
once thought of framing as a "religious play" but which in many
parts reads like a novel, it is hinted that the dry-nurse has
taken more trouble than the parents over the little boy's early
religious instruction (1973, 1:6). But those who wished to argue
that mothers should suckle their own babies and directly super-
vise their older children often found it advantageous to show
the average wet-nurse as drunken and the average dry-nurse
as irresponsible. While it is likely enough that some were so, it
is plain that the move to represent nurses in general in this
way was predetermined by the nature of the case which the
writer was seeking to make.

Early eighteenth-century periodical essays and related works
such as *The Family Instructor*, which likewise deploy fictional
forms for the exploration of social issues, often show themselves
to be in conscious reaction against the ethos of the still-
influential form of stage comedy and against what their authors
see as the spread of that ethos into everyday life. Sometimes,
as in Steele's *Tatler* review (16 April 1709) of a performance of
The Country Wife, the writer will present a well-loved comedy
as a "very pleasant and instructive Satyr" on "the Vices of the
Town" (Steele 1987, 1:30–31). At other times, however, an attack may be mounted on the whole ethos of Restoration comedy,
as in the same author's well-known *Spectator* piece for 15 May
1711, where the arch-rake Dorimant from Etherege's *The Man
of Mode* is described as "a direct Knave in his Designs, and a
Clown in his Language" instead of the fine gentleman he has
generally been taken for. An essayist who approaches a play in
this way is taking it (rightly or wrongly) as a rival branch of
conduct-literature, one whose spell over audiences is strong and,
if baneful, must be broken (cf. Fletcher 1934). In reaction
against the ethos of the comedies, the *Tatler, Guardian,* and
Spectator essays, as well as those from Defoe's *Review,* offer a
family-oriented discourse in which childhood and domesticity,
ridiculed in the comedies, appear in a more favorable light. But
the contrast between comic and noncomic texts is far from absolute. Both bring into play the same situations and the same
choices, though each gives the material a different slant. Neither group, moreover, fails to allow for contradictory or mixed

responses. There are traces of concern and even guilt in the mainly irresponsible discourse of comedy, and traces of dismissive humor in the ostentatiously moral periodical essays. The celebrated promise in *The Spectator*'s tenth number (12 March 1711) to "enliven Morality with Wit, and to temper Wit with Morality" was not given in vain. Here again, as in the humane comedies of Durfey or Farquhar, there is a noticeable fear of leaving irreverent wit too far behind.

A less attractive feature of the periodical essays is that their generally sympathetic approach to children is contaminated by feelings of self-interest, with the child presented as potential rewarder of the family, town, and nation that fostered it. A common manifestation of this is the notion of procreation as a source of future warriors, potential contributors to the greatness of the British nation (Perry 1991, 206–8). We have already noticed the breezy, but always slightly uncomfortable, association between breeding and recruiting in comedies such as *All Mistaken, The Recruiting Officer,* and *The What D'Ye Call It;* but the same devil-may-care comic note is also struck in works explicitly aimed at influencing social thinking and social praxis. The notorious marriage-broking parson Alexander Keith, in his attack on Lord Hardwicke's Marriage Act of 1753, claimed that the hasty, impulsive marriages permitted under the old law were good for England. Moll and Dick would go together to the fair: by midnight they would be married and in each other's arms, "[be]getting a soldier or seaman for the service of their king and country" (1753, 18; cf. Boucé 1982, 29). Keith, of course, had a vested interest in representing hasty marriages as an asset to the nation: he had made his living from celebrating them until Hardwicke's act put them outside the law (Howard 1964, 1:443–44). But he clearly felt that others would understand and approve the point he was making about impulsive marriages as a source of needed population, and his confidence was probably justified. The argument he used seems to have commended itself at times even to Henry Fielding, a more humane and disinterested commentator, who invoked the connection between recruiting and breeding both in comic fictions and in serious pamphlets on social issues.

Although in his teenage years he once referred to his baby brother as a "shitten brat" (Battestin 1989, 23), Fielding as a grown man liked children. In his *Covent Garden Journal* (2 June 1752) he distinguished "two glorious Benefactions, I mean that to the Use of Foundling Infants, and that for the Accommodation

of poor Women in their Lying-in" (1988[a], 251) from a host of
rival charities which were not worth supporting, and elsewhere
in his writings he showed concern both for the born and for
the unborn child. But even as he pleads for better treatment
of children, Fielding sometimes finds himself resorting to the
argument that today's healthy infant is the lusty serviceman of
fifteen years hence:

> What must become of the Infant who is conceived in *Gin?* with the
> poisonous Distillations of which it is nourished both in the Womb
> and at the Breast. Are these wretched Infants (if such can be sup-
> posed capable of arriving at the Age of Maturity) to become our
> future Sailors, and our future Grenadiers? (1988[b], 90)

Such rhetoric may recall to us Simone de Beauvoir's analysis
of attitudes toward children still prevalent in the twentieth century: "It must be said," she writes, "that the men with the most
scrupulous respect for embryonic life are also those who are
most zealous when it comes to condemning adults to death in
war" (1972, 468). It is especially disturbing to find Fielding, in
his pamphlet on the increase of robbers, suggesting that babies
must be nourished well now if they are to fight well later, for
in expressing this view he is incongruously (and probably unconsciously) echoing a speech which in *Tom Jones* he attributes
to the bluff, insensitive Squire Western. After a breach of the
peace provoked by one of Tom's tumbles with Molly Seagrim,
Parson Thwackum tells the Squire that he should rid the parish
of trollops. Western retorts: "I would as soon rid the Country of
Foxes. . . . I think we ought to encourage the recruiting those
Numbers which we are every Day losing in the War"
(1:5.12.267). It is a time-honored maxim: what war ravages,
procreation must replace. The further implication that the new
breed will die in its turn on new battlefields is seldom directly
expressed but can hardly fail to be understood.

An equally revealing instance of this topos is Addison's essay
in the 11 July 1713 *Guardian* on the peace celebrations of that
year, in which charity-children took part:

> For my Part, I can scarce forbear looking on the astonishing Victo-
> ries our Arms have been crowned with to be in some Measure the
> Blessings returned upon that National Charity which has been so
> Conspicuous of late, and that the great Successes of the last War,
> for which we lately offered up our Thanks, were in some Measure

occasioned by the several Objects which then stood before us. (Steele et al. 1982, 366)

Addison follows this up by remarking that "there is scarce an Assizes where some unhappy Wretch is not Executed for the Murder of a Child," and suggests that "the Guilt is equal, tho' the Punishment is not so" in the case of those "who by Unnatural Practices do in some Measure defeat the Intentions of Providence, and destroy their Conceptions even before they see the Light." He does not quite say that children saved from these fates, and charitably supported by the nation, should pay their debt by joining the army when they grow up, but he does not stop far short of saying so.

A similar sense of enlightened self-interest seeps into other writings about the charity school movement. Peter Coveney aptly quotes a sermon of 1706 which complained that "the greatest disorders in any neighborhood do most commonly proceed from the folly of children." Without charity schools, the preacher warns, "the poor, ragged children would swarm like locusts on our streets" (quoted in Coveney 1957, 28). (The opening sequences of Defoe's *Colonel Jack* consider the same situation from the street-boy's point of view.) Eighteenth-century rhapsodies on charity children are more often covert hymns to social order than appreciations of childish vitality and spontaneity: in their emphasis on decency and conformity they exemplify those attitudes which later provoked the "Holy Thursday" poems of Blake. But there are important exceptions, one of the most striking being, astonishingly enough, the *Guardian* for 11 July 1713, whose opening we have already quoted. At first, as we have seen, Addison's essay adopts a serious and ostentatiously conformist tone, inviting its readers to infer a causal link between charity to poor children and success in battle. Soon, however, a remarkable transformation comes over the essay. The writer turns away from his praises of British victories and from invectives against abortion, infanticide, and contraception, and ends with a suggestion designed (it almost seems) to let the impulsive begetters and conceivers off scot free. In Europe, he points out, there are hospitals where parents can leave children they cannot keep. Could not England benefit from a similar institution?

It often happens that the Parent leaves a Note for the Maintenance and Education of the Child, or takes it out after it has been some

Years in the Hospital. Nay, it has been known that the Father has afterwards owned the young Foundling for his Son, or left his Estate to him. . . . Many are by this means preserved, and do signal Services to their Country, who without such a Provision might have perished as Abortives, or have come to an untimely End, and perhaps have brought upon their guilty Parents the like Destruction. (Steele et al 1982, 367)

While there is still a hint that some of the children will be expected to pay for their upbringing with "signal services to their country," there is also another note in this part of the essay which we may characterize as redemptive rather than retributive, comic rather than serious. It predominates in the passage where Addison describes the arrangements in continental hospitals for the reception of foundlings:

In the Walls of these Hospitals are placed Machines, in the Shape of large Lanthorns, with a little Door in the side of them turned towards the Street, and a Bell hanging by them. The Child is deposited in this Lanthorn . . . [Later] the proper Officer comes and receives it without making further Enquiries. The Parent or her Friend, who lays the Child there, generally leaves a Note with it, declaring whether it be yet Christned, the Name it should be called by, the particular Marks upon it, and the like. (Steele et al. 1982, 367)

Modern research (Fildes 1988, 150) confirms the accuracy of the representation.

It is impossible to ignore the swift plunge of Addison's overtly didactic essay into the world of comedy. Not only is there a powerful emphasis on forgiveness and redemption rather than punishment: there is also an obvious delight in the aleatory. The skeletal plot envisaged by Addison is close to one frequently found in Roman comedy or, for that matter, in English comic novels as they were to develop shortly after Addison's death. In improvident youth parents lose or desert a child. Subsequently, when they are better able to aid and foster it, it is miraculously restored, perhaps to achieve distinction in later life. The device whereby a machine in the shape of a lantern spirits the baby away until the parents are ready to claim it seems designed to put in train this typically comic process. It is amusing to see the upright Addison, normally so preoccupied with socially responsible behavior, giving his blessing to this happy-go-lucky scheme.

Evidently, then, essayists such as Addison and Steele, as well as overtly comic writers such as Farquhar and Gay, succeed best in their handling of childhood and parenthood when they achieve a blend of comedic and concerned responses. A similarly satisfactory balance is achieved by the journalist Ned Ward in his account of a night-patrol undertaken in a London parish. The watchmen hear a noise which sounds like the howling of cats. But

> by the Help of a Watchman's Lanthorn, who met us in the Passage, we discover'd a Hand-Basket from whence we conceiv'd proceeded this ingrateful Discord. *Hey day*, says the Watchman, *What, in the Name of the Stars, have we got Here? The unhappy Fruits of Some-Bodies Labours I'll warrant you, who had rather get ten Bastards than Provide for one.* He opens the Wicker Hammock, and finds a little lump of Mortality crying out to the whole Parish to lend him their assistance.

The child has a rhyme pinned on his breast explaining that the father was a sailor and the mother a whore and appealing to those who find the child to have him cared for:

> Have Mercy upon me I Pray,
> And carry me out of the Weather;
> For all that my *Mother* can say,
> The *Parish* must be my *Father.*

The watchmen all laugh at this. Their leader pronounces judgment:

> *I'll warrant 'tis some poor Poets Bastard, Prithee take it up and lets carry it to the Watch-house fire. Who knows, but, by the Grace of Providence, the Babe may come to be a second Ben Jonson? Prithee, Jeffrey, put the Lappit of thy Coat over it, I'll warrant 'tis so cold it can scarce feel whether 'tis a Boy or a Girl.* Away trooped his Dark Majesty, with his Feeble Band of Crippled Parish Pensioners, to their Nocturnal Rendez-vouz, all tick'l'd with the Jest, and as Merry over their hopeful Foundling, as the *Egyptian* queen over her young Prophet in the Rushes. (Ward 1954, 2:9–10)

What is, perhaps, most significant about Ward's story is the range of responses it brings into play. On the one hand the watchmen show a hearty benevolence toward the baby as a representative of new life. For them the discovery of the infant, the contingent result of someone's "labors," is a joke, but not an especially sour joke. They seem to feel some disapproval of people who "would rather get ten bastards than provide for one," but this is by no means their dominant reaction. Quite soon, indeed, the men find themselves entertaining proprietary feelings about the child, which they like to think of as "their" hopeful foundling. Bastards, according to their folk belief, are often more vigorous and talented than other children: the baby which has been left at the mercy of fortune may become a prophet or a poet, a Moses or a Ben Jonson. The watchmen, then, behave rather like the old shepherd who finds and adopts the young Perdita in *The Winter's Tale*. Theirs is a knowing laughter, a cheery tolerance, a guarded affection.

4

Education

The texts discussed in the last chapter address social issues in widely differing ways, mingling comedy, satire and denunciation, entertainment, advice, and polemic in different proportions. The same is true of the texts to which we now turn, those devoted to the education of children. The most important is Locke's *Some Thoughts Concerning Education* (1693). The book is mentioned or cited, usually with approval, by innumerable writers throughout the eighteenth century, including not only professional educators but periodical essayists, novelists, and even writers of comedy. Before Locke's time thinking on education had been dominated by contradictory, yet coexisting, beliefs in childhood innocence and in original sin (Pattison 1978). Neither theory leaves much of a mark on Locke, though he prefers the idea of natural innocence to that of natural corruption, warning parents against "poison[ing] the Fountain" and "corrupt[ing] the Principles of Nature" in children (1968, 139). While admitting that particular children have different natural bents (66.159), Locke emphasizes the child's receptivity to education and insists that its mind is free of innate ideas. These opinions are taken up by the novelists who follow (Gibson 1975, 35).

Locke is distinguished by, among other things, the sharpness of his observation of children of all ages, down to the very youngest. As a tutor at an Oxford college he would naturally have had opportunities to observe young teenagers, since in the seventeenth century it was normal for colleges to admit boys at that age; and he also did some tutoring in private families. As a physician he was in attendance at the birth of the baby who was to become the third Earl of Shaftesbury, while as an educator he influenced this and other members of the family in countless ways (Locke 1968, 44–46). In his writings his concern for born and unborn infants is reflected in his warning to women not to lace themselves tightly during pregnancy, and his recommendation that babies wear loose garments instead of the traditional swaddling clothes which restricted their freedom of movement (123–24; cf. Dewhurst 1954). Locke notes that, though a child has no innate knowledge of the danger of fire, it responds instinctively to the beauty of flickering flames. He also knows that a six-month-old child can distinguish between different adults and may object to being held by a stranger (222). This willingness and ability to notice the details of infants' behavior, and to make distinctions between children of different ages, sets Locke apart from most previous writers, and may explain why parents from influential families so often turned to him for educational as well as medical advice. It was a request of this kind which gave rise to his book on education (4).

Locke's advice about the ways in which children of different ages should be treated is moderate and practical. While admitting that "No Body can think a Boy of Three, or Seven Years old, should be argued with, as a grown Man" (181), Locke advises parents to watch the child's development carefully and to begin using rational persuasions as soon as it is capable of understanding them: "Children," he counsels, "are to be treated as rational Creatures" (152). At the same time he wants allowance to be made for "the Natural Disposition of their Childhood," "the natural Gaiety of that Age" (157). His tolerant comment on the adolescent or young adult is that "Youth must have some Liberty, some Out-leaps" (203). He deplores the lack of suitable literature for children; the growth of children's literature in the later eighteenth century, and the presence of a welcome element of playfulness even in the more moralistic works, have been plausibly attributed to his influence (Pickering 1993, 14). Locke warns fathers, too, not to be impatient with their sons for not thinking at twenty as their seniors think at fifty (203). Of the relationship between pupil and tutor he observes that "all their time together should not be spent in Reading of Lectures, and magisterially dictating to him . . . Hearing him in his turn, and using [sc. accustoming] him to reason about what is propos'd will make the Rules go down the easier" (204). This last idea of "making the rules go down easier" pervades Locke's whole treatise: he disapproves of "Beating, Chiding, or other Servile Punishments," and recommends "as much Indulgence as [the children] make not an ill Use of" (147).

Some of this can be traced back to Montaigne or even Ascham; but Locke articulated it far more fully, and it gained a new force and wider acceptance in his time. When we read a sentence like, "I consider [children] as Children, who must be tenderly used, who must play, and have Play-things" (143), we know that the historical period identified by Philippe Ariès, in which people had no clear concept of childhood as a distinctive state of being, is nearing its end. Locke was no Jean-Jacques Rousseau or J. M. Barrie: his appreciation of the childhood state was not of such a kind as to make him wish for it to be artificially prolonged. But Locke did show considerable fondness for children and childhood for their own sakes: from him we hear no patrician sneers at the "noise and impertinencies" of the young.

Locke considered most parents bad educators of their children. While more apt than a modern commentator like Stone to find evidence of parental (especially maternal) fondness in genteel society of his time, he feared that this fondness was often capricious and misdirected (138–39). Overprotectiveness was one of his favourite targets. In a wealthy family, he observed, the child was seldom out of sight of some adult: this well-meant supervision, if continued too long, prevented it from learning to fend for itself (122). Children, Locke recommended, should be encouraged to learn to go about alone; they also should be encouraged to acclimatize themselves by playing in sun and wind without hats. (The philosopher grumbles a little about the unlikelihood of fond parents being willing to follow this advice) [121].) A related problem is spoiling. Many parents overindulge the "pretty Perverseness" of the toddler (138). Then when the children grow "too big to be dandled," so that their parents "can no longer make use of them as Playthings," the adults begin to complain of tendencies which their own folly has encouraged, insisting that "the Brats are untoward and perverse" (139). Lovelace in *Clarissa* conjectures that this may be what went wrong with his own early upbringing: "I have seen parents (perhaps my own did so) who delighted in those very qualities in their children while young, the natural consequences of which (too much indulged and encouraged) made them, as they grew up, the plague of their hearts" (Richardson 1932, 3:64–65). In some cases, Locke noted with disapproval, early spoiling was succeeded by excessive punishment, which in turn made the victims dull and inactive (Locke 1968, 148). (This last sequence of events unfolds relentlessly in the eleventh chapter of Smollett's *Peregrine Pickle*.) Unfortunately, Locke observed, some parents came to like the "unnatural Sobriety" which flogging produced in their children, since the victims would now "make no Noise, nor give them any Trouble" (150).

Locke preferred children to be gently but firmly checked from their early years so that punishments could be kept to a minimum later. He envisaged a steady growth toward a state of freedom, responsibility, and self-determination which would make children and parents satisfactory companions for one another. The usual method of upbringing, he suggested, had the opposite effect: it spoiled children in infancy and repressed them later. The child who had been first spoiled and then rejected by its parents would be thrown back on the company of servants, from whom it would pick up bad habits. Those subjected to this process would grow up cunning, furtive, resentful of their parents, addicted to wine and lechery, and inclined to wish that their fathers would hurry up and die (139–46).

This scenario is made the more plausible by the fact that it can be traced in other contemporary discourses, as different from one another as from Locke's treatise—in Restoration comedy, for example, and in the literature of good conduct and religious instruction. In the anonymous, and enormously influential conduct book *The Whole Duty of Man,* the father is adjured to remember that, "since he was the instrument of bringing [his children] into the world," he must provide properly for them once they are in it, rather than spending all his substance on his "own riots, and excess." This lesson seems to have taken considerable time to penetrate parents in the upper ranks of society, at least as the novelists portray them. As late as 1796 Robert Bage, in his novel *Hermsprong,* presents as one of his central characters a nobleman who lets his daughter Caroline be brought up by a female relation, so that he can have his own house free for gambling parties. When Caroline nears maturity, her father promptly assumes the most tyrannical control over her life, disregarding the Lockean precept that a father who pays no attention to his children during their early years forfeits the right to exercise control over them when they grow up (Bage 1979, 3:32–33, 162–63, 173). The narrator, without naming Locke, upholds the Lockean ideal, presenting it as if it were a radical new idea, still stoutly resisted by conservatively minded men.

Locke also warns parents against heaping up money and property to go to their children once they themselves are dead, while refusing them adequate maintenance in the meantime: this "lessens the childs affection to his parent, nay, sometimes it proceeds so far, as to make him wish his death" ([Allestree] 1977, 300). The latter idea gave rise to what soon became a stock joke: in *The Recruiting Officer,* for example, young Captain Plume, meeting his friend Worthy in solemn mood, inquires facetiously, "What ails thee, Man? . . . Has your Father rose from the Dead, and reassum'd his Estate?" (Farquhar 1988, 2:44)

Locke's sensitivity to the possibility of bad relations between parents and children did not lead him to conclude that children should be taken away from home and educated at public schools. He could see that "being abroad" might make the child "bolder, and better able tó bustle and shift amongst Boys of his own age"; also that "the emulation of Schoolfellows, often puts Life and Industry into young Lads." But on the whole he felt that boarding schools were likely to instill more bad lessons than good ones:

> You must confess, that you have a strange value for words, when . . . you think it worth while, to hazard your Son's Innocence and Vertue, for a little Greek and Latin. For, as to that Boldness and Spirit, which Lads get amongst their Play-fellows at School, it has ordinarily such a mixture of Rudeness and ill-turn'd Confidence, that those misbecoming and dis-ingenuous Ways of shifting in the World must be unlearnt [after leaving school], and all the tincture wash'd out again, to make way for better Principles. (1968, 165–66)

Rousseau enlarged on this perception and inveighed against spoiling the innocence of children by premature socialization and filling their heads with rules which they were not yet ready to understand.

In the novel, the question of the best type of education for a boy—and it is boys who, both in Locke's treatise and to a lesser extent in novels of the period, occupy most of the writer's attention—was one of the most energetically canvassed. In handling it, novelists were far from slavish in their adherence to Locke. Sarah Fielding's *Adventures of David Simple,* for example, directs some Lockean satire at adults who treat "their Little-ones in such a manner, as if they were laying Plots to procure their hearty Aversion to the End of their Lives," and advances the anti-Filmerian view that parents should not treat or regard their posterity as slaves (1973, 134). In the inset story of Camilla (134 ff.) the narrator is careful to show the parents "delighted" with the "little childish Remarks" of their offspring; the brother and sister "passed [their] Childhood in all the Happiness that state is capable of enjoying; and the only Punishment [they] ever had for any Fault, was that of being sent from [their] Parents' sight." But at the age of nine the boy is dispatched, contrary to Locke's advice, to a public school. "It was with great difficulty," the narrator comments, "[that] these fond Parents were induced to part with him; but they thought it was for his Good, and had no Notion of indulging themselves at his Expence." Here it is the desire to hold on to a child, rather than the desire to send him away, which is thought to indulge the parents' wishes to the child's detriment. In the real-life Fielding family Sarah's elder brother Henry was sent away to Eton, so family tradition might be held to sanction the practice; but in *Tom Jones* Henry shows the wise Mr. Allworthy keeping his two nephews at home to be educated by private tutors. In such cases the evolving plot, with its representation of the success or failure of different educational methods, acts as a comment, favorable or unfavorable, on Lockean precepts.

One impulse for which we may search in vain in Locke is the wish to direct against the propertied classes of his time a blanket accusation of frigidity in their behavior toward their children. The fact that Locke moved in Whig rather than Tory circles and wrote his book on education for Whig rather than Tory squires may have had much to do with this: Locke is quick to detect feelings of hostility and aggressiveness toward offspring in the work of the Tory Sir Robert Filmer but not in the lives of his Whig patrons. However, he is prepared to criticize other aspects of childrearing practice, including some of those prevalent in the group to which his patrons belonged, when it seems necessary to do so.

Locke's chief complaint is not that parents lack fondness but that their fondness is impulsive and capricious, uninformed by any satisfactory theory of education or (to put it another way) of continuous child development. Thus at times he sounds as if he would prefer to see children taken out of their parents' hands and given into the charge of enlightened tutors like himself: in particular, he intimates that misguided practices in the earlier stages of upbringing can lead to ill-feeling later. He stresses the need to lay foundations early for the friendship and mutual respect between parent and child which should prevail in later years.

Locke's belief that early spoiling led to a later revulsion of feeling against the child, and his implied recommendation of a stand-off period when the child would spend most of its time with a tutor, seems to have made an especially strong impression on creative writers. Swift's Lilliputians are, apart from their preference for boarding school education, remarkably Lockean in their educational ideas:

> The Nurseries for Males of Noble or Eminent Birth, are provided with grave and learned Professors . . . [The boys] are never suffered to converse with Servants, . . . whereby they avoid those early bad Impressions of Folly and Vice to which our Children are subject. Their Parents are suffered to see them only twice a Year; the Visit is not to last above an Hour; they are allowed to kiss the Child at Meeting and Parting; but a Professor, who always standeth by on those Occasions, will not suffer them to whisper, or use any fondling Expressions, or bring any Presents of Toys, Sweet-meats, and the like. (1965, 61)

Here, as is usual in *Gulliver's Travels,* the text keeps its own counsel. There is no clear sign as to how far we should approve or disapprove this particular Lilliputian practice: the reader is dared to decide. Lilliputian education is clearly more austere than Locke would have wished, yet the idea of keeping a rein on parental fondness is certainly present in Locke's text. The same Lockean distrust of spoiling is echoed more unambiguously in Smollett's *Peregrine Pickle* (1751), where the narrator observes that a sudden lapse in his mother's affection did Peregrine good in the long term: he was spared her potentially harmful indulgence, being left instead to the management of a sympathetic junior teacher at one of his schools (1969, chap. 11, 13).

The diverse recommendations in *Some Thoughts on Education* were developed, then, in strikingly varied ways. While writers showed appreciation of Locke's new approach, they also tended to extrapolate on his teachings in directions dictated by their own preconceived ideas. Often the divergence from Locke seems to be due to some inhibition on the part of the parent against the affective, concerned, and involved concept of fatherhood that Locke propounds. In novels, there are moments when a parent's interest in educational theory is made to seem like a substitute for direct involvement in the life of the child. The most flagrant example, of course, is *Tristram Shandy,* a book notoriously influenced by Locke, where Walter Shandy writes a "*TRISTRA-paedia,* or system of education" for Tristram, but is always somewhere else whenever a crisis occurs in his son's life.

The perception behind Sterne's portrayal of the personal relationship, or lack of relationship, between Walter and his son is that father-son relationships are inherently difficult. (It was all very well for Locke to prescribe: he never had children of his own.) A striking real-life example of the problem is to hand in Lord Chesterfield's letters to his son. Ronald Paulson, commenting on the letters, rightly suggests that in Chesterfield the impulse to restrict the child's liberty is almost as strong as the impulse to grant it (Paulson 1979, 140: cf. Fliegelman 1982, 40ff). "If you will do everything that I would have you do till you are eighteen, I will do everything that you would have me do ever afterwards." "I shall love you extremely, while you deserve it; but not one moment longer" (Stanhope 1959, 21). "I do not, therefore, so much as hint to you, how absolutely dependent you are upon me; that you neither have, nor can have, a shilling in the world but from me; and that, as I have no womanish weakness for your person, your merit must and will be the only measure of my kindness" (14–15).

These are quotations chosen by Paulson, and his selection is perhaps unfair to Chesterfield. The Earl did, after all, take far more pains over his son's education than most noblemen of the time would have done, especially for a bastard who could not inherit his father's title. Against the stern note sometimes struck in the letters we should set the fact that such concerned, detailed, and thoughtful letters were written at all. It is, of course, transparent that Chesterfield longs to form his son into an improved version of himself—witty, urbane, charming, at home in the best company. But it is equally clear that the attempt was an almost total failure and doomed to be so from an early stage. The young man grew up shy and awkward, making a far from brilliant marriage without his father's knowledge or consent (ix). The father-son relationship, therefore, fell far short of the Lockean ideal of close friendship and mutual confidence. But there is fondness as well as sternness in the letters. While the anxious parent presses his son to learn rhetoric, history, and languages at what would now be considered an excessively early age, he does heed—if a little grudgingly—Locke's injunction about letting children be children, play, and have playthings. It is, he tells the boy, "very proper and decent that you should play some part of the day ... fly your kite or play at ninepins," and he shows indulgence to his son's liking for cricket and for caged birds. But it is difficult for a modern reader not to feel that Chesterfield thinks of these gestures as concessions to weakness: the vigilance of the parent-preceptor is never really relaxed. The remarks about kites and ninepins are closely followed by the warning, "I am sure you desire to gain [your tutor's] approbation, without which you shall never have mine" (1).

The tendency to give with one hand while taking away with the other persists in those letters which were written during the boy's late teens. When the young man reaches the age of eighteen his father exhorts him to enjoy this "happy and giddy time" in his life," but he cannot resist immediately adding a warning about adherence to morality (150). Here as always we can see what difficulty Chesterfield finds in overcoming his jealous possessiveness or abandoning his chosen roles of preceptor and overseer. A few months earlier he is to be found wishing, in an enjoyable flight of fancy, that he could use Gyges' magic ring to make himself invisible and transport himself to Venice, where his son is staying in the course of his grand tour; but the fantasy soon relapses into the usual warning that the father's love depends absolutely on the son's good behavior: "If all . . . things turned out to my mind, I would immediately assume my own shape, become visible, and embrace you; but, if the contrary happened, I would preserve my invisibility, make the best of my way home again, and sink my disappointment upon you and the world" (107–8). Here the writer struggles manfully to accept the fact that his son is old enough to make his own decisions and his own mistakes; but the shadow of the stern parent standing at the young man's shoulder, ever ready to disapprove of any departure from the prescribed program, remains.

Paulson seems to feel that Chesterfield's approach to his son's education exemplifies the teachings of Locke. In fact it represents a distortion of Locke, regressing some way toward the frigid aristocratic model of fatherhood which is criticized in so many contemporary texts. In a letter to a son, a disclaimer of any "womanish weakness for [his] person" (15) seems harsh and overemphatic, reminiscent of the ridicule which rakes in Restoration drama reserved for public demonstrations of fondness for wives and children by the citizenry. For a father to insist that "to talk of natural affection is talking nonsense" (21) is to turn a notion of the arbitrary and provisional nature of family ties, which Locke had used to counteract the tyranny of patriarchy, against the child. Locke had argued that fathers did not acquire rights over children by the mere act of begetting them, but only by fostering and care: Chesterfield turns this argument round to establish that a child has no right to affection from its father unless it behaves, and develops, in the manner he wishes. So while Chesterfield clearly thinks of himself as a disciple of Locke, he is in some ways typical of those tendencies against which Locke and his followers reacted: he seizes on those of Locke's precepts which can, with a little interpretive dexterity, be made to bear a conservative or repressive interpretation. In our own day we are emerging from a period where Locke's writing has been represented as repressive, and entering one where Locke is seen as the heir to earlier, and stimulus of later, revolutionary thought (Ashcraft 1987; Fliegelman 1982).

One area in which Locke's thinking may at first seem more conservative is his attitude toward women. His advocacy of the rights of mothers, already noted, is clearly undertaken partly in order to make a point against Filmer; and his *Some Thoughts Concerning Education* gives disappointingly little attention to the special needs of girls. The book on education was written in the first instance for a landed gentleman, Edward Clarke, who wanted advice on the education of his heir, an eight-year-old boy: this no doubt helps to explain its gender bias. (Locke 1968, 4ff) But when Clarke's wife asked for a complementary program of education for her daughters, Locke sent only a brief and rather condescending letter in reply.

One reason for this, no doubt, was Locke's belief that little distinction needed to be made in the education of the two sexes. "I have said He here," he observes at one point in *Some Thoughts on Education,*

> because the principal Aim of my Discourse is, how a young Gentleman should be brought up from his Infancy, which, in all things will not so perfectly suit the Education of Daughters; though where the Difference of Sex requires different treatment, 'twill be no hard matter to distinguish. (117)

The differences turn out to be few in number: "some though no great difference" should be made between girls' education and that of boys, "for making a little allowance for beauty and some few other considerations of s[ex], the manner of breeding of boys and girls, especially in their younger years, I imagine should be the same" (117 n). In his letter to Mrs. Clarke, Locke concedes that girls should play in the shade rather than in the sun, and that it is "not fit that girls should be dabbling in water as your boys will be" (344–45). However, from the context it is not hard to infer that these are concessions to Mrs. Clarke's prejudices:

Locke would in fact prefer his rules for diet, exercise, and exposure to the elements to apply to girls as well as boys:

> I should rather desire in my wife a healthy constitution, a stomach able to digest ordinary food, and a body that could endure upon occasion both wind and sun, rather than a puling, weak, sickly wretch, that every breath of wind or least hardship puts in danger. (344)

To frame precepts for women in terms of what one would wish one's wife to be is admittedly patronizing. But Locke's tone here is partly explained by his attitude to the recipient of his letter. His opinion of women as a sex was much higher than his opinion of Mrs. Clarke as an individual. His friend Lady Masham had, Locke claimed, taught herself Latin with the aid of a Latin Bible, and passed her knowledge on to her son Frank: Locke hoped that other mothers would do the same (288 and note). But from Mrs. Clarke, an annoyingly conventional type of wife and mother, Locke did not expect so much.

Locke's references to women in *Some Thoughts Concerning Education* are few in number, but mostly appreciative. One of his arguments against sending boys away to school is that the practice of educating girls at home does not make them "less knowing or less able Women" (166). When criticizing the rote learning of Latin imposed on unhappy boys, he notes how much more easily their sisters, using a more direct and natural method, learn French:

> When we so often see a French Woman teach an English Girl to speak and read French perfectly in a Year or Two, without any Rule of Grammar, or any thing else but pratling to her, I cannot but wonder, how Gentlemen have overseen [sc. overlooked] this way for their Sons, and thought them more dull or incapable than their Daughters. (269)

This tactic of showing how women can in favorable circumstances achieve more than men is one that Locke uses several times. We have already noted the passage in which he shows how a quick-witted woman can learn Latin with minimal help and teach it to her son: elsewhere he shows how a boy's mother, "despised, 'tis like, as illiterate for not having read a System of Logick and Rhetorick," may succeed better at "expressing herself handsomly in English" than a country schoolmaster "who has all the Tropes and Figures in *Farnaby's Rhetorick* at his

Fingers' ends" (299–300). Although he does betray suspicion of
mothers who spoil their children and his book on education gives
so much more attention to the education of boys than of girls,
Locke is far more sympathetic and tolerant in his attitude to
females than, for example, Rousseau (cf. Kerber 1980, 15–27;
Yolton 1985, 57–58).

In Locke's work, however, the female and the feminine are
not foregrounded to any great extent. When he does give them
prominence, he does so as part of his program to discredit rigid
aristocratic patriarchy, whose most obvious consequence at the
family level is frigidity and distrust on the part of the father
toward those whom he represents to himself as subordinates
rather than as loved ones. Among Locke's disciples, some, notably Rousseau, regress in the direction of distrust for women
and children while others, notably Steele, boldly validate physical and emotional warmth and even, to some extent, the feminine. Steele not only writes essays in praise of breast-feeding
and of the affection between parents and children: he is
also more prepared than Locke was to take the deconstruction
of patriarchy to its logical conclusion, arguing that daughters
should not automatically be considered less important than
sons. In *Spectator* no. 196, Steele reminds his readers that a
sensible daughter may bring more credit to a family than a
boorish son, adding, however, that boorishness in sons may be
attributable less to their own shortcomings than to their fathers' "severity and distance."

The first great male novelists likewise show even less prejudice against women than Locke: while their figurations of families and childhood place some emphasis on male children, that
emphasis is less than overwhelming. Defoe adopts female perso-
nae in *Roxana* and *Moll Flanders* and evokes Moll's childhood
in as much detail as Colonel Jack's. In Fielding's *Amelia*, the
child who is given most prominence is Booth's eldest girl. In
Richardson's *Pamela*, the only child whose feelings are explored
in any detail (apart from Pamela herself, who at fifteen is on the
border between childhood and adulthood) is Mr. B.'s illegitimate
daughter, Miss Goodwin. In *Clarissa* one daughter outshines all
the rest of her family: her excellence, her desire and potential
for deciding her own destiny and learning to exist as an entity
apart from her family are unforgivable only in the eyes of her
frigid and undiscerning relatives. In *Sir Charles Grandison*, it
is the hero, in his negotiations with the della Porretta family
over his possible marriage to Clementina, who shows insuffi-

cient concern for girls when he agrees that the daughters of the marriage, but not the sons, shall be brought up as Roman Catholics. But the concession exposes Sir Charles to some sarcasm from the other parties to the negotiation, who sardonically enquire why he should show such concern for the souls of the boys and such apparent indifference to those of the girls. The reader seems intended to conclude that this is one of the few occasions when Sir Charles is in the wrong. The needs, rights, and natures of girl children were not, then, ignored in eighteenth-century texts, fictional or otherwise. It is true that some writers pay more attention to male children than to their sisters; but this bias is far less pronounced in the novel than in most other forms of discourse and is less strong overall than might have been expected in such a strongly patriarchal society.

The opposite bias, indeed, characterizes Sarah Fielding's *The Governess* (1749). This novel is a landmark in a number of ways. It is an early and distinguished example of fiction actually written for children. (For discussions of early children's literature as opposed to literature about children, see Pickering 1981 and Summerfield 1984.) It is full of practical ideas about education and personal development; its fictional world is one into which no important male character, and only one important adult female, intrudes. The governess of the title is Mrs. Teachum, a clergyman's widow who runs a school with nine pupils, deliberately refraining from taking more for fear of neglecting any. While she knows she must maintain authority in the classroom, she likes to think that her pupils will cast off their reserve before her during leisure hours: she will "at times become the Companion of her Scholars" (Fielding 1968, 248).

Predictably, the story is moralistic and didactic: the dedicatory letter dwells on the importance for young women of "keeping down all rough and boistrous Passions" (87). Less predictably, there is no heavy preaching and, in fact, very little direct reference to religion. Still more surprising is that, while the teacher's views and precepts are given some attention, much more goes to interaction between the girls. In one of the inner stories a foolish maid tells a little girl that it is an indignity to submit to being taught by another child, but both inner and outer tales set strongly against this prejudice. The book's main character is Jenny Peace, the eldest of Teachum's pupils, who is "but fourteen Years old"—"none of the rest [having] yet attained their twelfth Year." Jenny often finds herself called upon to maintain harmony among the others: she sets about educating them to live tranquilly together. The most successful method of doing this proves to be the telling of stories. Some are fairy stories, involving giants and magic. But Jenny's most fruitful idea is to persuade each girl, in turn, to tell her own life-story.

Mrs. Teachum's comments on Jenny's techniques of management are revealing. She is a little worried by the possible effects of fantasy on children: she reminds Jenny in private that "Giants, Magic, Fairies, and all sorts of supernatural Assistances in a Story, are only introduced to amuse and divert" (166). Later she adds: "If the Story is well written, the common Course of Things [will] produce the same Incidents, without the help of Fairies" (276). However, the governess is not a Gradgrind *avant la lettre:* she makes no attempt to forbid tales of the marvelous altogether, contenting herself with reminding the girls that such things should be treasured chiefly for their allegorical meanings. When Jenny asks permission to read a second fairy-tale to the others, Teachum graciously tells her that, since she has clearly understood what she was told on the last occasion, she "may be trusted almost in any-thing" and may "follow her own Judgment and Inclinations" in amusing her friends (216).

This time, though, an objection is raised by one of the other girls: Polly Suckling suggests that "it would be better to read some true History, from which they might learn something; for she thought Fairy-Tales were fit only for little Children." Jenny cannot "help smiling at such an Objection's coming from the little Dumpling, who was not much above Seven years of Age" (217–18). Instead of abandoning the story, she tells another to justify it, this time an autobiographical one. Several years before, a raree-show ("A show carried about in a box: a peep-show"—*Oxford English Dictionary*) came to the village where Jenny lived. The other children in the parish were anxious to see it, but six-year-old Jenny "had taken it into her Head, that it was beneath her Wisdom to see Raree-Shows." Eventually her mother, surprised that the child had refused to see the show though she had been given permission, wormed out the reason and laughed Jenny out of her "Pretence of Being wise": she herself, she confided, had seen the show, and it was "really very comical and diverting" (217–19). Jenny was left to chide herself for missing, out of sheer pride, an entertainment which she would have enjoyed. Evidently Sarah Fielding was anxious that the case for fantasy and popular entertainment, to be argued so passionately in later centuries by writers as diverse as Dickens and Bettelheim, should not go by default.

Jenny's procedure of having the girls relate their life-stories is equally revealing. At first it seems incongruous to ask such small children to engage in autobiographical exercises: what can they possibly have to tell? (Some of the girls' stories, indeed, turn out to be very brief: Lucy Sly's lasts just over a page, and ends with the words, "This is all I know of my Life hitherto"— 201–3.) Why, then, does Mrs. Teachum so heartily approve of the exercise? She certainly does so for, while remarking that she would not like to interfere with the children's freedom of speech by being present when the stories are told, she asks Jenny to put them in a book and bring it to her later. Having read it, she expresses herself pleased that the children have "all confessed their Faults without Reserve; and the untowardly Bent of their Minds, which so strongly appear'd before the Quarrel [the event which began the book], has not broke out in these their little Histories" (314).

It is the word "confess" that betrays Sarah Fielding's intention. The scheme with which she credits Jenny fulfills the same function as the spiritual autobiographies of the seventeenth century: the girls' exercise in self-analysis is calculated to further spiritual health and amendment. But each child finds instruction in the others' tales as well as her own. Sukey, after hearing Patty's story, congratulates Jenny warmly on her scheme:

> "What Thanks can I give you, my dear Friend, for having put me into a Way of examining my Heart, and reflecting on my own Actions; by which you have saved me, perhaps, from a Life as miserable as that of the poor Woman in Miss *Sukey*'s Letter!" (206)

It would be unwise to make extravagant claims for *The Governess*. Its moral purpose is at times intrusive and its use of fantasy frustratingly constrained. But the book is full of details of relationships between children and parents, children and teachers, children and other children, even children and animals. A neglectful private governess, instead of disciplining the little girl in her care, prefers to accuse "the Dog, or the Cat, or any-thing she could lay the Blame upon," sooner than own that her charge is at fault: she even admires the little girl for her "Cunning and Contrivance" when she takes the hint and begins to accuse others of her own misdeeds, getting a foot-boy whipped for smashing a china cup which she herself has broken (201–2). One little girl at Mrs. Teachum's lived until she was six years old in a family where "no-body took much Notice of us, whether we knew any-thing, or whether we did not" (209–10). On an excursion into the country from the school, the governess, "so far from laying [the girls] under a Restraint by her Presence, encouraged them to run in the Fields, and gather Flowers; which they did, each Miss trying to get the best to present to her Governess" (212–13). At the end of the same walk there is a feast of strawberries and cream at a dairy kept by a gray-haired old lady "troubled with the Palsy." Polly Suckling tactlessly asks her "Why she [shakes] her Head so?" while Patty Lockit says she hopes her own hair will "never be of such a Colour." The more mature Jenny Peace is understandably "afraid they [will] say something to offend the old Woman" (213).

In short, the book reflects not only a growing interest in education, with an emphasis on the avoidance of repressive methods of teaching and upbringing, but also a growing awareness of the diversity of incidents, interests, and problems which may occur in the life of a child. This widening of the range of fictional references to children and of creativity in representing the childhood state was to continue throughout the second half of the eighteenth century.

5

Fathers

In Restoration stage comedy, the aura of wit and vivacity that surround the rake make it easy for audiences to laugh at his jokes against offspring, and from there it is a short step to acceptance of his attitudes and behavior as tolerable or even admirable, an aspect of his love of freedom and his refusal to be confined. But from the last decade of the seventeenth century a few comic dramatists begin to activate their audiences' sympathy for children as part of a more general program of revising or subverting the values of earlier comedies. And in the years from 1709 to 1713 Addison and Steele, who in their periodical essays often seem bent on repudiating the values of traditional comedy, go further. For them the uncaring father is not an exuberant scamp but a monster. His desertion of women and offspring is no longer suggestive of wit, vitality, or exuberant theatricality: instead it is shown to signify a deficiency in humanity, a failure of love.

In the emerging novel anxiety over the figure of the rejecting father is acute. The most psychologically convincing example is also one of the earliest: Dorante, the wayward husband in Mandeville's *The Virgin Unmasked* (1709), a book which deserves more prominence in the history of the novel than it has generally been given. (Fielding borrowed the title *The Virgin Unmasked* for one of his plays, and the narrative of Mrs. Fitzpatrick in *Tom Jones* closely resembles one of Mandeville's main inset stories.) Dorante, as his name suggests, resembles the rakes of Restoration comedy; but his attitudes and behavior, instead of being treated with amused tolerance, are seen with the fascination of horror. Dorante gains the affections of a rich man's daughter and marries her without her father's consent. At first he hopes that the old man will come to accept the marriage: when this hope fails he resolves to make money out of his wife by another method, ordering her to sell her favors to a rich nobleman. "If not," he warns, "I can keep you no longer; turn out with your Brats" (Mandeville 1975, 64). When Aurelia refuses, her spouse taunts her with not knowing what is good for her:

> "Some Babes are fond of their own Bubby [teat], tho' it be never so good for 'em to change their Milk: have you never seen them, when they are put to a strange Breast, how they'll scratch and tear, cry their little Hearts out, and rather Starve, than draw it? This is your Case exactly, and there is as much Wit in the one as there is in the other." (65)

The rake, as here represented, sees a woman's mentality as barely distinguishable from that of a child. Both are temperamental and perverse; both refuse the advice of the husband/ father, who thinks he knows what is best for them. This assimilation of woman to baby is not casual or even unconscious: in Dorante's speech to his protesting wife the analogy is drawn out lovingly and at fantastic length. The resulting flight of wit equals, or surpasses, those attributed to the rakes in stage comedy:

> "You are just like the Children, that can play a hundred pretty Tricks, if they please; when you are alone with them, they'll act them over and over again, till you are tired; but to oblige and divert your Friend, you shan't make 'em show one, though you kiss'd their Breech; and instead of doing as you bid 'em, they'll run into a Corner to hide their Faces, and pray what is the reason? the same as yours, forsooth they are ashamed; prithee leave being so Childish, and consider you are a Woman, and have two Children of your own." (65)

What is perhaps most striking here is the detailed observation, the specificity of the knowledge of children attributed to the rake. He knows about the precautions taken to accustom a baby to more than one teat, so that it can still be reared if its nurse or mother dies or finds her milk drying up. He is well acquainted, too, with the bashfulness of slightly older children when asked to perform their "pretty tricks" before company. But familiarity with children has brought contempt rather than affection: the rake's critique of "brats" is all the sharper for being so firmly grounded in experience. Mandeville, be it noted, does not try to deprive the rake of his traditional gift for wit and satire. But he ensures that there will be no temptation for the reader to empathize with Dorante: neither the closeness of his observation nor the sparkle of his wit can conceal the harshness of his rejection of women, offspring, and the whole world of tenderness, scruple, and reciprocal responsibility.

In comedy, there is a certain shamefaced enjoyment of the irreverent expressions which rise to the rake's lips whenever he thinks of children, and even of his hopeful predictions that his bastards may die: we are made to feel that these utterances need not be taken quite literally, that they are a necessary part of a swashbuckling pose. In Mandeville, they suddenly become literal representations of a believable psychological state in which the father refuses to acknowledge the child as in any sense part of himself. For Lucinda, the spinster-narrator of Mandeville's cautionary tale, there is nothing surprising in this: it is axiomatic that men mostly dislike both women and children, and only cultivate their acquaintance for selfish reasons. A man in Lucinda's last tale confesses without embarrassment to a married friend that he hates the "fiddle faddle of a great many Women in a House, and the bawling of Children" (206). Later the same man comes under suspicion for paying too much attention to the young son of a pretty woman, who for her part believes that "Men, for the Generality of 'em, care but little for other Peoples Children, most always think them troublesome, and hardly ever take Pleasure in bearing those little Impertinencies, which the best of them will be guilty of." (207) Her diagnosis is correct: the man only gives presents to her little boy as a preparative to seducing her.

The most uncompromising passage in the book concerns the death of Aurelia's son. The father, Dorante, comes home drunk; he and his wife have a row. The child, who sleeps in the same room, is awake and overhears his father threatening his mother:

> "My dear Boy ... made no doubt, but [his father] was going to execute his Threatenings; and making all the haste to him ... took hold of his Leg, with abundance of Tears, entreating him not to hurt his Mother. *Dorante*, ... looking back upon the begging Posture of the Child, and disliking [that] he should show so much Concern for me, Maliciously resolved to Frighten him throughly. ... what! Sirrah, said he, would ye help your Mother against me? Come, I'll make away with your Mother." (97)

The passage conveys vividly the disparity in understanding between child and adults. The wife knows that her husband is playing a game—though a cruel and dangerous game—and decides to let him have his way: his feelings of frustration and inadequacy will be dissipated if he can reassert his position as master in his own house. But the child is too frightened, and too inexperienced, to understand the situation:

> Immediately [Dorante] ... ran to his Sword, and Drawing it, he came to me seemingly in a great Fury: I observed the Humour [he] did it in, and apprehending no Danger at this time, I lay still ... I heard *Dorante* say, what ails the Boy? The Rascal is making Mouths; ... I look'd up, and saw my Child in Fits: I did what I could to recover him [but the fits persisted] ... The next Day *Dorante* went his journey, without taking any notice, either of me, or the Child. [The fits] ... left him the Night following; but then he fell into so Violent a Fever as carried him off the Seventh Day after. (96–97)

We saw earlier that Freud, in *Civilization and Its Discontents,* diagnosed a resentment on the part of lovers at the intervention, or even presence, of a child. In Mandeville's tale the child intervenes tragically, not in a scene of love, but in a domestic quarrel. His intervention gives rise to a painfully convincing piece of writing of a kind seldom attempted in later fiction. In Richardson and Fielding small children are sometimes objects of concern and even sources of dissension between their parents: occasionally they take part in the action to the extent of carrying messages or asking questions. But only Mandeville attempts a scene in which a decisive intervention, which sets parents and offspring in a dynamic, threefold relationship, is initiated by a preadolescent child. It is a situation full of difficulty, but also of promise, for the writer of fiction. Yet the difficulty seems to have stifled the promise: the motif is one which Mandeville's immediate successors neglected to explore.

Even Defoe, innovative novelist as he was in many respects, makes little more than a gesture toward it. In *Colonel Jack* (1722) the protagonist gives an account of his birth and beginnings, which resembles the comedy scenario where a rake or whore fobs off unwanted children to a nurse but is more circumstantial and perhaps closer to social practice. The father can afford "a good piece of Money" for the nurse, or rather foster mother. But both he and the mother (who "kept very good Company"—perhaps a euphemism for living as a high-class prostitute) are chiefly anxious to get rid of the child, and to avoid blackmail approaches from people who know their secret:

"My Father ... charg'd [the nurse] that if I liv'd to come to any bigness, capable to understand the meaning of it, she should always take care to bid me *remember, that I was a Gentleman,* and this he said was all the Education he would desire of her for me, for he did not doubt ... but that sometime or other the very hint would inspire me with Thoughts suitable to my Birth." (3)

Here, as in the stage comedies, the father seems less than desolated at the prospect that the child may die before he comes to maturity. If the boy lives, he intimates, the most effective incitements to success will be regular reminders of his notional status as a gentleman: these are, he says, "all the Education he would desire" for the boy. This looks like a version of the old notion that the father has fulfilled his duty to the child simply by begetting it: blood—provided that the child knows enough about its antecedents to be inspired to live up to them—will always tell. It is a convenient pretext for providing the child with no other inheritance, leaving him to fend for himself in later life.

In this novel, then, the failings of the child's parents are made more obvious than in the stage comedies, but they are not in the end visited on the offspring: Jack neither dies in infancy nor ends on the gallows, though his early circumstances seem to make either fate quite likely. Instead he prospers and becomes, after many vicissitudes, the gentleman he always claimed to be, so that his father's prediction that pride of birth will spur him to achievement is, oddly enough, fulfilled. This last plot device has some of the escapism of comedy. It removes the need for that relentless exploration of the consequences of rakery which, in Mandeville, leads to dynamic—even tragic— interaction between parents and child.

Gulliver's Travels presents a different case. Because it is an allegory with an episodic plot it is seldom thought of as a novel: Ian Watt, in his classic study (1957), does not discuss it, and W. Austin Flanders, more recently, gives it only the briefest mention (1984). It has taken Michael McKeon to set it in its true place beside *Robinson Crusoe* as a distinguished example of early novel writing (1987, 338–56). *Gulliver's Travels* traces, at length and in detail, the development of one fictional figure and also explores the instability of the self. It is reasonable to attribute psychological complexity to Gulliver and to see his attitude toward families and familial life as one of his most fully realized characteristics. In particular Swift evokes, almost as strikingly as Mandeville, the nausea of the rejecting adult male in the presence of children and babies. (For another approach, see Traugott 1984.)

One of the protagonist's most disconcerting experiences in the land of the giants is his encounter with a Brobdingnagian infant:

> When Dinner was almost done, the Nurse came in with a Child of a Year old in her Arms; who immediately spyed me, and began a Squall that you might have heard from *London-Bridge* to *Chelsea;* after the usual Oratory of Infants, to get me for a Play-thing. The Mother out of pure Indulgence took me up, and put me towards the Child, who presently seized me by the Middle, and got my Head in his Mouth, where I roared so loud that the Urchin was frighted, and let me drop; and I should infallibly have broke my Neck, if the Mother had not held her Apron under me. (Swift 1965, 91)

This time the speaker is not a rake but one who is, in his own country, a husband and father. He has submitted tamely to society's requirement that he shall marry and breed ("Being advised to alter my Condition, I married Mrs. Mary Burton"—20) and even thinks of himself as a fond father. Yet his resentment wells up in a description of infant behavior whose pungency is increased by its wealth of evocative detail.

The circumstances, of course, are exceptional: the tiny Gulliver may be forgiven for his terror and nausea when the monstrous baby puts him into its mouth or seems about to drop him from a great height. However, his sarcastic reference to "the usual oratory of infants" betrays his feeling that the young giant's behavior is typical of babies in general; and the sharpness of his delineation of the less lovable traits of young children approaches that of Mandeville's married rake. Moreover, the revulsion extends beyond the selfishness, masterfulness, and caprice of infants (which had been commented on even by Locke) to the apparently natural and amenable process of suckling:

> The Nurse to quiet her Babe made use of a Rattle, which was a Kind of hollow Vessel filled with great Stones, and fastned by a Cable to the Child's Waist: But all in vain, so that she was forced to apply the last Remedy by giving it suck. I must confess no Object ever disgusted me so much as the Sight of her monstrous Breast. (91)

A leading characteristic of passages like these is their satiric humor, which arises from an incongruity between different points of view. If we adopt Gulliver's own viewpoint, we may feel inclined to share his horrified fascination with the giant's child. On the other hand the simple but potent device of making Gulliver tiny in comparison with the other human figures always works to distance us from his comments and remind us of their self-regarding nature. Perhaps the crowning irony is that Gulliver himself, contemptuous as he is of the childhood state, is treated very much like a child or baby during his sojourn in Brobdingnag: the equation between childishness and tiny size is unhesitatingly made. Gulliver is given a nurse, Glumdalclitch, who is herself no more than nine years old (95); from her he learns his letters out of a manual written for young girls (100). Although he resents being treated in this way, he unconsciously plays up to his role, showing off to his nurse as a real child would do. One of his deepest humiliations occurs on a walk in the country, where he tries to show off by jumping over a cowpat: to his mortification he "unfortunately jump[s] short" and finds himself in the middle up to his knees. He is cleaned by a footman, reproved by his nurse, and laughed at later by the courtiers when the story is told (124).

The childishness of Gulliver's behavior here is unmistakable (though at other times he will write patronizingly of his nurse Glumdalclitch, who he says is fond of trinkets and keepsakes "as Children at her Age usually are"—114). Equally undignified, because equally damaging to his image of himself as a mature and self-sufficient being, is the incident where a monkey, mistaking Gulliver for "a young one of his own Species," carries him up to the roof of a high building, holding him "as a Nurse doth a Child she is going to suckle," and stuffing him with nauseating food (122–23). At such moments what Gulliver seems to resent most strongly is ridicule: for an adult nothing can be more distressing than to be as helpless as a baby and to be treated accordingly.

Since Gulliver's own feeling for children is, as we have seen, by no means warm or sympathetic, there is a certain comic justice in the indignities he suffers: we are reminded of *Love for Love,* where Valentine resents the domineering ways of his father Sir Sampson but is by no means exemplary in his attitude to his own (illegitimate) young. At the end of the voyage to Lilliput, when Gulliver begins to hope that he may finally get home, he expresses delight at the prospect of "once more seeing [his] beloved Country, and the dear Pledges [he has] left in it" (79), but before the end of the chapter he admits: "I stayed but

two Months with my Wife and Family; for my insatiable Desire
of seeing foreign Countries would suffer me to continue no
longer" (80). This vacillation between the longing to return
home and the compulsion to leave soon becomes a pattern, with
Gulliver repeatedly breaking resolutions to stay in England
with his family and forsake the sea. It begins to look as though
his feeling for his wife and little ones is culturally imposed
rather than spontaneous. Sea voyages do for Gulliver what enlistment in the army does for beleaguered married men in the
comedies: they free him from the tedium and restriction of
everyday married life.

   Even at the end of the first book, at a point where this pattern
has not yet established itself, Gulliver's description of children
as "dear pledges" of conjugal love sounds suspiciously formulaic.
It is hard not to recall that Satan uses the same phrase in *Paradise Lost* to describe his offspring Death—whom at first sight he
found "detestable"—in a deeply sophistical and self-interested
speech. Swift's protagonist, who uses the expression at the end
of his first voyage, will later reach a state where, instead of
feeling fond of his children, he experiences the most antifamilial
reaction of all:

> When I began to consider, that by copulating with one of the Yahoo-
> Species, I had become a Parent of more, it struck me with the utmost
> Shame, Confusion and Horror. (289)

   In *Gulliver's Travels* the figure of the author is unusually well
hidden behind that of the unreliable narrator: from internal
evidence it is hard to make a reliable deduction as to Swift's
judgment on Gulliver's misoprogenitive nausea. In other
eighteenth-century novels such feelings are treated with disapproval or even revulsion. But though not endorsed they are presented as disturbingly common: almost every novel has a
character who is allowed to express them, and even justify them
in the terms so familiar from Restoration plays. For example,
in the first edition of the second part of Richardson's *Pamela*
(1742) Sir Simon Darnford, represented as a former friend of
Wycherley and thus as the avatar of the superannuated Restoration rake, refers to his daughters as "little Bastards, . . . that
were father'd upon him for his Vexation" (Richardson 1741–42,
3:78). There are indications in the text that retribution is coming upon Sir Simon for his manifold offenses against the family:
his youthful sins catch up with him in the form of painful at-

tacks of gout, besides which the old man is mortified by his growing awareness that he has somehow become extraneous to his family and, indeed, a burden to them. However, the fact that Sir Simon's rejection of issue is given such forceful expression shows that even at this relatively late date the nausea of parenthood, and the related but less intense feeling that children are better kept at a distance, have not disappeared from the culture or from its imaginative writing. Although not approved they are clearly understood.

A question which both fiction and social commentary raise at this time is the extent to which a father should personally look after, and care for, his children. George Booth, the nonconformist Earl of Warrington, seems to be representative in concluding that a father should not be expected to look after babies, toddlers, or girls. "In their most tender Age," he wrote, "the care then due to [children] is such, as the Father is not at all capable of performing ... There are numerous Parts of the Business and Thought necessary to the due Education of them, especially of the Daughters, as a Man cannot, and some which would be indecent for the Father to seem to have any regard to" (Booth 1985, 7).

In fiction, the reaction of Dorante in Eliza Haywood's *The Fortunate Foundlings* (1744) when he finds twin infants abandoned in his garden is typical of what a novelist finds it plausible to attribute to a humane man at this date. "Whatever stands in need of protection," he tells himself, "merits protection from those who have the power to give it," and accordingly he adopts the children. On leaving home he gives orders for their nurture, "not in a cursory or negligent manner," but with care and foresight. When he goes "down to his estate" (which he generally does "two or three times a year"), he always sends for them and expresses "great satisfaction" at their good health; when they reach "an age capable of entertaining him with their innocent prattle" he begins to be fond of them, but still puts them both out to school as soon as they are old enough. This relatively distant behavior calls forth from the narrator the admiring question, "What more could have been expected from the best of fathers?" (Haywood 1974, 3–6). Evidently such efforts are as good as can be expected, and better than most men would have reached to. Even Captain Booth in Fielding's *Amelia,* who is shown caring for his children and romping with them, has to admit to the friendly clergyman Dr. Harrison that he has left their religious instruction to his wife (1983, 360; cf. Smallwood 1989, 114).

The very suggestion that a man might take on the formal instruction of his children comes, in such contexts, as something of a surprise. In Defoe's *Family Instructor*, the wealthy middle-class father is made to feel ashamed that he has not attended to the religious instruction of his son; but the implication is that a minor miracle is needed to make a man in his circumstances do so, and modern studies of the period associate such behavior chiefly with dissenting ministers and professional educators (Marcus 1978, 43, 54–55; Pollock 1983, 111–15; Stone 1977, 465). To find it discussed by an aristocrat (admittedly a dissenter) such as the Earl of Warrington, or (in fiction) raised as a possibility for an army officer like Fielding's Captain Booth comes as a surprise. The fact that it was raised at all points to a searching re-examination of family roles.

However, radical questioning does not always lead to radical solutions: Warrington, for example, takes more account of the father's freedom than of the children's (or mother's) needs. While insisting on the husband's right to attend to such public or private concerns "as must necessarily employ his time, and draw his thoughts abroad, and which he should be criminal in neglecting," the Earl makes it clear that this exemption is not to be extended to wives. The mother, it seems, is "by Nature appointed to a more Domestick Life than the Father, to whom other Affairs become his more immediate indispensable Duty" (Booth 1985, 6–7). Thus while the new concern for children assigns fresh responsibilities to mothers—including not only breast-feeding but early education—it initially permits, and even encourages, fathers to avoid caring for girls or younger boys, and to transfer much of the responsibility for older boys to a tutor. It is with Richardson and Fielding that this attitude, in turn, comes to be questioned. In their novels it is not enough for the father-husband not to reject or abandon his children: he should, it is implied, help to care for them.

Richardson's first heroine, Pamela, encounters the problem of the financially responsible but emotionally frigid father quite early in her relationship with Mr. B. The child-figure in the first part of *Pamela* is Miss Goodwin, B's illegitimate daughter, and the story of her conception is a version of an old comic intrigue of premarital seduction. The girl's mother, Sally Godfrey, left England after her daughter's birth and married a West Indian colonist. At the time of the action this former mistress has passed out of B's life, but her child remains to remind the reader of the consequences of the rake's pranks. To Pamela, in a moment of self-revelation, B confides:

> "I am far from making a Boast of, or takeing [sic] a Pride in, this Affair: But since it has happen'd, I can't say, but I wish the poor Child to live, and be happy; and I must endeavour to make her so." (Richardson 1741–42, 2:366–7)

So, at least, the first edition; but in later versions Richardson toned the passage down to omit the hint that a man in Mr. B's situation might secretly wish for the child to die (1974, 2:295). The early version is the more honest: we have seen how often the consciousness of high infant mortality intrudes itself upon the fictional rake, with the thought giving rise to a guilty longing.

To Pamela, however—at least at first—it is B's overt paternal care for the little girl that is evident, not his suppressed hostility. When B. takes her to see Miss Goodwin at boarding school for the second time, and shows signs of fondness for her, Pamela is impressed:

> "How commendable is this his love to the poor child, compar'd to that of most libertines, who have no delight, but in destroying innocence; and care not what becomes ... of the unhappy infants." (3:354)

This last reflection is conciliatory, even sentimental: Pamela tells herself that B has accepted his responsibilities and that all is well. But difficulties, in the shape of fresh patterns of rivalry, quickly arise. B, seeing that his wife has taken to Miss Goodwin, announces:

> "You must not talk to me of [the child's] coming home, after this visit, Pamela. How should I stand the reproaches of my own mind, were I to see the little prater every day before me, and think of what her poor mother has suffer'd on my account?" (3:356–57)

This is part of a technique which Richardson regularly uses to suggest B's dexterity in rationalization—his ability to deceive others, and perhaps himself, into thinking he is acting from worthy motives when in fact he is talking himself into doing what suits him best. No doubt the model reader is meant to take the squire's contrition over his daughter as sincere; but it is still clear that B is denying the child (and Pamela) what they most need and want. "The moment Mr. B. handed me out of the chariot," Pamela records on the occasion of her second visit to the school, "Miss Goodwin ran into my arms with great eagerness, and I as tenderly embraced her" (3:353–54). Incited by Pamela, Miss Goodwin tells B: "You should, in pity, let me live with you, sir; for I have no papa, nor mamma neither: they are so far off" (3:355). This fictional child wants more than food, clothing, and education: she wants an identity, a home, and loving parents.

In many respects the story of Miss Goodwin relates closely to stage comedy. Even Pamela's affection and care for the child recall *The Recruiting Officer,* where the rake's future wife takes an interest in the children he has had by his lowly mistress. The most significant difference between the comedy-children and Miss Goodwin is that the latter is no longer a baby. This means that instead of being a mere counter in the game she can become a participant: she can comment on, and intervene in, the lives of older people. Though her exercise of these functions is in practice severely limited—she takes part in no scene as dramatic as the scene between mother, son, and father in *The Virgin Unmasked*—it does represent an attempt by Richardson to register the new sensitivity of his time to the emotional needs of children, to their different stages of development, and to their existence as living and feeling beings.

The one problem that Richardson avoids is that of how, or whether, Miss Goodwin discovers whose daughter she really is. B has no hesitation in confiding the secret to his wife, though she might well have felt threatened by it. But Miss Goodwin herself is not told: Richardson lets B draw attention to the girl's ignorance of her parentage by telling Pamela that her "niece" is still in the dark (2:290, 295). Recognition scenes, in which characters encounter long-lost relations or discover the truth about their ancestry, were a commonplace in literature from the time of Sophocles or Plautus to Richardson's own day, and readers of *Pamela* perhaps had a right to expect one. From the records of the Foundling Hospital we know that eighteenth-century children, poor as well as rich, were as inquisitive about their parentage as orphans are today (McClure 1981, 237), while in fiction the problem of revealing an orphan's family background was one which was soon to be acknowledged. (In Frances Burney's *Evelina* the protagonist's foster father informs another character, "I have thought it necessary she should herself be acquainted with the melancholy circumstances of her birth. . . . I would not leave it in the power of chance, to shock her gentle nature with a tale of so much sorrow"—Burney 1958, 17.) But Richardson never shows B. confronting the problem of letting Miss Goodwin know that she is his daughter: in this instance, exceptionally, the novelist silently ignores an issue which his own narrative has raised.

In the second part of *Pamela,* which follows the protagonist into the period of her marriage with Mr. B, a child will become the focus for much graver tensions. Antagonism develops soon after Pamela conceives. In the earlier part of the novel B has enjoyed joking with his wife about changing her shape (2:159); but this may point more to pride in his own masculinity than to desire for children. And B, unlike Mirabell in *The Way of the World,* cares more for his wife's figure than for his child's health: ignoring Locke's warning against strait-lacing, he requires Pamela to lace herself tightly while pregnant, a demand which draws a reproof from his sister Lady Davers. While he insists, in one of his conversations with Pamela, that "no man has a greater affection for children" than he has (4:13), his sentence concludes with a long concessive clause showing why Pamela's first child should nevertheless be left with a nurse. Most of his overt reasons are connected with his desire to enjoy intellectual pursuits with his wife and to take her on parties of pleasure, which is flattering to Pamela in one way but distressing in another. Only gradually will B acquire a sense of the value of children and of the dangers a woman encounters in "perpetuating the family and name of her husband" (as a friend of Pamela's puts it). In some respects, as in his manner of arranging for a midwife, he is considerate (4:95). Yet there are times when he seems to have little idea of what is due to the conceiving, bearing, and fostering mother.

From the outset, for example, he resists Pamela's request to be allowed to suckle her own baby. His fondness for her looks makes him anxious to prevent her relapsing into "carelessness of person," as he has seen even "very nice" [sc. fastidious] women do during nursing. His program of improving Pamela's mind by French and Latin lessons has only just begun; suckling will interrupt it. "Let the nurse's office," he begs,

"have your inspection, your direction, and, when I am abroad, your greatest attention, if you please: but when I am at home, even a son and heir, so jealous am I of your affections, shall not be my rival in them: nor will I have my rest broken in upon, by your servants bringing to you, as you once propos'd, your little-one, at times, perhaps, as unsuitable to my repose, and your own, as to the child's necessities." (4:10–11)

B's concern for Pamela's intellectual development seems enlightened; his admission of his own loving jealousy is disarming. But the reader cannot help inferring that with B—as with most rakes—it is selfishness which prevents him from allowing Pamela to suckle her child. B has always feared those who might rival him in his wife's affections. Now he is threatened by a rival of the most insidious kind, a helpless and demanding one, with a presumptive right to disturb the intimacies of himself and his wife at any hour (cf. Doody 1974, 91–98; Stone 1977, 426–7). He does his best to think and speak of the child in the newly fashionable language of concern—"the little one" rather than "the brat"—but he cannot help regarding it in the way a comedy rake would have done; namely, as a threat to his and Pamela's glamor, freedom, and youth. The comedy rakes sent their illegitimate offspring to wet-nurses in villages on the outskirts of London: in real society it was still common for people of good family to have their children, legitimate as well as illegitimate, nursed off the premises. Mr. B, as Pamela's parents remind her in a consoling letter, is at least "not averse to have the child in the house" (4:16). But he cannot resist the temptation to forbid Pamela to suckle the baby. Her son must not thrust her husband out of her life.

Mr. B wins the battle about breast-feeding, but his nose is still out of joint. In the later stages of Pamela's pregnancy he begins a flirtation with an alluring countess. When he learns of the birth of his son, he observes pointedly, "If my Pamela is safe, the boy is indeed welcome" (4:99). A little later Pamela confides to her sister-in-law that her husband has little enthusiasm for the child:

He once said, as I would have presented the crowing infant to his arms, and hoped he would have kissed him, rejecting him, as I thought, Give him to his nurse, (indeed he said, my dear), it is time enough for me to mind him, when he can return my notice, and be grateful. Was not this, madam, a very slighting manner of expression? (4:109)

Pamela's own hurt feelings prevent her from reading her husband's accurately. B is not annoyed merely because the infant, so fond of and demanding on its mother, is indifferent to him. His sharpest grievance is the interruption the child is causing to his familiar intercourse with Pamela. This worries him even before the birth, and provokes him afterwards to threats and innuendoes born of hurt pride. When Pamela reminds him that the wives of biblical patriarchs suckled their own children, B retorts that those patriarchs "had several other wives" to console them for the temporary absence of one (4:11). After the birth, describing a trip to Oxford (shared with the countess but not with Pamela), B observes provokingly, "I had a partner too, my dear, to represent you." When Pamela replies submissively, "I am much obliged to the lady, sir, whoever she be," her husband continues, "Why, my dear, you are so engaged in your nursery! Then this was a sudden thing, as I told you" (4:125). The right to organize a party of pleasure on a sudden whim is, to B, emblematic of a youthful freedom which parenthood threatens: he cannot resist reminding Pamela that she is now less able to share these pleasures than she used to be.

When Billy falls ill and Pamela is distracted with worry, B gives her fair words but allows himself, at parting, a sharper thrust than any he has yet ventured:

> He is very kind; and Billy not being well, when he came in, my grief passed off without blame. He has said a great many tender things to me: but added, That if I gave myself so much uneasiness every time the child ailed anything, he would hire the nurse to overlay him. Bless me, madam! What hard-hearted, what shocking things are these men capable of saying! The farthest from their hearts, indeed; so they had need. For he was as glad of the child's recovery as I could be. (4:131–32)

We have heard "overlaying" mentioned before, in just this callous and casual way, by the rake Valentine in *Love for Love*.

It is the rake's adjustment to marriage in all its aspects—including parenthood—that is responsible for that brief section of the second part of *Pamela* in which a dull and mechanical sequel almost turns into a great novel. B's flirtation with the countess; his trips away with her, of which Pamela is allowed to hear a little, but not too much; the adolescent rakish patter about polygamy: all these are skillfully interleaved with scenes involving Pamela's pregnancy, lying-in, and early motherhood. All point to the same thing: Mr. B is not in love with the countess; he is not out of love with Pamela; he is jealous of the baby for coming between him and his wife. He has torn himself from

a bachelor existence, where he was adored by women and free
to come and go as he pleased, to marry Pamela. His return to
his old habits after the baby's birth is an implicit reproach to
his wife: "I gave up my freedom to marry you. You ought, in
gratitude, to spend a little more time with me."

To Pamela, of course, things appear differently. To her it
seems that the female, her aspirations controlled by a husband
obsessed with his prerogatives, is herself doomed to a condition
not unlike that of the helpless child:

> We are forced to struggle for knowledge, like the poor feeble infant
> who, as I describ'd in my first letter on this subject, is pinioned,
> legs, arms, and head, on the nurse's lap; and who, if its little arms
> happen, by great chance, to gain freedom, and offer but to expand
> themselves, are immediately taken into custody, and pinn'd down
> to passive behaviour, by the tyrannical nurse. (4:277)

Pamela is a student of Locke's theories of upbringing and education, and her metaphor of the helpless baby is presumably inspired by Locke's attack on the practice of swaddling. However,
there is something not merely Lockean but almost Blakean in
her protest against unnatural tyranny and confinement. The
child and the woman are conceived as potentially free spirits,
with the swaddling clothes as emblems of the bondage imposed
by a repressive culture. The context concerns the acquisition of
knowledge (or its prevention), but the unmistakable implication
is that the tyrant-father-husband is also impelled to keep his
wife, mistress, and children "swaddled" in other ways.

Ironically, however, Richardson's text sometimes points to a
possible reversal of this relationship. We have already alluded
to the wish of the male to find in the wife or mistress a symbolic
mother, with the suggestion that this identification becomes impossible once she, by bearing his children, introduces him into
the repressive cycle of family responsibilities (Kristeva 1974,
453). Precisely this insight is implicit in the second part of *Pamela* in Richardson's handling of Mr. B. At one time, B. tells
Pamela, he was not "at all solicitous whether [his] name was
continued or not by [his] own descendants" (3:161). From B.'s
imagined viewpoint, this would exemplify his fine contempt for
social conventions and his insistence on preserving his personal
freedom. But there are counterindications that identify his feelings about children as symptoms of immaturity: evidently he is
nervous of having children because he himself is still something

of a child. The notion of B. as infant with Pamela as mother is pervasive. It lies, for example, behind B.'s choice of metaphor when he begs Pamela not to nurse her own baby:

"I advise you, therefore, my dearest love, not to weaken, or, to speak in a phrase proper to the present subject, *wean* me from [my] love to you." (4:14; Richardson's emphasis)

B is constantly afraid that Pamela will use the "wire-drawing ways of [her] sex" (4:10) to attain an undue dominance over him, to reduce him to a child-like state of dependence. The danger seems especially acute to him once Pamela has a real child to play off against her husband, the metaphorical child. As mother and baby grow together, the husband is liable to shrink and fall away. In this atmosphere of insecurity, the confinement chamber and the nursery become theaters of war: one parent or other, it begins to seem, must be defeated and reduced to dependent status. In this context B.'s flirtation with the countess appears as a stratagem to maintain control. Nor is it simply a defensive move designed to assert independence from Pamela. At one point it is carried to the extreme of an assault on Pamela's own territory, the home, and even to what Pamela interprets as an attempt to carry off her baby. B. brings the countess home on a visit, and the latter asks to see the child:

I rang. Polly, bid nurse bring my Billy down.—My, said I, with an emphasis. . . .
Will you give master to my arms one moment, madam? said the Countess.
Yes, thought I, much rather than my dear Mr. B should any other. (4:137)

The overt fear to which Pamela is admitting here is that the countess and B. may have a child if their liaison ripens into actual adultery. But there are other sources of insecurity also. "Give Master to my arms" is ambiguous: "Master" is a fond way of referring to the baby, the son and heir, but for Pamela it could also allude less openly to Mr. B., whom she continued to call "master" long after she ceased to be his servant in the literal sense and became his wife. To the risk that the task of mothering B. senior may be taken from her is added the possibility that her own baby may be absorbed into a triangle of relationships from which she will be excluded. Giving the countess her baby to hold is an experience which makes Pamela more than uneasy:

> I yielded it to her: I thought she would have stifled it with her warm kisses. Sweet boy: Charming creature! And pressed it to her too lovely bosom, with such emotion, looking on the child, and on Mr. B, that I liked it not by any means. . . . I wonder'd the dear baby was so quiet . . . I would have had him just then cry, instead of me. . . . I grudged it, to think her naughty lips should so closely follow mine. [And later] . . . O be contented, too lovely, and too happy rival, with my husband; and tear not from me my dearest baby, the beloved pledge of our happier affections! (4:137–40, 150–51)

In comedy, characters scheme to transfer children to other characters. In the second part of *Pamela* the child is coveted by two rival women, and his transferability is a source of unease. Pamela's Billy, handed from mother to nurse to prospective stepmother, sets up no cry of protest. Evidently he has as yet no affections so specific and so deeply imprinted that they cannot be changed. It suits B. that Pamela should absorb this truth. He wants her to learn that, if she attempts to use Billy to gain dominance over her husband, the child can be taken away from her and given to someone else. Overtly, this threat is an extreme example of the callousness of the imperious male. Covertly, it is B.'s reproach for a lost world of courtship where he could uninterruptedly enjoy the company of the woman of his choice. (The visit of the countess is followed by yet another request to Pamela to leave Billy and come with her husband on a party of pleasure.) The whole procedure evokes the panic of B. as an always-indulged son, whose access to the mother-figure is threatened by the birth of a younger sibling. B's awkward gestures are, in their way, manifestations of his love: he resents Pamela's maternal attentions to Billy because he wants to be mothered himself. And Pamela, in her unuttered speech to the countess, implicitly admits that his fears are justified: "O be contented, too lovely, and too happy rival, with my husband; and tear not from me my dearest baby." In the last resort Pamela can dispense more easily with her husband than with her child.

In earlier literature, such as the ironically entitled *Ten Pleasures of Marriage,* the rituals of christening and lying-in were satirized as opportunities, eagerly seized by the wife, to exploit the husband financially while shutting him out emotionally. But a thoroughgoing thematization of the child as potential rival to the husband had to wait for the eighteenth-century novel. In the second part of *Pamela* it moves close to the center of the book.

Fielding's *Joseph Andrews* (1742), originally conceived as a parody of *Pamela,* moved ideologically closer to it in the course of composition. Here both childhood and paternity are once again seen to elicit contrasting responses. Two of the most likeable characters, the country-loving Mr. Wilson and the quixotic Parson Adams, show exemplary fondness for their children, but outside their families the survivalist attitudes of comedy often prevail. Gaffer Andrews, who learns that Joseph is not his son after all but that Fanny is his long-lost daughter, has no objection to giving up the boy but is chary of taking on the girl: "'Well,' says Gaffar *Andrews,* who was a comical sly old Fellow, and very likely desired to have no more Children than he could keep, 'you have proved, I think, very plainly that this Boy doth not belong to us; but how are you certain that the Girl is ours?'" (Fielding 1970, 305). Earlier, Andrews's wife has revealed that gypsies stole her healthy child and substituted a sickly one while her husband was away on army service. She managed to nurse the foster child back to health; when her husband returned he "said he was a chopping Boy, without ever minding his Age." "So I," Gammer Andrews belatedly confesses to the Gaffer, "seeing you did not suspect any thing of the matter, thought I might e'en as well keep it to myself, for fear you should not love him as well as I did" (305).

Partly this is a device to smooth a bumpy stretch of plotting, but like most lost child devices in literature it also embodies a genuine point about the attitudes of some parents toward their children. Old Andrews's cheery, irresponsible approach is typical of comedy, as Fielding himself hints when he calls Andrews a "comical, sly old Fellow." Andrews fails to notice such trivia as age differences in children; and he is quite prepared to engage, when he gets the chance, in a comic contest to get rid of his own offspring without taking anyone else's in return. (Here, as elsewhere, Fielding transfers to a lower-class character some functions that used to belong to the well-born stage rake.) Andrews is an irresponsible begetter who pays little heed to children: here as in other novels there is a hint that a man who is no more than this is in some sense extraneous to the family. The gaffer evidently spent a long period away from his wife and child, during which he contributed nothing to their welfare; his wife, as she tells the assembled company, was obliged to manage as best she could:

> "Times growing very hard, I having two Children, and nothing but
> my own Work . . . to maintain them, was obliged to ask Relief of the
> Parish; but instead of giving it me, they removed me . . . fifteen
> Miles." (305)

It is the mother who has to stand the hardship. (For the hardships of real-life wives and mothers while husbands were at
war, see Stone 1990, 142–43.) The father, who comes home after
the worst is over and fails even to notice a discrepancy in the
child's age, gives his offspring little but his name: it is hardly
an injustice if, through a contrivance of his wife's, this name is
given to a child he never begot.

No great weight of authorial censure descends on the Gaffer
for his breezy insouciance about his offspring. Fielding forgives
him, apparently, on the same grounds that Bernard Shaw felt
he could forgive the poor for their attachment to drink: the conditions of his existence invite it. Sharper satire is reserved for
frigidity toward children on the part of richer men. In *Joseph
Andrews* the protagonist of the inset narrative of Leonora has
a parent who "pass'd in the World's Language as an exceeding
good Father." His neighbors attributed his rapacious inclination
to "rob and plunder all Mankind" to "a desire of raising im-
mense Fortunes for his Children"; but in fact he looked on children as "an unhappy Consequence of [his] youthful Pleasures;
which as he would have been delighted not to have had [sic]
attended them, so was he no less pleased with any opportunity
to rid himself of the Incumbrance." Far from heaping up money
for his offspring, he regarded them as

> Rivals, who were to enjoy his beloved Mistress [money], when he
> was incapable of possessing her, and which he would have been
> much more charmed with the Power of carrying along with him:
> nor had his Children any other Security of being his Heirs, than
> that the Law would constitute them such without a Will, and that
> he had not Affection enough for anyone living to take the trouble
> of writing one. (113)

The rich man's cunning is not a function of comic vitality, as
that of old Andrews partly is, but of the anticomic qualities of
lifelessness and lovelessness. He is cheating himself as well as
others. He is ignoring a natural obligation between parent and
child; he is losing love and getting only money in return.

In *Joseph Andrews,* then, affection for children is one of the
clearest marks of difference between good and bad characters.

Often, it is true, Fielding's way of encoding this message seems stilted or sentimental: phrases like "little darling" and "little prattler" are overworked. But in a book which acknowledges the existence not only of the irresponsible comic stance but also of much darker attitudes, the warmth and solicitude toward children of characters like Wilson and Adams is a relief. In addition, there is an implied critique of that central figure of earlier comedy, the lively young rake. This figure, Fielding implies, has the potential to develop in either of two contrasting ways. Leonora's father turns into a miser, who sees children as a tiresome consequence of his youthful pleasures; Mr. Wilson matures into an affectionate parent who sees the loss of a beloved son as a punishment for his misspent youth. *Joseph Andrews* keeps in play the notion of children as a liability—particularly, for those that are fond of them, an emotional liability. But it also, like so many other novels of its time, suggests that bairns may be blessings, and that love for them is characteristic of the truly human being.

The figure of the rejecting father, like so much else in early eighteenth-century fiction, finds its culmination in Richardson's *Clarissa* (first edition 1748: third, much-revised edition 1751). This novel undertakes, in a more thoroughgoing way than any before or since, the subversion or deconstruction of the traditional comic plot. Its exuberant villain, Robert Lovelace, is a comic rake whose contrivances issue in tragedy. In his attitudes to his offspring, as well as in his attitudes to women, Lovelace epitomizes the abjection of the gay and irresponsible seducer who ostentatiously refuses to be tied down to family life.

Rakes, as we have often noted, are seldom enthusiastic about taking responsibility for babies and infants. However, no comic hero likes to be thought of as an outright enemy to new life: most are happy to bestow at least a kind word on a "brave boy" who cheekily imposes himself on the world as a result of a casual amour. Lovelace goes further: he likes to think of his care for his children as

a distinction in my favour from other rakes; who almost to a man follow their inclinations without troubling themselves about consequences. In imitation, as one would think, of the strutting villain of a bird, which from feathered lady to feathered lady pursues his imperial pleasures, leaving it to his sleek paramours to hatch the genial product in holes and corners of their own finding out. (Richardson 1932, 3:243)

There is a powerful irony in the mid-sentence change from disparagement of the barnyard cock, and the cock's counterpart in the social world, to entanglement in the alluring metaphor. Lovelace begins by execrating the "strutting villain of a bird": he ends by exalting it to imperial status and imaginatively identifying himself with it. Elsewhere he rhapsodizes, "A cock is a grand signor of a bird!" (2:67–68). This drift from a stance of compassion and responsibility to one of cheerful freebooterism is characteristic of the movement of Lovelace's thought.

As manifestations of the life-force—or, more precisely, as extensions of his own masculine vigor—children appeal to Lovelace. Shortly before Clarissa's first escape, when he has held her captive for some time, he takes delight in imagining his beautiful prisoner with "a twin Lovelace at each charming breast, drawing from it his first sustenance" (2:477). In the first edition the vision is even more lyrical and a great deal more earthy: Clarissa is imagined "pressing with her fine fingers the generous flood into the purple mouths of each eager hunter by turns" (Richardson 1985, 706). Much later, after the rape, Lovelace longs to hear news of the "charming, charming consequence" of the event, a pregnancy that will bring him "one charming boy by this lady" (Richardson 1932, 3:242–43). But his motives for wanting children are mixed. He enjoys the idea of Clarissa suckling twin Lovelaces not merely because he is stimulated at the prospect of life, reproduction, and growth, but also because the needs of a child are a means of ensuring the dependency of the mother. A Clarissa burdened with twin bastards would be gratifyingly obsequious to the father, "full of wishes, for the sake of the pretty varlets, and for her own sake, that I would deign to legitimate; that I would condescend to put on the nuptial fetters" (2:477). And there is another, yet more unworthy, motive for wanting Clarissa to become pregnant: "Should she *escape me,* and no such effect follow, my revenge on her family, and, in *such* a case, on herself, would be incomplete" (3:243). (For discussion of some of these quotations from a different point of view, see Perry 1991.)

Through Lovelace's own discourse his picture of himself as a generous and caring father is exposed as a fantasy. Writing of his conduct toward the son that a former mistress died in giving birth to, he has this to say:

I have contrived to see the boy twice, unknown to the aunt who takes care of him. . . . The boy is a fine boy, I thank God. No father need be ashamed of him. He will be well provided for. If not, I would take care of him. He will have his mother's fortune. They curse the father, ungrateful wretches! but bless the boy. (2:148)

Lovelace enjoys cursing the dead woman's family for their ingratitude to the man who has given them a grandson, yet he finds it convenient to let them have the trouble and expense of the child's upbringing. This feeling is discernible in most of his many utterances on the subject of children. Though he crows more loudly than other rakes about the delights of lusty offspring, and boasts of his care for them, his practice as outlined in the text is that of any other barnyard cock. In spite of his lordly condemnations of avarice, he is far from being a generous provider for his dependents: he is happy for the consequences of his exuberant sexual activity to be taken care of by someone else.

The rake's construction of his own existence as one of bracing freedom and bold independence is always in danger of replacement by the reader's construction of it as one of lack, of insufficiency, of immaturity, of the fear of growing up. Lovelace disarmingly reveals his fear of maturity, with its attendant emotional and financial involvements, in an account he gives of one of his dreams. (For a metafictional interpretation of the dream see Castle 1984.) In this dream Clarissa, convalescent from the illness that follows the rape at Sinclair's brothel, is lured away to another house where the penetration is repeated, this time with less obstinate resistance on her side:

Then, as quick as thought, . . . ensued recoveries, lyings-in, christenings, the smiling boy, amply, even in *her own* opinion, rewarding the suffering mother.

Then the grandfather's estate yielded up, possession taken of it: living very happily upon it: her beloved Norton her companion; Miss Howe her visitor; and (admirable! thrice admirable!) enabled to *compare notes* with her; a charming girl, by the same father, to her friend's charming boy; who, as they grow up, in order to consolidate their mammas' friendships (for neither have dreams regard to *consanguinity*), intermarry, change names by Act of Parliament, to enjoy my estate—and I know not what of the like incongruous stuff. (3:250–51)

For the rake, this is a vision of paradise: a pastoral scene of fertility and renewal from which the male parent is deliciously, intriguingly absent. The women and children—Clarissa, her friend Anna, the two babies, Mrs. Norton the old nurse—make up a self-sustaining community, living comfortably on the income of Clarissa's grandfather's estate. The male child is at once the consequence of the rape and its reparation. (The rake, though he does not want the trouble of children himself, assumes that women and married people all want them: we have already seen Lovelace cursing the family of a former mistress, who died in childbed of his illegitimate son, for their lack of gratitude for the present of a healthy male child.) More delightful still, the boy and girl will marry; and the law, which forbids both the marriage of siblings and the inheritance of bastards, will be manipulated to allow the children to have their father's estate.when he dies. The incestuous nature of the union between brother and sister is an extra titillation: where more conventional minds see incest as a dire and fateful consequence of rakery (cf. Nelson 1992), Lovelace sees it as refreshing and life-renewing, symptomatic of a return to the freedom of primitive times.

Lovelace's picture of Anna and Clarissa on the country estate, like his earlier vision of Clarissa as the meek mother suckling vigorous twin hunters, belongs to the genre of mythological painting. It depicts a little paradise, a closed ecological system, which owes its being to the absent Lovelace—the maker and giver who, godlike, can withdraw from his creation, leaving it to grow and renew itself without his care. Most audacious of all is the way Lovelace's vision blends Clarissa's Christian fantasy of a retired, chaste, charitable country existence with his own dream of untrammeled libertinism attended with no harmful consequences. (The scene filled with christenings and "the like incongruous stuff" is a follow-up to an earlier one in which Clarissa and her "*old* nurse . . . *old* coachman . . . and two or three *old* maidservants . . . (for everything will be old and penitential about her)" will live "very comfortably together, reading *old* sermons, and *old* prayer books; and relieving *old* men, and *old* women" [3:177].)

Lovelace's pleasure in the idea of children is always mastered by his fear of the reality. That may explain why his visions of parenthood are so often distanced by translation into terms reminiscent of painting or sculpture. This is true of the disturbing visions—of which there are several—as well as the more inviting ones. Some time after the rape, at a juncture when Lovelace (though he does not know it) has in fact lost all chance of marrying Clarissa, he indulges in a satirical fantasy of himself and the lady going to church in some future married state. The thought of them kneeling together, with their numerous family, reminds him irresistibly of a piece of seventeenth-century monumental statuary, with a horde of stone children clustering round two equally rigid parental figures:

> The honest cavalier in armour is presented kneeling, with uplifted hands, and half-a-dozen jolter-headed, crop-eared boys behind him, ranged . . . all in the same posture—facing his pious dame, with a ruff about her neck, and as many whey-faced girls all kneeling behind *her* . . . (3:316)

To figure in a tableau of this kind would be to fall from the enviable estate of a Lovelace to the miserable condition of a conventional patriarch like Clarissa's father: a "gloomy tyrant," as Lovelace delights to call him, ruled (though he does not realize it) by his wife and son by turns. Harlowe's gout has imprisoned him in his morgue-like house with his mostly chilly family; his constant fear is that the unruly Lovelaces of the outside world will break in to steal his ducats, his daughter, or both. Yet his joy in his daughter, his greatest treasure, was mixed even while it lasted; for, as Lovelace admiringly notes, she outshone the rest of the family and transcended their low and sordid ideals. To her father, no less than to Lovelace, Clarissa is a problematic individual. Each senses that she constitutes a challenge to his own supremacy: the challenge is one that neither man can meet. This reminds us that the concept of the child has a certain elasticity about it; even when grown to maturity, a child is still one's offspring. While little children can involve their parents in trouble, boredom, responsibility, and expense, grown-up sons and daughters bring new causes of anxiety: their lives and personalities take on an independent existence, passing rapidly beyond their parents' control.

Lovelace's sketch of petrification by domestication is a caricature; caricature, like farce, is often used to distance the unthinkable by ridicule. Lovelace, anxious to dispel his personal nightmare, labors to exorcize it with his satirical pen. Less real to him, but still disturbing, is the vision of a horde of children who, instead of resembling the figures on a monument, grow up as intoxicatingly unruly as their father:

> At last, perhaps, when life shall be turned into the dully-sober stillness, and I become desirous to forget all my past rogueries, what comfortable reflections will it afford, to find them all revived, with

equal, or probably *greater* trouble and expense, in the persons and manners of so many young Lovelaces of the boys; and to have the girls run away with varlets perhaps not half so ingenious as myself! (3:474).

This envisages a Lovelace reduced, not to the condition of Clarissa's father, but to that of another gouty elder, his own uncle Lord M. The old peer, pathetic ruin of a former rake—like Sir Simon Darnford in *Pamela,* he used to be a friend of Wycherley (3:323)—is confined to his house and the company of his female relatives. His imaginative poverty is betrayed by his love of platitudinous proverbs; his only excitement—and chief torment—is provided by the exploits of his unruly nephew. Lovelace, it appears, feels rather less awed by the prospect of turning into a Lord M than he does at the thought of becoming a James Harlowe Senior: marginally, he would rather be tormented by children who inherit his own high spirits than rigidify in the company of a family characterized by Clarissa's supposed coldness. But he is still unwilling to think of his children superseding and replacing him, of their maturing into worthy successors and rivals. It consoles him to imagine the girls eloping with less distinguished rakes than himself; the boys' adventures, servile imitations of his own, will hurt his pocket more than his pride.

Lovelace's fears of paternity and marriage run deep and are often expressed in devious ways. Perhaps the subtlest manifestation of them occurs in the passage where he likens Clarissa to Semele and himself to her lover, Jupiter:

> There was, I believe, a kind of frenzy in my manner which threw her into a panic like that of Semele perhaps, when the Thunderer, in all his majesty, surrounded with ten thousand celestial burning-glasses, was about to scorch her into a cinder. (2:98)

At first sight this is simply an awesome evocation of Lovelace as master of Clarissa and disposer of her destiny—a godlike Lovelace, resplendent but terrible bringer of fire and light. Semele was consumed with fire because she rashly asked to see her divine lover in his real shape—to know him, to classify him, to tie him down. Lovelace hints that if Clarissa tries to do the same to him she will be punished in some analogous way. But this is not all. In his retelling of Semele's story Lovelace leaves something out: the birth of the young Dionysus from Semele's ashes (Braudy 1974). He cannot assimilate the idea of new birth into his self-gratifying version of the myth. Offspring may, in the short run, provide living proof of a man's vitality, but in the long run they threaten it: in classical myth, which is often at the back of Lovelace's mind as he acts out his godlike or heroic roles, young gods and heroes repeatedly thrust doting parents from their thrones. This fate, as it happens, never overtook Jupiter, with whom Lovelace likes to compare himself. But Lovelace cannot wholly ignore the possibility of his own decline from a youthful, encroaching, magisterial Jupiter, enjoyer of women, king of gods and men, to an old, sulky, muttering, avaricious paternal deity like James Harlowe, "old AUTHORITY," thundering from his remote palace while the wine of life is poured and drunk elsewhere—a "gloomy tyrant whose only boast is his riches," impotent, a jailer, suspicious and resentful of the godlike young.

It is with Lovelace that Richardson, and the eighteenth-century novel, achieve their finest figuration of the rogue male who rejects parenthood and family life. One reason for this is Richardson's skill in reactivating the connotations which surrounded the rake in stage comedy while at the same time showing the baneful consequences, in terms of heartlessness and lovelessness, that the rake's approach to life can entail. Mandeville's presentation of Dorante in *The Virgin Unmasked* is admirable and convincing, but it is unremittingly serious: it lacks the comic dimension which Richardson imparts to his most triumphant male creation. It would be ungracious not to laugh with Lovelace, even in his most outrageous moments of anti-familial fantasy: he is, in his way, an exuberant comic figure. But he is also sinister. His comic energy and demonic pranks resemble those of Edmund in *King Lear:* within the fictional world they have dire consequences for other characters. Nowhere is this more apparent than in Lovelace's appropriation and development of the old comic arguments against marriage and family life.

Not all representations of fathers in the eighteenth-century novel are negative. Booth in Fielding's *Amelia,* though weak and feckless in other ways, never wavers in his love and care for his children; while in the novels of Smollett it is, as we shall see, the father rather than the mother who normally presides over the idyllic scene at the end of the book. In the meantime the uncle (an obvious substitute father) looks after the young man as he moves through the harsher scenes of his childhood and early manhood. (It always is a young man: girl children and female education are of almost no interest to Smollett.)

After 1750, there is an increasing tendency to suggest that fathers, foster fathers, and male teachers can after all be expected to give personal attention to the education of children, including young children and older girls. Sarah Scott's *Description of Millenium Hall* (1762) is transitional in this respect. Early in the novel a man who adopts a beautiful young woman decides, as Dorilaus in Eliza Haywood's *Fortunate Foundlings* had done in a similar situation, to send her to school, "very prudently judging, that his house was not a proper place for education, having there no one fit to take care of a young person." He is aware also that there are "minute feminine details" which will need to be attended to but "of which he [is] too ignorant to acquit himself well" (1974, 37–38). The narrative implicitly commends this decision, for the man later becomes amorously interested in his ward and persecutes her with his advances: evidently she was better away from him. However, later in the novel, in the inset story of Miss Selvyn, a little girl's education "devolve[s] entirely on her father," who, "well qualified for the part," becomes "himself her tutor," with such success that "at twelve years old she excel[s] all the young ladies of the neighborhood of her own age" (193). Another male character "takes a great deal of pains in the education of his two sons, while their mother spends almost the whole year in town, immersed in folly and dissipation" (253). By the time of *Mansfield Park* (1814) it is considered plausible to represent even a frigid parent like Sir Thomas Bertram as taking the trouble to "examine" a child—even a girl child and poor relation like Fanny Price—in French and English, though it is clearly implied that Sir Thomas's inquisitions were a terrifying ordeal for the girl herself (Austen 1970, 282).

In the first half of the eighteenth century, however, the rejecting or abandoning father looms large in the world of the English novel; and while he sometimes keeps part of the glamour formerly attached to the stage rake, who abandoned and disowned children with such fine insouciance, he emerges overall as a strongly negative figure.

6

Mothers

In the twentïeth century, the word "motherhood" has become a metaphor for all that is universally loved and revered. Even in the male-dominated world of public meetings the expression "motherhood motion" is used to denote a resolution which nobody will want to oppose. Yet this feeling is not as timeless or universal as it might seem. Dorothy Dinnerstein, in an influential book published in the 1970s, writes of "our species' fundamental ambivalence toward its female members," and attributes it in large measure to "the fact that the early mother, monolithic representative of nature, is a source of ultimate distress as well as ultimate joy." In questioning how far mother-love is biologically determined and how far it is subject to the strengthening or weakening influence of culture, the same writer notes that "the bodily machinery of motherhood works strongly to bind women to their young." Yet Dinnerstein is also sensitive to the possibility of a mother's hostility toward her offspring—"There is of course no such thing as a wholly benevolent mother, with no antagonism whatsoever to the child as an autonomous being"—and even more to the opposite danger, that a mother's overwhelming influence may stifle the growth of maturity and self-expression in her children: "Motherhood . . . gives us boys who will grow . . . into childish men, unsure of their grasp on life's primitive realities. And it gives us girls who will grow . . . into childish women, unsure of their right to full worldly adult status" (1987, 79–81, 111).

Both modern validation and modern questioning of the maternal role and function had their counterparts in the seventeenth and eighteenth centuries. Patricia McGraw detects a "prevalent belief in the strength of maternal love" in the period, but then has to explain the popularity of novels like *Roxana* and *Moll Flanders* whose central figures behave at times as rejecting mothers. She suggests plausibly that "many, if not most, parents harbor occasional fantasies about being rid of dependent children." In novels, she conjectures, "the depiction of unmotherly mothers is used, in part, as a strategy to shock readers and increase sales. . . . Novelists sought to demonstrate that maternal affection was not necessarily inherent" (91, 105, 118). A more recent writer, Patricia Crawford, notes that in the early modern period a mother's inability to love a child was sometimes treated as a sign of mental disorder (1990, 41).

We have seen that Sir Robert Filmer, champion of the rights of fathers, neglected those of mothers. Other political philosophers did not. Hobbes concluded that in the state of nature, where marriage did not exist and where paternity was decided by the mother's word, dominion over the child must have fallen to the female parent, not to the male. (For Filmer, Hobbes, and Locke on this topic, see Kerber 1980, 16–19 and Staves 1979, 140). Locke, in the first of his two treatises on government, chided Filmer for quoting the biblical injunction "honor thy father" while suppressing the continuation "and thy mother" (Locke 1967, 167). In *Some Thoughts Concerning Education* he emphasized the importance of maternal care, both during babyhood and in the early stages of learning (1968, 288).

Most of the male writers who followed Locke concurred with him in stressing both the symbolic and practical value of maternal care. In 1739 the Earl of Warrington represented the "Care and Education of Children, both with respect to their Bodies and Minds," as being "by *Nature* given" to the mother "in a much greater Proportion than to the Father" (Booth 1985, 6). In the same year an anonymous writer styling himself "Philogamus" (lover of matrimony) attributed to women an "inexpressible desire" for children: this irresistible longing he thought necessary for the preservation of the human species, since it helped women to endure "such Dangers and Difficulties [in bearing and raising offspring], as would be almost impossible to undergo without it" (Philogamus 1985, 67). Tom Brown, in the preface to his translation of Louis de Gaya's book on marriage, announced that members of "the Fair Sex" all know "that nothing is troublesome to 'em, that tends to the keeping a Child as it should be" (1704, A2v).

Women writers, while sometimes appearing flattered by the new valuation of motherhood, occasionally pointed to the negative aspects of the role assigned to them. Mary Astell, perhaps the best-known early English feminist (though she was neither the first, nor the only one), satirized men's extravagant expectations of the ideal wife and mother (Perry 1986, 143). The gentle-man in search of a wife, she observed, looked for "one to manage his Family, an House-keeper, a necessary Evil . . . One who may breed his Children, taking all the care and trouble of their Edu-cation, to preserve his Name and Family" (Astell 1986, 105). One of Astell's modern champions, Ruth Perry, detects an asso-ciation in her writing between sex and death, due partly to the frequency of deaths in childbirth at this period. Perry also sug-gests that many seventeenth-and eighteenth-century women with a talent for writing found it impossible to exercise their art and simultaneously carry out duties as wives and mothers (Perry 1982). Astell, however, described the education and even suckling of children as important and satisfying tasks, which women ought to accept. If mothers of high rank "had a due regard to their Posterity," she wrote, "they wou'd not think themselves too Good to perform what Nature requires [sc. breast-feeding], nor through Pride and Delicacy remit the poor little one to the care of a Foster Parent" (1986, 144). As for education, women were well fitted to carry out this duty pro-vided that they were allowed to acquire a convenient fund of learning of their own:

> Great is the influence we have over [men] in their Childhood. . . . If a Mother be discreet and knowing as well as devout, she has many opportunities of giving such a Form and Season to the tender Mind of the Child, as will shew its good effects thro' all the stages of his Life. . . . If she do not make the Child, she has the power to marr him, by suffering her fondness to get the better of discreet affec-tion. (167)

For Astell, indeed, it makes sense for women to accept the role of educators of children since it will give them a responsible role in society and a pretext for demanding proper education and training for themselves. Astell's most treasured project was a kind of Protestant nunnery which would provide for its mem-bers, according to their individual tastes, either a temporary respite from marriage or a permanent refuge from it; and she saw the education of children as one of the mainstays of this hypothetical community. Expanding on Locke, she explains that the "foundation" of a child's education, "on which in a great measure the success of all depends," ought to be

> laid by the Mother, for Fathers find other Business, they will not be confin'd to such a laborious work, they have not such opportunities

of observing a Child's Temper, nor are the greatest part of 'em like
to do much good, since Precepts contradicted by Example, seldom
prove effectual. (177)

The dismissiveness toward men exemplified in the last comment does not fully disguise the essential conservatism of the
argument. The father may be allowed to escape most of the
responsibility for the child's upbringing: it will be shared between the mother, the carefully chosen nurse, and the single
woman teacher. Astell's claims for women do not, then, differ
essentially from Locke's: at times she even uses the masculine
pronoun "he," as Locke does, when referring to children in
general.

Despite its acceptance by some women writers, the notion
of motherhood propounded by men was somewhat patronizing.
Philogamus's praise of women's courage in risking their lives
to bear children is accompanied by an unflattering assumption:
"The most chaste Virgin in the World can scarce contain herself
at the Sight of a beautiful Child; but is ready to devour it with
her Kisses; without which Tenderness, it were morally impossible to preserve the Species." The form of expression betrays
the writer's underlying conception of women as fundamentally
sensual and passionate creatures. Their impulse to conceive,
bear, suckle, kiss, and fondle babies is seen to derive from a
sensual passion "which we rudely, and wrongfully term Lust,"
but which is evidently to be thought of as analogous to lust.
Their propensity for bearing and raising children is seemingly
not owing to choice but to a desire programmed into them by
nature (Philogamus 1985, 8). The writer is concerned to validate
women's passionate feelings for children, and to champion the
loyal wife and mother against the "Strumpet" who may lure her
husband away from her. But the gesture by which he asserts
the importance of the role of the wife and mother within the
affective family simultaneously limits its scope: "Women were
principally designed for producing the Species, and Men for
other greater Ends" (12). Apparently this writer would have
agreed with comments like that of F. R. Leavis in our own century who, writing of the remoteness of modern civilization from
natural rhythms, concluded: "It is not easy today to accept the
perpetuation and multiplication of life as ultimate ends" (1963,
79). Such limited means of fulfillment might suffice for women,
but not for men.

The new recognition of the mother's role in upbringing and

education was accompanied, too, by an acute anxiety lest she
might, in practice, betray or overcome her natural impulses,
neglecting her duty or going about it in the wrong way. The
Earl of Warrington, having established to his satisfaction that
other duties will (and should) often take a father away from his
children, seems inclined to pass responsibility for their education on to the mother. But then, as if determined to assign the
best of both worlds to the husband and the worst of both to the
wife, he goes on to lament that if a father does concern himself
with the education of his children their mother, whose relationship with them is by nature so much closer and more intimate,
may undo what her husband has achieved:

> When a Father [is] . . . linked to a Woman . . . who . . . is not only
> totally remiss in taking Care of her Children, but corrupts their
> Morals by the evil Influence of her Indiscretions or Malice, and who
> must be so constantly amongst them; she may, and probably will,
> in a few Hours, outweigh and defeat all or great Part of the good
> Effects of many Months or Years Labour and Study of the Father
> for the good of his Children. (Booth 1985, 8)

Transposed into the discourse of comic fiction, this would resemble Walter Shandy's perennial complaint that his plans for his
son are frustrated by the impulsiveness and irrationality of his
wife and female servants. In its original context it betrays the
discontents of an eighteenth-century noble household riven by
internal rivalries and strife.

In the discourses of social commentary and philosophy, then,
we may often detect a tendency to take from women with one
hand what has been given with the other. Commendations of
the model mother are often followed by allusions to the bad
mother in her various guises. The overfond mother will spoil
her children by overindulgence or corrupt them by her evil influence. The woman who prefers not to have children, or who
entrusts them in their early years to a succession of potentially
unreliable nurses, risks being considered unwomanly and unnatural, though the privilege of a social or political life unham-
pered by the distractions of offspring is readily conceded to
fathers. Thus the new ideology often is used as a way to confine
women to their nurseries or (if they refuse to be so tied) chide
them for neglect of their duties.

The possibility of a woman preferring childlessness over
motherhood, treated with unquestioning disapproval in most
controversial works, was more searchingly explored in the new

discourse of prose fiction. It is revealing to find a woman writer
Mary Manley, expressing doubts (in her role as fictional narra
tor) about the universality of maternal love, which she describes
somewhat nervously as "that meritorious Tenderness, common
to all the Female-kind, and only less to be found in the Human
Where Reason, if not destroys, yet weakens instinct" (1971
1:567). What is noticeable here is that, while the innate and
universal character of maternal feeling is not directly denied
there is a recognition that the conditions of human existence
can weaken or break the bond between mother and child.

A more thoroughgoing, and more uncompromising, treatmen
of the problem of motherhood is found in Bernard Mandeville's
The Virgin Unmasked. This book, considered from another
viewpoint in an earlier chapter, does not at first sight look like
a legitimate novel: if anything it bears more resemblance to
early pornography (Vichert 1975, 1). The title is deliberately
titillating and the form, as in pornographic works like the *École
des Filles* (ca. 1655) or *The Whore's Rhetoric* (1683), is that of a
dialogue between an older woman who gives advice about life
and a younger one who questions her. But the aim of Mande
ville's older woman, Lucinda, is not to instruct her niece
Antonia in whoredom: it is to warn her against all sexual
involvement, including marriage. To illustrate her argumen
Lucinda tells cautionary tales which anticipate later develop
ments in the novel through their preoccupation with the fine
detail of interpersonal relationships and their determination to
explore, with a thoroughness unknown to stage comedy, the dy
namics of the nuclear family and the possibility of happiness
in marriage.

In stage comedies the brief, sardonic comments on pregnancy
and breeding dropped by female characters had invited the in
ference that well-bred young women were informed about such
things. But in Mandeville's book Lucinda, the lively spinster
narrator, assumes—apparently correctly—that her niece is ig
norant and innocent, looking forward to marriage and mother
hood not only as the natural destiny of her sex but also as more
or less unalloyed pleasures. Lucinda feels obliged to acquain
her niece with the negative aspects of both.

Lucinda herself does not dislike children: though she some
times affects disdain by referring to them as "brats" she gives
herself away elsewhere by expressions like "a mannerly Child
of an engaging Humour, whom [the parents] were deservedly
fond of" (206), and she has clearly been a generous friend to

her niece during the latter's childhood years. Yet she makes a powerful case for regarding childbearing and motherhood as a curse, and pregnancy as a loathsome and potentially fatal disease:

> Is it not a Thousand pitys, to see a Young Brisk Woman, well made, and fine Limb'd? as soon as she is Poyson'd by Man, Reach, Puke, and be Sick, ten or twelve times in a Day, for a Month or Six Weeks; and after that, Swell for Seven or Eight Months together; till, like a Frog, she is nothing else but Belly. . . . Be assured, that the Bearing, as well as Bringing forth of Children, wasts Women, wears 'em, shakes, spoils, and destroys, the very Frame and Constitution of them. (119–23)

The speech continues in the same vein for several pages. Its very vigor and luxuriance prevent it from being taken too seriously: partly it is an enjoyable exercise in paradox or rhetorical exaggeration. Yet there is an irreducible referential element, bearing with it a telling comment on a condition experienced by most human females. The same is true of Lucinda's comments on breast-feeding. "When Aurelia's Daughter was a Maid," she recalls for her niece's benefit, "she was talk'd of every where, for having an extraordinary fine Bosom; let her now compare once her Breasts to yours, and see, which are the firmest" (119). The comment is made in a discourse framed as a fiction, but we know that similar discussions were being conducted in other contemporary discourses, such as Steele's essays, which had only the most rudimentary fictional frame and were offered explicitly as social commentary. In the same way Mandeville's text, though it does not require the reader to swallow Lucinda's doctrines whole, does offer itself as an intervention in contemporary debates about living: the tales Lucinda tells are meant to stimulate processes of discovery and evaluation.

Lucinda's warnings against pregnancy and the other biological consequences of motherhood form more or less separate sections at the beginning and middle of the book. The exemplary tales she tells later focus not so much on pregnancy and suckling as on maternal love. The main conclusion is that love for their children exposes women to the blows of fortune and the malice of enemies. Though a spinster, Lucinda knows how hard it is not to love one's child; she herself, as we saw earlier, is sensitive to the charms of other people's offspring despite her pragmatic, dismissive pose. But the burden of her tale is that "fondness

to their Brats" typically makes women vulnerable to seductive
flattery, or locks them into unhappy domestic ménages from
which they would otherwise break away (34). In the main story
of Aurelia it is said at one point that she would have liked to
leave her husband, "but what could she do with her Children,
whom she Doated on? . . . She resolved to bear with any thing,
rather than leave her Dear Babes" (86).

Elsewhere Aurelia is made to recount how, when she was
staying with her mother-in-law in the absence of her husband,
the former did her best to sow dissension in the family by exploiting Aurelia's preference for her son over her daughter:

> I know 'tis wrong, to make a Distinction in our Inclinations between
> Children; Parents should distribute their Love with a Just, and
> equal hand among them; but here I could not help it; my Daughter
> through Illness was very Froward [sc. perverse, hard to handle];
> and afterwards, the Grand-Mother giving her more Liberty, than I
> would have allowed her, grew a Ramping Girl; and having gain'd
> her by little Gifts, which, as I was kept [Aurelia was kept short of
> money by her husband], I was not able to bestow; the Old Woman
> took great Delight to see, that she could draw her from me. (94)

As the analysis of this sinister family situation proceeds, the
reader sees more and more clearly that a situation involving
children can be just as compulsively narratable as any other.
The intrigues and rivalries become steadily more complex,
partly because each of the two children, even at this early age,
has a distinct and unmistakable "character." Aurelia's mother-
and sister-in-law work insidiously, not only on Aurelia's feelings
of guilt at preferring her son to her daughter, but also on the
girl child's willingness to be lured away from her mother:

> They would always teaze me, in telling me I did not Love her:
> Heaven knows it was false; but how could I show so much Love to
> her, who not Contented to be, where she could get nothing, was
> always with my Mother-in-Law; as I could to my dear Sober Boy,
> that despising their Bribes of Tarts, and Sweet-Meats, with which
> they coaxed his sister from me, would hardly ever leave me. (94–95)

Here the situation elicits a profusion of detail and a depth of
observation of interpersonal relationships which epitomize
what we have since come to expect from a novel. It is puzzling
that later novelists, skillful as they were in delineating the plots
and schemes of adults and in exploring the ethical codes which

they tried to follow in their dealings with one another, did not follow Mandeville's lead in exploring the dynamics of relationships involving children. But such is the case. In a surprising number of instances children in the early novel, like those in stage comedy, are babies, too young to speak for themselves; even when children old enough to talk are introduced, as they sometimes are, their words, actions, and choices are never as carefully articulated, or their influence on the dynamics of the family as subtly displayed, as in Mandeville's innovative book.

Mandeville's Aurelia, though she is used by the narrator to illustrate the snares into which motherhood may lead an unfortunate woman, is never portrayed as a frigid, rejecting, or abandoning parent. In later novels, however, these less positive maternal stereotypes begin to appear. The protagonist of Defoe's *Colonel Jack* (1722), for example, observes:

> My Mother kept very good Company, but that part belongs to her Story, more than to mine; all I know of it, is by oral Tradition thus; my Nurse told me my Mother was a Gentlewoman . . . and she (my Nurse) had a good piece of Money given her to . . . deliver [my father] and my Mother from the Importunities that usually attend the Misfortune, of having a Child to keep that should not be seen or heard of.
>
> My father it seems gave my Nurse something more than was agreed to at my Mother's request, upon her solemn Promise that she would use me well, and let me be put to School. (Defoe 1965, 3)

The mother's concern for the child, even in her son's slightly apologetic account, sounds minimal. Her chief anxiety seems to be to dispose of him so that she may resume her life of pleasure as quickly as possible: in this and other respects she can be seen as a female recasting of the comedy-rake, or a novelistic version of the carefree, irresponsible society woman of stage comedy and satire. In *Moll Flanders* (1722) and *Roxana* (1724), Defoe's two celebrated novels with female protagonists, this figure will take on more complex forms. Moll and Roxana will appear, at different moments in their respective novels, both as freebooters and as settled wives or mistresses; both will be swayed alternately by the impulse to abandon, and the impulse to foster, their children.

Moll Flanders, as many critics have noticed (Lerenbaum, 1977; Miller, 1980; Shinagel, 1969), repeatedly abandons babies. She leaves her first two, without regret, to the care of her first husband's family, describing them in the familiar comic terms

as a piece of property which is more of a liability than an asset
to its possessor:

> My two Children were indeed taken happily off my Hands, by my
> Husband's Father and Mother, and that by the way was all they got
> by Mrs. Betty. (Defoe 1976, 59)

Of her third child Moll reports casually, "*I had had one by my
Gentleman* Draper, *but it was buried*" (64): she is relieved at the
death of this infant, for its father has left her no money. Next
Moll walks out on her Virginia children, admitting to a "real
desire never to see them . . . any more" (91). However, all these
children apart from the dead one have been born of incestuous
unions (Brooks 1969), which makes Moll's indifference or revulsion more understandable. In the case of the Virginia family
her disgust when she discovers the forbidden relationship is in
proportion to the love she once bore the fruits of it: "had things
been right" she would never have left them (Defoe 1976, 91).
As it is she delays her flight from her husband/brother—much
against her own will—for fear that the children, when known
to be born of incest, may be prohibited by law from inheriting
their father's money (96).

Moll's discourse, then, is marked by maternal fondness. She
will sometimes express relief that a child is dead, but unlike
some of the stage-comedy heroes she never wishes that a healthy
child would die. Of her son by her Bath lover, "a fine, lovely
Boy, above five Years old" (122), she reflects:

> I was greatly perplex'd about my little Boy; it was Death to me to
> part with the Child, and yet when I consider'd the Danger of being
> one time or other left with him to keep without a Maintenance to
> support him, I then resolv'd to leave him where he was; but then I
> concluded also to be near him my self too, that I might have the
> satisfaction of seeing him, without the Care of providing for him.
> (125)

The last phrase suggests that Moll wants the pleasure of the
child without the expense, yet it does credit her with an awareness that there is pleasure to be had: this sets her apart from
those feckless comic figures who give no sign of parental feeling.
When Moll feels no affection for a child, she shows no hesitation
in admitting the fact; this, by the law of differentiation that
operates in all discourse, adds weight to her protestations of
love for her favorites.

This same law of differentiation operates in the distinction drawn between Moll and Mother Midnight, midwife and trader in stolen pleasures, the next most important character in the novel. The Mother's attitude to babies is wholly businesslike. She forbids husbands and wives to sleep together under her roof because, though she "care[s] not how many Children [are] born in her house," she will "have none [be]got there if she [can] help it" (170). She frankly prefers still births and miscarriages to live deliveries because they save christening fees (166). When Moll is found to be pregnant, Mother Midnight offers her a dose to procure a miscarriage: when Moll rejects it with horror the older woman advises her to send the baby, when it comes, to a hired nurse. By this means, she claims, she has saved "many an innocent Lamb, as she call'd them, which would otherwise perhaps have been Murder'd" (168). But Moll mentally dismisses this as sales talk: the wet-nursing system is "only a contriv'd Method for Murther; that is to say, a killing . . . Children with safety" (173):

You give a Piece of Money to these People to take the Child off the Parents Hands, and to take Care of it as long as it lives; now we know, Mother . . . that those are poor People, and their Gain consists in being quit of the Charge as soon as they can; how can I doubt but that, as it is best for them to have the Child die, they are not over Solicitous about its Life. (175)

Comedy displays a carefree attitude to the infant (abandon it and someone will find it and look after it), modulating into a hostile one (with luck it may have the decency to die). Moll's meditations encompass the theme that hard comedy excludes: the importance of fostering, particularly maternal fostering, to the very survival of the individual and thus of the species. Each child, Moll reflects, is "born into the World helpless" and can be raised only by an adult's "Care and Skill." Without this, half the children that are born would die "tho' they were not to be deny'd Food"; half of those that remained would be cripples or fools. Affection is "placed by Nature in the Hearts of Mothers" to make them bear the "Care and waking Pains needful to the Support of their Children" (173–74). Yet in spite of these expressed convictions Moll keeps finding herself passing children to foster mothers. Even the beloved child of her Lancashire husband cannot be permanently protected: there comes a time when Moll can pay no more to the nurse and has to write to Mother

Midnight to beg that "the poor Child [may] not suffer" for its
mother's misfortunes (197).

When Moll abandons her offspring she does so in the interests
of her own comfort and survival. She is well acquainted with
the figure of the poor debtor's wife, who "perhaps [has] not Half
a Crown for herself, and three or four Children" (65): hers is
not a mode of living that Moll can accept. Instead she adopts
(though not without guilt) a strategy closer to that of the comic
characters. Once out of sight, the child is to some extent out of
mind: at least the mother can console herself with the thought
that providence, or the affection of a nurse with a little more
humanity than most, may provide (177). Since historical records
show that some hired nurses did show devotion to their charges
(McClure 1981, 94, 129), we need not dismiss Moll's vision of a
loving and caring nurse as a mere sophistry or self-delusion.
But neither Moll herself nor the reader can feel satisfied with
this solution. It is a source of profound unease.

Insofar as she inhabits the comedy world, Moll must accept
not only the system of disposing of children but also Mother
Midnight, the agent of disposal. In her comic aspect the old
contriver functions as an ally: in another genre—that of folk
tale, say—her function would be evil, like that of the stepmother
in *Hansel and Gretel,* with her acolyte the anonymous baby-
farmer standing in as the witch. But *Moll Flanders* is never
quite a comedy, never quite a tragedy, never quite a folk tale or
fable. It is a novel of contingency, relying on its indefinition for
effect. By allowing Moll to inhabit different generic or percep-
tual worlds alternately (or even simultaneously), it successfully
suggests the flux, the uncertainty, the lack of a stable conceptual
frame that characterizes ordinary human life. Mother Midnight, accordingly, is an ambivalent figure, part surrogate
mother to Moll, part desecrator of Moll's own maternal feelings.

Moll's success as a survivor in her early years is due in large
part to her sexual attractiveness. Her youth and beauty, while
she has them, are at best a source of livelihood, at worst productive of unsupported offspring. But in her forty-eighth year it
begins to be time, as Moll euphemistically puts it, for her to
leave off child-bearing. (The allusion to the menopause, often
missed, is noted by Lerenbaum [1977, 111–15] and Miller [1980
162, n. 17].) So Moll changes from a liver on stolen pleasures
to a liver on stolen goods. This change of life brings about a
further hardening process: as thief Moll finds that children and
those in charge of them are ideal victims. Sometimes she reflects

that she may be stealing from a "poor widow like [herself], that had pack'd up these goods to go and sell them for a little Bread for herself and a poor Child," but her own necessities silence her self-reproaches (Defoe 1976, 193). In the notorious passage where she steals from a "pretty little Child [that] had been at a Dancing-School" she admits: "The Devil put me upon killing the Child in the dark Alley, that it might not Cry." In the event she manages the theft without murder, and later tells herself that she has "given the Parents a just Reproof for their Negligence in leaving the poor little Lamb to come home by it self" (194). Later victims include "a young Lady big with Child" (201), frightened by a jostling crowd, and a "poor Woman half out of her Wits" with fear who is escaping from a burning house with a bundle and two little children: in the latter case Moll delivers the 'poor Lambs' to a neighbor as promised but walks off with the bundle (which contains valuables). As we have seen, this comic parallel between a swaddled child and a bundle containing more materially valuable commodities can be traced at least as far back as Middleton (1969, 44–47).

None of these traces of comic freebooterism, however, quite nullifies Moll's protestations of continuing care for children. It is true, of course, that her use of such expressions as "poor Lambs" during her thieving phase sounds just as hypocritical as Mother Midnight's did earlier in the book, while her comment on her "just reproof" to the parents of the little girl she robbed is ludicrous. But Moll is made to sense that callousness to children is for her a kind of nadir, as is indicated by her rather guilty insistence that she still felt a residual affection for them: "I had a great many tender Thoughts about me yet, and did nothing but what, as I may say, meer Necessity drove me to" (195). It is misguided to adopt, as some critics have done, a public prosecutor's approach toward Defoe's fictional protagonist, seeking to discredit every expression of fondness and, when that tactic fails, claiming that Moll's reflections are "out of character." The reading which results is distressingly, and unnecessarily, flat. Defoe credits Moll, not with a single self but with at least two selves: one conventional yet lively, the other vivacious, deviant, but not totally ruthless.

Which phase of Moll's being, though, is to be regarded as the more authentic? The comic, survivalist response may at first seem more spontaneous; but then, as Dorothy van Ghent seems to suggest, its denial of motherhood can equally well be regarded as an affront to the sensual life or (as Julia Kristeva would put it) the semiotic phase of being (Kristeva 1974). Comic triumphs, such as the disposal of children whom one cannot afford to keep, are victories not for the sensual but for the mental life: they are triumphs of cunning, of reason. The idyll, where sensual pleasures come into their own and where the connotations of childhood and breeding are positive, is as a literary or experiential mode opposed to the comic: it relaxes over its pleasures, whereas comedy takes its triumphs on the run. What Moll, as a comic or picaresque character, fails to experience is the joy of motherhood, the pleasure in feeding and touching ascribed to female characters by writers as different as Shakespeare and Richardson. Defoe, as we shall see, is not unaware of the existence of this complex of feelings, but in *Moll Flanders* it is experienced chiefly as a brooding absence.

An open reading of *Moll Flanders* will not reveal Moll as a monster. It will show her to possess enough maternal feeling to know what she has missed by her (largely forced) abnegations of the maternal role, with her initial receptivity to the charms of children steadily dulled by the necessities of her life. However, while there is truth in the notion that the model reader will forgive many of Moll's more callous actions because they are committed under the pressure of necessity (though a sharp critique of Moll's attempt to plead necessity is offered by Novak [1963, 78 ff.])—it is also true that Defoe shows acquisitiveness gaining a grip on Moll until she is prepared to steal others' property, abandon her own children, and take advantage of other women who are burdened with infants, even when such ruthlessness has temporarily ceased to be necessary for her survival. (It is this process that accounts for the tragedy of Roxana as well as the near tragedy of Moll.) The hardening process is shown at work in Moll's bigamous and/or incestuous marriages, her whoring, and her stealing, as well as in her increasingly callous attitude toward the young. Perhaps, then, Moll can best be seen as a comic character who moves, at crucial moments, perilously close to the tragic pole.

The tensions incident to the mother-child relationship are even closer to the heart of the tragedy of *Roxana* than they are to that of the novel of contingency, *Moll Flanders*. Roxana's parting from her first family, prepared for from the opening pages, is much more heartrending than Moll's from hers. Roxana's first husband is rich but foolish: as his bankruptcy approaches, his wife finds the prospect of imminent poverty doubly alarming because she has now "five Children by him; the only

Work (perhaps) that Fools are good for" (Defoe 1964, 10). The last tart comment revives an old joke about the fool's tireless sexual vigor, but laughter is checked by the narrator's sober evocation of consequences. Roxana is left with her "Family of Children on [her] Hands, and nothing to subsist them" (13) and with the prospect of having her "Children starve before [her] Face" (14). Her husband's married sisters, "well perceiving" that she is "in a Condition that [is] likely to be soon troublesome to them" (15), avoid her, and there is nobody else on hand to help. At one moment Roxana's mind is assailed with the ultimate horror: "We had eaten up almost everything, and little remain'd, unless, like one of the pitiful Women of *Jerusalem*, I should eat up my very Children themselves" (18).

In practice the worst prospect that the world seems to hold for these children in the early pages of Defoe's novel is that they will be forced to go on parish charity. But Roxana, like Moll, realizes (and at a much earlier period of her life than Moll does) what this is likely to entail:

A hundred terrible things came into my Thoughts, viz. of Parish-Children being Starv'd at nurse; of their being ruin'd, let grow crooked, lam'd, and the like, for want of being taken care of; and this sunk my very Heart within me. (19)

Yet Roxana, like Moll, soon finds her heart hardened toward the children by the misery of her own circumstances: she ends by sending her confidential servant Amy to dump them on her sister-in-law. Amy easily hoodwinks the maid who opens the door:

Sweetheart, said she, pray go in and tell your Mistress, here are her little Cousins come to see her . . . Here, . . . take one of 'em in your Hand, and I'll bring the rest'; so she gives her the least [sc. smallest], and the Wench goes in mighty innocently, with the Little One in her Hand, upon which *Amy* turns the rest in after her, shuts the Door softly, and marches off as fast as she cou'd. (19)

What commands attention here is the speed with which the discourse of picaresque comedy swamps that of the new gentility. The wheedling appellation "sweetheart" and the sight of the "little cousins" innocently holding hands are cynically exploited to dupe the unsuspicious maid. To the mistress of the house, when she finds out what has happened, the practical consequences of the trick are immediately apparent. It is not the

language of tenderness that rises to her lips. Instead she
screams to her husband, "I have order'd them to be set in the
Street, without the Door, and so let the Church-Wardens take
Care of them. . . . Let her that brought them into the World look
after them if she will; what does she send her Bratts to me
for?" (20).

Superficially the scenario resembles that of the comedies and
farces. An indigent person proves deft and cunning enough to
saddle a richer and more secure one with superfluous children:
the more brats there are, the greater the comic triumph when
they are disposed of successfully. But the slight shift of tone
contrived by Defoe is enough to turn hilarity into nightmare.
In comedy, convention dictates that the victim of the child-
dumping, however reluctant at first, shall eventually accept the
task of fostering: the audience is allowed to assure itself that
the infants will thrive. But Defoe closes off the route to this
cheery comic resolution. We are told at once that the aunt accepted responsibility with a bad grace and only because her
husband insisted; later on when Roxana, wealthy and belatedly
concerned, seeks out her abandoned sons and daughters, she
hears that their aunt treats them "barbarously," making them
"little better than Servants in the House, to wait upon her and
her Children" (189).

The youngest son has been put out to a trade. This sounds
better than nothing—it is a livelihood, at least—but Roxana's
maternal feelings are alarmed when she learns that it is "a very
laborious hard-working Trade, and he is but a thin weak Boy"
(191). The boy's sister, Roxana is horrified to learn, has been
put into domestic service. The distraught mother resolves to
trace the girl at all costs:

> I was too tender a Mother still, notwithstanding what I had done,
> to let this poor Girl go about the World drudging, as it were, for
> Bread, and slaving at the Fire, and in the Kitchen, as a Cook-Maid;
> besides it came into my Head, that she might, perhaps, marry some
> poor Devil of a Footman, or a Coachman, or some such thing, and
> be undone that way; or, which was worse, be drawn in to lie with
> some of that coarse cursed Kind, and be with-Child, and be utterly
> ruin'd that way; and in the midst of all my Prosperity this gave me
> great Uneasiness. (197)

Ironically the house in which the girl has taken service turns
out to be Roxana's, where the truant mother has been living
the life of a courtesan. The daughter, living unrecognized in her

mother's household, is corrupted, not by the blandishments of a "coarse, cursed" footman or coachman, but by the example of a "coarse, cursed" whore, Roxana herself.

Roxana's story becomes a kind of female version of the Oedipus legend: the banished child comes back, unrecognized, into its parent's life in fatal circumstances. It is this foolish, loving, confused daughter-servant who is to be the ruin both of her mother and herself. Her childish innocence was exploited and imposed on by Roxana and Amy when they dumped her on her aunt. The process is furthered when she becomes infatuated with their way of life during her period of service in the house of Roxana the courtesan, whose identity she does not guess until later. The tragic climax is reached with her murder at Amy's hands at the end of the novel.

The process of the text lays steadily more blame on Roxana, more than was ever laid on Moll. Yet Roxana, like Moll, is given moments of deep reflection on the consequences of transgression against the institution of the monogamous, child-rearing family. After the birth of her son by a wealthy lover, a German prince, she meditates:

> Great Men are, indeed, delivered from the Burthen of their ...
> Bastards, as to their Maintenance: This is the main Affliction in
> other Cases, where ... either a Man's legitimate Children suffer
> [financial loss], ... or the unfortunate Mother of [the bastard] has
> a dreadful Affliction, either of being turn'd off with her Child, and
> be left to starve, &c. or of seeing the poor Infant packed off with a
> Piece of Money, to some of those She-Butchers, who take Children
> off of their Hands, as 'tis called; that is to say, starve 'em, and, in a
> Word, murther 'em. (79–80)

The context confers on this speech an appearance of objectivity. Roxana herself is not poor at the time. Her royal lover is rich and dotes on the child: he will "sit and look at it, and with an Air of Seriousness sometimes, a great while together." But thoughts of the difficulties which other bastards face, and from which her son is exempt, only lead Roxana to ponder other problems, less obvious than poverty or neglect, that he may face in later life. It is as if her thoughts moved steadily through the territory of wealth and security to a frontier of danger that logically must be reached: "Whatever the Merit of this little Creature may be, he must always have a Bend on his Arms; the Disaster of his Birth will be always, not a Blot only to his Honour, but a Bar to his Fortunes. . . . Nay, if it lives . . . the Infamy must descend even to its innocent Posterity" (81).

Needless to say, all this is partly propaganda on behalf of legitimacy and Christian marriage. But there is nothing illogical or strained in attributing such thoughts to Roxana in the situation in which she finds herself. And the process of brooding on the consequences of bastardy generates further insights into parent-child relations, and into the links between the individual as an infant and the same individual as a fully socialized adult. The baby is a "lovely, charming Child" (80): this reminds Roxana of the old tale, belonging equally to the comic and to the tragic tradition, that bastards are more talented and vigorous than other children. But the discourse of responsibility supervenes when the mother wonders how her son will feel about himself when grown up, and in particular how his self-image will be shaped by the circumstances of his birth and upbringing. Here the child has ceased to be a mere extension of the parent: he begins to be thought of as an individual whose selfhood is separate and to some degree continuous. The early years of upbringing are asocial, but he will eventually have to be introduced into the social world. Here his identity, his social passport as it were, will be inscribed with discriminatory marks that relate the history of his origins. This shaming heraldry, which a poor person's son might escape altogether, is ineluctably imposed on the bastard of an eminent man.

With Roxana, as with Moll, moments of clear perception and intuitive sympathy for children alternate with callous and dismissive comments. When her second child by the Prince dies her feelings are mixed, but relief is uppermost:

> I brought him another Son, and a very fine Boy it was, but it liv'd not above two Months; nor, after the first Touches of Affection (which are usual, I believe, to all mothers) were over, was I sorry the Child did not live, the necessary Difficulties attending it in our travelling, being considered. (104)

Later Roxana admits that she might prefer not to have any more children: "I did not," she confides, "forget that I had been Rich and Poor once already, alternately; and that I ought to know that the Circumstances I was now in were not to be expected to last always; that I had one Child, and expected another; and if I bred often, it wou'd something impair me in the

Great Article that supported my Interest, I mean . . . Beauty"
(105).

Superficially this reasoning looks very like Moll's. But in fact
Roxana's hardening process has gone further by this point than
Moll's ever did. Her reflections on the inconvenience of offspring
put her in the same class as the frigid couples in Defoe's *Conjugal Lewdness* who complain of the "noise and impertinencies"
of children and do their best to avoid breeding. Her plea of necessity is discredited when she voluntarily adopts the way of life
of a London courtesan, even though she has a fortune of her
own and an offer of marriage from a wealthy Dutch merchant.

The affair with the merchant, and Roxana's treatment of their
child, is especially revealing. Her refusal of the merchant's offer
of marriage condemns their child to illegitimacy, a prospect
which troubled her when she was dandling the prince's son but
which she tries to make light of now. The merchant, for his part,
is desolated that "any thing that [is] to call him Father, should
. . . be call'd Bastard" (158). Years later, when he meets Roxana
again, he will reiterate that he "look'd back on . . . the Cruelty
of [her] Treatment of the poor Infant . . . with the utmost Detes-
tation" (226). Roxana's own attitude toward the child is that of
a guilty person toward one whom she knows she has injured:

> It is with a just Reproach to myself, that I must repeat it again,
> that I had not the same Concern for it, tho' it was the Child of my
> own Body; nor had I ever the hearty affectionate Love to the Child,
> that he had; what the reason of it was, I cannot tell; and indeed I
> had shown a general Neglect of the Child, thro' all the gay Years of
> my *London* Revels. . . . I scarce saw it four times in the first four
> Years of its Life, and often wished it would go quietly out of the
> world; whereas a Son which I had by the Jeweller, I took a different
> Care of, and showed a differing Concern for. (263)

Thus the social world and its constraints have their effects on
a presocial relationship: Roxana's maternal feelings are neu-
tralized or contaminated by her guilt over a breach of propriety.
Nor is it merely propriety that is involved: the child will suffer
materially from his mother's decision. In isolation, sexual transgressions can be harmless, morally neutral; when they are accompanied by parenthood they are big with consequence.

What seems at first sight to distinguish *Roxana* most clearly
from *Moll Flanders* is its plotting; on a closer examination plotting and ethos are seen to be inseparable from one another.
Moll Flanders is a rambling tale: characters from earlier parts

sometimes reappear in later parts, but throughout there is a
sense of randomness, of contingency rather than fate. *Roxana*
is a tragedy in which the protagonist's behavior toward her children precipitates her fall (see Hume 1970). A fault that invites
retribution is her increasing enjoyment, once she has been
forced out of her initial married state, of illicit relationships.
The retribution duly comes: when she traces her first family
after a lapse of years she is debarred from mixing with them,
for she can "by no means think of ever letting the Children
know what a kind of Creature they ow'd their Being to, or giving
them an Occasion to upbraid their Mother with her scandalous
Life, much less to justifie the like Practice from my Example"
(205). Her hubris manifests itself when she rejects marriage
with a merchant in the hope of becoming courtesan to a king:
in the process she shows her willingness to sacrifice a child. Her
nemesis is another child, whom she left far from willingly on
the collapse of her first marriage, and whom she unwittingly
employs as a servant during her career as the so-called Fortunate Mistress. Roxana has neglected the care of her children,
not in order to avoid starvation, but in order to live a life of
which she is secretly ashamed.

Indicative of the increasing understanding of parent-child relations at this period is the fact that what Susan, the daughter
abandoned to poverty and servitude, is shown to want primarily
from Roxana is not money but identity, family, acknowledg-
ment, connections, love. When she learns that the servant Amy
is the one who brought money for herself and her siblings, Susan
is seized with "a strong Fancy that Amy [is] really her Mother"
(266) and protests at her refusal to admit it. "What have I done,"
Susan asks, "that you won't own me, and that you will not be
call'd my Mother? . . . Don't disown me now you have found me;
don't hide yourself from me any longer; I can't bear that. . . .
It will break my heart" (267). Gradually, however, she pieces
together the story of her real mother's departure for France and
return to England; and at last she bursts out to Amy, in a moment of ill-fated intuition, "That if she [is] not her Mother,
Madam Roxana [is] her Mother, . . . and then all this that Amy
[has] done for her, [is] by Madam Roxana's order" (270). From
this time onwards Susan pursues the woman whom she is now
convinced is her mother: worse, she seems anxious to confide to
others "all that her Head cou'd retain of Roxana, and the days
of joy which [she] had spent at that part of the town" (283). It
would be fatal for Roxana's Dutch merchant, now her husband,

to know that Roxana once abandoned him to live the life of a high-class courtesan.

By this time Roxana, even when her security is threatened, finds herself unable to repress maternal feeling. At times, when her daughter shows a maddening accuracy of recall, the mother will allude to her coarsely as a "young Slut" (288) and insist that she is behaving "like a Child." Yet when they meet there is a surge of tenderness:

> I was ready to sink when I came close to her, to salute her; yet it was a secret inconceivable Pleasure to me when I kiss'd her, to know that I kiss'd my own Child; my own Flesh and Blood, born of my Body, and who I had never kiss'd since I took the fatal Farewel of them all. . . . Much ado I had, not to abandon myself to an Excess of Passion at the first Sight of her, much more when my Lips touch'd her Face; I thought I must have taken her in my Arms, and kiss'd her again a thousand times, whether I wou'd or no. (277)

There is a quiet emotional intensity in this, a willingness to abandon the text to an evocation of sensual and bodily rapture, that we seldom find in Defoe: here at least there is nothing in the rhetoric to suggest hesitation, hypocrisy, or lack of involvement on the part of the character who speaks. Earlier, Roxana's maternal affection is seen to generate not only physical longing and sympathetic identification but also, when the defense of a child is at stake, an uncontrollable vindictiveness and ferocity:

> Amy was so provok'd [by Susan's untimely conjectures], that she told me, in short, she began to think it would be absolutely necessary to murther her: That Expression fill'd me with Horror; all my Blood ran chill in my Veins, and a Fit of trembling seized me. . . . "And I," says I in a Rage, "as well as I love you, wou'd be the first that shou'd put the Halter about your Neck, and see you hang'd, with more Satisfaction than ever I saw you in my Life; nay," says I, "you wou'd not live to be hang'd, I believe, I should cut your Throat with my own Hand." (270–71)

But Amy cannot share Roxana's newly found maternal feeling: she remains true to the abandoning model of womanhood which Roxana has renounced. Thus this hitherto faithful servant becomes a copybook example of what René Girard has described as the inauthenticity of desire, in which individuals adopt the desires of others as their own (1965). Prompted by Roxana herself, Amy has always taken it for granted that nothing, including motherhood, must stand between her mistress and the life of riches, glamour, and festive celebration. Now, abruptly, Roxana herself requires that this comedic pursuit of pleasure, untrammeled by family ties, be abandoned. Amy for her part resents and rejects her mistress's new demand: intent on following the old way through to the end, she officiously pursues Susan in what she conceives to be Roxana's best interests. It is strongly hinted that the murder of Susan is carried out in the end.

A distinctive feature of Moll's and Roxana's lives is discontinuity. Both characters repeatedly disguise themselves, change location, or move between a respectable bourgeois life and one that depends on vice or crime. One function of their offspring is to call this chameleon existence into question. Children cry out for continuity: children are continuity. On the other hand, as Freud and others show, reproduction has a tendency to subordinate the individual to the species and to emphasize her or his subjection to repetition and death (Brown 1970, 24; Freud 1961, 108). The mother-child tie in particular is one which neither can escape definitively. Moll loses her mother and her name in infancy, but finds them when she accidentally marries her half-brother and takes her blood-mother as a mother-in-law. Roxana's daughter insistently claims kinship when she discovers, in later life, that her chosen role model (the Fortunate Mistress) and her lost mother are the same person. It is as if, in a world of contingency, one tie at least must be seen as necessary and inalienable. The latent relationship between mother and child is reactivated in circumstances that punish both for their transgressions against continuity, which is as much as to say for their offenses against the family. If Moll is punished less harshly than Roxana it is because Moll always opts for marriage when she can—even the formality of a bigamous marriage is made to seem like the tribute that vice pays to virtue—whereas Roxana deliberately degrades marriage, delaying it as long as possible.

What follows from this is that neither Moll nor Roxana can be plausibly regarded as a triumphantly fulfilled comic figure, revelling in festive license and in emancipation from social rules. When either character abandons children she is shown to do so with regret (for offspring whom she loves) or revulsion (when the children remind her of an unhappy or disastrous relationship). In these two narratives, then, there is none of the carefree exuberance of the abandoners of offspring in Restoration comedy. Nor, on the other hand, does either novel offer descriptions of idyllic suckling or familial feasting. The nearest either text comes to an evocation of joy in physical contact is Roxana's description of the furtive kiss bestowed on her grown daughter, a child soon to be sacrificed in the interests of her mother's selfish, yet joyless, existence. Moll's delight in meeting her rich and handsome Virginia son after a lapse of years seems unfeigned, but is far from constituting the "reintegration of maternity" that Nancy Miller claims for it (1980, 18). The man who is Moll's husband at this point is not the father of this son (Moll having lost contact with his child many years earlier); and the Virginia son, whom she has rediscovered, is a respectable landowner to whom she dare not confide her history. (She neglects to tell him that the gold watch she gives him is stolen; she does not spend her last years in his company.) When she decides to stay with her Lancashire husband, she has to abandon her project of settling down with her son: the insidious and (as Defoe would see it) unnatural choice between a husband and a child is one that she is still having to make at the end of her life as she has repeatedly done during earlier years. Reintegration is precisely what Moll never achieves: marriage and parenthood, comedy and idyll, settled and picaresque modes of living are never reconciled.

Why this might be so may perhaps be deduced from a short but telling scene in a slightly later novel, Fielding's *Joseph Andrews* (1742). In the twelfth chapter of book 3, Fielding introduces a distinctly shifty mother-figure, an innkeeper's wife. This woman tells the social-climbing steward Peter Pounce that she would not mind seeing her husband ruined as he deserves, but that she has "three poor small Children, who [are] not capable to get their own Living; and if her Husband [is] sent to Gaol, they must all come to the Parish, for she [is] a poor weak Woman, continually a-breeding, and [has] no time to work for them" (Fielding 1970, 242). Here Fielding seems to be juggling deftly with several comic and satiric ideas. One is the familiar comic notion of children as a liability; but there is also another, compensating idea of them as a means of eliciting sympathy from strangers and influential people.

More insidiously, the mother's concern for her children seems poised to become accepted as the whole duty of woman, displacing other traditional obligations. The landlady clearly feels that she can consign her husband to the devil without exciting her guests' disapproval; she will still appear in a good light provided that she shows a proper concern for her offspring. All that redeems the husband, apparently, is his capacity for begetting children, which makes up for his other deficiencies: "If it was not for that Block-Head of his own, the Man in some things [is] well enough; for she [has] had three Children by him in less than three Years, and [is] almost ready to cry out the fourth time" (242). In this speech the distinction between sexual pleasure and prolific childbearing becomes blurred: the speaker presents them as part of the same continuum, with the implication that the male who provides them is good for little else. Indeed the upshot of the speech is that it is the husband, rather than the children, who is dispensable. We may agree that the landlady is joking, enjoying some pert fun with her guests; but it is a sign of the times that she feels she can get away with this kind of joke. In an earlier period a fictional character of this type might have jested at the expense of her "brats": now she jests at the expense of her spouse.

Fielding's portrayal of the landlady exemplifies that uneasiness over the prestige and importance of motherhood which we found ourselves considering at the beginning of this chapter. On a small scale it parallels Defoe's presentation of Moll Flanders and Roxana: admiration for the woman's comic resourcefulness and for her willingness to manipulate the responses of others in her own favor coexists with nervousness about the phenomenon that the character represents. There is an echo here of the old fear of the cuckolding wife, whose superior cunning and highly charged libido reduce her menfolk to ciphers. An extension or variation of the traditional topos shows the woman concerned above all with security for herself and her children, compared to which the welfare or even continued existence of the husband is relatively unimportant. Susan Staves is undoubtedly right in detecting in the discourse and behavior of eighteenth-century males a fear that "the balance of power in domestic relations was shifting from husbands to wives in ways which were both unfair and socially disruptive" (1990, 163). An obvious outcome of this concern was a reluctance on the part of novelists to present mothers and mother-figures without satirizing them or, at least, playing down the positive connotations of their role.

A more striking and more extended instance of this disquiet over maternity occurs in the early chapters of Smollett's *Peregrine Pickle*. Its first manifestation involves a woman who is not an actual mother but a surrogate, one whose desire for motherhood remains, to the last, frustrated, and constantly exposes her to ridicule. When the bachelor Gamaliel Pickle moves from the city to the country, his sister Grizzle becomes

> engrossed by a double care, namely, that of finding a suitable match for her brother, and a comfortable yoke-fellow for herself. Neither was this aim the result of any sinister or frail suggestion, but the pure dictates of that laudable ambition, which prompted her to the preservation of the family name. (Smollett 1969, 13)

The repudiation of any "sinister or frail suggestion" behind Grizzle's behavior sounds ironical. Other pointers in the text combine to indicate that Grizzle does indeed yearn for sexual and sensual fulfillment; there is more than a suspicion that Smollett, like "Philogamus," sees women's "inexpressible Desire of Children" as an aspect of a wider sensuality. Grizzle's wish to see her brother married is made to seem like a sublimation of her own desire for marriage: at Gamaliel's wedding, for example, she pushes herself forward to such an extent that she becomes "the principal figure" of the festivity, almost eclipsing the bride (17). However, while Grizzle's promotion of her brother's marriage seems partly owing to self-interest, her longing for a child in the family seems genuine enough. When her sister-in-law becomes pregnant Grizzle drives her to distraction with her attentions, which are offered not for the expectant mother's own sake but because Grizzle regards her as "the vehicle which contain[s], and [is] destined to convey her brother's heir to light." The prospective aunt begs Mrs. Pickle not to eat a peach in case the child in her womb should suffer: no sooner is the request complied with than she changes her mind, recollecting "that if her sister's longing [is] baulked, the child [may] be affected with some disagreeable mark, or deplorable disease" (21).

Grizzle's propensity for making herself ridiculous by her solicitude continues after Peregrine's birth. When Mrs. Pickle takes over the care of the child, which she does as soon as she is well enough, her advanced methods fill her sister-in-law with alarm. Peregrine's mother orders

> that the bandages with which the infant had been so neatly rolled up, like an Aegyptian mummy, should be loosened and laid aside, in order to rid nature of all restraint, and give the blood free scope to circulate; and with her own hands she plunged him headlong every morning in a tub-full of cold water. (28)

Locke would have endorsed Mrs. Pickle's rejection of swaddling clothes, which restrict the child's freedom of movement: he would likewise have approved her exposure of her baby to cold water (1968, 117–19). And the model reader of Smollett's novel must also be meant to commend these methods of baby care, for despite Grizzle's apprehensions they succeed. The dip in the cold tub

> seemed so barbarous to the tender-hearted Mrs. Grizzle, that she . . . opposed it with all her eloquence, shedding abundance of tears over the sacrifice when it was made . . . She was deceived, however, in her prognostic; the boy, instead of declining in point of health, seemed to acquire fresh vigour from every plunge, as if he had been resolved to discredit the wisdom and foresight of his aunt, who, in all probability, could never forgive him for this want of reverence and respect. (Smollett 1969, 28–29)

At this point it may seem that, while Grizzle is being made ridiculous by her insistent interference and by her predilection for old-fashioned methods, both she and her sister-in-law are being presented in a positive light from the point of view of their shared devotion to the baby. But in fact Smollett is preparing a remarkable narrative reversal in which the young Peregrine will lose, first the love of his surrogate mother, and then that of his real one.

The wound to Grizzle's pride when Perry's glowing health discredits her forecast turns her neurotic anxiety over the boy's welfare to a vindictive dislike. During his infancy

> she was known to torture him more than once, when she had opportunities of thrusting pins into his flesh, without any danger of being detected. In a word, her affections were in a little time altogether alienated from this hope of her family, whom she abandoned to the conduct of his mother, whose province it undoubtedly was to manage the nurture of her own child. (29)

Smollett, then, turns Grizzle's impulses toward maternal fostering and care into a joke: he seems to do everything to prevent his reader from interpreting them in a way that would excite sympathy for the character. Locke had exercised a withering irony on mothers who resisted his recommendation that children be regularly exposed to cold water: "How fond Mothers are like to receive this Doctrine, is not hard to foresee. What can it be less than to Murder their tender Babes to use them thus?

What! put their Feet in cold Water in Frost and Snow, when all one can do is little enough to keep them warm?" (1968, 119). Smollett, following Locke's lead, mocks Grizzle's impulse to protect Peregrine from cold dips as an instance of misguided tenderness; this and her wish to keep him swaddled are presented as instances of her wrongheaded faith in old-fashioned methods. When her attempts to influence the child's upbringing are frustrated, she turns against him, relenting only at a much later stage of his life when it becomes apparent that his mother has cast him off.

It is notable that Smollett, as narrator, shows signs of guilt about his negative presentation of Grizzle's maternal impulses: at one point he moves to counter the accusation that his manner of portraying her is "uncharitable" (1969, 16). Yet throughout the early chapters he labors to fortify his text against any more inward, sympathetic, and psychologically oriented analysis. Grizzle remains a caricature: both her sexual and maternal longings are mocked by the narrator and frustrated by the movement of the plot. Not content with ridiculing her attempts to preside over her sister-in-law's pregnancy and early motherhood, Smollett subjects her to the humiliation of a false pregnancy when she herself finally marries. After this disaster she pettishly repudiates all maternal feeling: she "c[an]not bear the sight of a child, and tremble[s] whenever the conversation happen[s] to turn upon a christening" (51).

The explanation for all this seems to be that mothering, in Smollett, is closely linked with smothering. The maternal impulse is shown as possessive and repressive, fatally associated with a frenetic desire to organize and dominate other people's lives. Thus the spinster Grizzle is shown trying to dictate to her sister-in-law about the upbringing of her own child; and when Grizzle herself finally secures a husband, she sets about "a scheme of reformation she [is] resolved to execute in the family," (44) spoiling the idyllic existence that the ex-sailor enjoyed with his old shipmates Hatchway and Pipes before his marriage. She is punished for these encroachments on the freedom of others by becoming a target of ridicule; significantly, her worst humiliation takes the form of a false pregnancy. After this disaster

> she found very few people disposed to treat her with those marks of consideration which she looked upon as her due. This neglect detached her from the society of an unmannerly world; she concentred the energy of all her talents in the government of her own house,

which groaned accordingly under her arbitrary sway, and in the brandy-bottle found ample consolation for all the affliction she had undergone. (51)

The idea that in this novel the yearning for motherhood is associated with an unhealthy tendency to dominate is confirmed by the symmetry which exists between the surrogate mother and the real one. Structurally, it would seem logical for Smollett to balance the figure of the overbearing Grizzle with a more gentle and yielding female character, but in practice he does the opposite. Perry's mother, in fact, proves as anxious to be mistress in her own house as Grizzle herself. Just as Grizzle disturbs the domestic peace of Commodore Trunnion, who is "teized and tortured" into marrying her (32), so Miss Sally Appleby, on marrying Gamaliel Pickle, promptly "assume[s] the Reins of Government" in the family (18). A necessary prelude to achieving control over Pickle and his household is to humiliate her rival, the as-yet unmarried Grizzle, whom she maliciously relieves of favorite household duties such as "reprehending the servants."

In Mrs. Pickle's case, too, the desire to dominate is linked with deficiency in the performance of maternal duties: Smollett shows her caring efficiently for her eldest son in his early childhood, but later her care and fondness turn to neglect and dislike. The alienation seems to spring from mishaps that occur in the process of Perry's education. His first school mistress avoids "unnecessary severities" for fear of "disobliging a lady of fortune," but Perry's mother is in fact "not so blindly partial as to be pleased with such unseasonable indulgence" (53). This could be interpreted as a sensible attitude: Locke, for example, advised parents to avoid excessive sternness, especially beatings, but also recommended reining in the selfishness and willfulness of young children as the best way to avoid the need for harsh punishments later. In the case of Peregrine's mother, however, there is a lurking suggestion that she actually relishes the idea of her son undergoing corporal punishment. Her remedy for the first teacher's indulgence is to place Perry with a tutor whom she instructs to give his pupil whatever "correction" he may seem to deserve, and who does so with an excess of enthusiasm. Once Peregrine has been "regularly flogged twice a day" for eighteen months he predictably becomes "obstinate, dull, and untoward" (53).

It is at this moment that Smollett gives the first unequivocal sign of the mother's deficiency in natural affection:

> [Peregrine's] mother was extremely mortified at these symptoms of stupidity, which she considered as an inheritance derived from the spirit of his father, and consequently insurmountable by all the efforts of human care. (53)

Peregrine's blockishness is due to a mistaken method of upbringing; but his mother, who prescribed the method, concludes from its lack of success that the child is incapable of benefiting from any method of education whatsoever. From this time on she ceases to care for her son; the only relative who still feels deeply for him is his bachelor uncle, Trunnion, who "rejoice[s] over the ruggedness of his nature" as wholeheartedly as his mother resents her son's supposed stupidity.

The commodore's most positive intervention in Peregrine's life is to ask Mrs. Pickle to let him send Perry to boarding school (at his expense, not hers.) She complies because she is pregnant with another child who she hopes will "console her for the disappointment she ha[s] met with in the unpromising talents of Perry, or at any rate divide her concern, so as to enable her to endure the absence of either" (54). When warm reports of Perry's progress come home from school, his mother expresses only token satisfaction, remarking that schoolmasters always exaggerate the improvement in their pupils so as to bolster their own reputations. One reason offered by the narrative for this indifference is that, by the time Peregrine begins to do well at school, his mother has been "blessed with a daughter, . . . so that her care and affection being otherwise engrossed, the praise of Perry was less greedily devoured" (56).

Here, as so often in the early chapters of *Peregrine Pickle*, Smollett as narrator seems to catch the mother in a double bind. On the one hand he comments that the abatement of Mrs. Pickle's fondness was an advantage to her son, whose education "would have been retarded, and perhaps ruined by pernicious indulgence and preposterous interposition" (56). But he cannot bring himself to allow Mrs. Pickle any credit for restraining an impulse to spoil Perry: on the contrary, he represents her as behaving with almost inhuman frigidity toward her eldest son, while showing excessive partiality for her other children. By the time Perry comes home she has not seen him for four years, and "with regard to him" is "perfectly weaned of that infirmity known by the name of maternal fondness" (62). Indeed, when she actually sees Peregrine she rejects him, handsome and well-grown as he is, just as she has rejected as exaggerated his uncle's reports of his progress at school:

> Strange to tell, no sooner was he presented to his mother than her countenance changed, she eyed him with tokens of affliction and surprise, and bursting into tears, exclaimed her child was dead, and this was no other than an impostor, whom they had brought to defraud her sorrow. (64)

That Smollett should show Peregrine's mother behaving with such a conspicuous lack of maternal feeling is striking: it demands an explanation. The solution offered by one modern commentator is that what the text refers to as Mrs. Pickle's "unnatural and absurd renunciation," her "vicious aversion" from her son, is due to his having been conceived before marriage, in an affair with someone with whom his mother was intimate before she met her husband (Collins 1979). But this seems implausible. Why should a mother, in such circumstances, love the spurious child less than the legitimate ones? Eighteenth-century cultural codings suggest, if anything, the opposite conclusion: Bridget Allworthy in *Tom Jones,* for example, who has one legitimate child and one illegitimate one, shows a marked preference for the bastard (Fielding 1974, 1:139). And why, if Peregrine is to be thought of as a spurious issue, should the narrator remark that when the boy began showing "symptoms of stupidity" his mother considered them as "an inheritance derived from the spirit of his father," a conjecture which surely encourages us to identify the mulish Gamaliel Pickle as the male parent? Besides, if Smollett intended to hint at a mystery surrounding Peregrine's paternity, he presumably would have offered a solution to it at the end of the book, as Fielding does for the mystery surrounding his foundling hero. But in *Peregrine Pickle* Smollett gives no such solution, nor does the text offer any plausible rival to Gamaliel Pickle for the honor of fathering Peregrine. Besides, if the mother is to be thought of as resenting her child as spurious, why is she so fond and so careful of him during his first few years of life? The markers in Smollett's text do not, then, seem to point to Peregrine's illegitimacy. A better explanation for his mother's sudden dislike lies in the failure of her plans for his education. She rejects him because he does not turn out as she hoped and expected.

It can hardly be without significance that the male characters whom Peregrine encounters in his childhood—notably his crusty old ex-naval uncle and a judicious tutor at one of his three schools—exert a far more benign influence on his life than either his mother or his aunt. Indeed in Smollett's fiction Locke's bogeyman, the patriarchal tyrant with his arbitrary power and hostile, resentful attitude toward his offspring, generally yields place to the specter of the domineering, child-rejecting wife. As Michael Rosenblum has shown, the idyll at the end of a Smollett novel is customarily established with the aid of a father or father substitute: these figures of paternal power are benign, not repressive. In true Lockean fashion they "allow their sons to grow up—i.e., to become fathers in their turn" (1975, 573).

Emphasis on the negative aspects of motherhood is not, of course, characteristic of every eighteenth-century novel: Fielding's Amelia and Richardson's Pamela, to choose only the two most prominent examples, are exemplary parents. But it is notable that even Pamela, though to the average reader she does not appear to be scheming to achieve dominance within the family, is suspected by her husband of doing so; while in *Clarissa* Colonel Morden is made to say that in Anna Howe's case her husband will be fortunate if motherhood dampens her over-lively spirits, rendering her easier for her husband to control (Richardson 1932, 4:470). Thus while Richardson perhaps sees as exaggerated the typical male's fear of being smothered within marriage by the ambitions and high spirits of his philoprogenitive wife, he is aware that such a fear may exist.

Defoe, like Richardson, is prepared on occasion to situate his narrative in the mind of a female character and thereby offer his reader an insight into her (imagined) inner life. But while the male novelist behind the narrator is prepared to expose the dilemma of the destitute mother with sympathy and in detail he is not, in the end, prepared to let a Roxana or a Moll Flanders control her destiny and enjoy the best of both worlds, the world of secure marriage and the life of passion and procreation. Both women are shown seeking to do this; both, in the process, regularly deceive men whose behavior toward them has been generous. Among male novelists, then, there is a tendency to represent the prolific, self-fulfilling mother as an object of fear, an ambitious schemer intent on usurping the almost regal status in the family which the husband had traditionally enjoyed.

7

Affection: Sentiment versus Comedy

In stage comedy, as we have seen, there is seldom any systematic attempt to arouse moral disapproval of the compulsive seducer and reluctant parent. The novel presents a different case. It stands half way between stage comedy on the one hand and conduct books, periodical essays, and social tracts on the other. Like these last, it validates parental love and the desire for children: it enlists the reader's indignation against cruel and neglectful parents and against those who willingly, or without too much pain, allow themselves to be separated from their offspring. Yet the discourse of childhood in the early novel is seldom monologic: the mocking voice of comedy counterpoints the tones of responsibility, humanity, and concern. Artistically, this diversity is very necessary. There is always a tendency for affective writing about children to lapse into sentimentality, and in the cultural climate of the early eighteenth century the danger was especially acute. Reinscription of the old comedic, survivalist discourse as a kind of palimpsest within the discourse of sentiment brought a bracing and refreshing atmosphere to many novels.

Comedy, Susanne Langer has written, asserts "a brainy opportunism in face of an essentially dreadful universe" (1953, 331). When early fiction ventures into comedy it is often into the type that Langer has in mind. "An essentially dreadful universe" sometimes seems a fair description of the world of early eighteenth-century Britain as perceived by its finest artists: in particular, widespread indifference or hostility at the public level to children, parents, and prospective parents seems to have been exacerbated by the harshness of the laws of settlement and the cruelty and rapacity of parish officers, which are tirelessly satirized by writers of fiction. In Aphra Behn's novella "The Black Lady," for example, a young gentlewoman who finds herself pregnant flees from her native county to London. The woman who accepts her as a lodger explains to her the risk they both run:

> If the Overseers of the Poor (justly so call'd from their overlooking 'em) should have the least Suspicion of a strange and unmarried Person, who was entertained in her House big with Child, and so near her Time ... she should be troubled, if they could not give Security to the Parish of twenty or thirty Pounds, that they should not suffer by her ... or otherwise she should be sent to the house of correction, and her child to the parish nurse. (1967, 5:8)

This looks like a harsher and more realistic version of the drama sometimes played out in stage comedy, in which everyone, the parish officers included, competes to extort money from the luckless parent or to avoid taking responsibility for the child. As it happens Behn's novella likewise ends comically, but this time in a manner much more favorable to the child and its mother. The man who originally seduced the young woman comes to London to find her, and they agree to marry:

> So to Bed they went together that Night; next day to the *Exchange,* for several pretty businesses that ladies in her condition want. Whilst they were abroad, came the Vermin of the Parish, (I mean the Overseers of the Poor, who eat the Bread from 'em) to search for a young Blackhair'd Lady ... who was either brought to Bed, or just ready to lie down. (9–10)

The mistress of the house, having no wish to aid these "vermin" in the search, feigns ignorance and pretends to co-operate:

> The Landlady shew'd 'em all the Rooms in her House, but no such Lady could be found. At last she bethought herself, and led 'em into her Parlour, where she opened a little Closet-door, and shew'd 'em a black Cat that had just kitten'd ... and so dismissed 'em like Logger-heads as they came. (10)

In "The Black Lady" the fallen woman is, for once, reabsorbed into the kind of world in which "ladies in her condition" are taken on shopping expeditions to buy the "pretty businesses" that they want: the intrusive parish officers are cheated of their prey and made to look foolish. But while the persecutors of pregnant women are discomfited, they remain a menacing presence, and in this Behn's story is typical of the fiction of the time. In *Moll Flanders* the officers have to be paid off by Moll's protector, Mother Midnight (163); even in *Roxana* the protagonist recognizes their existence to the extent of remarking that her wealth and social standing exempted her from their harassment (164). Mentions of parish authorities in the novels, like those in the periodical essays, generally stress their rapacity and their propensity for abusing their authority. The picture given of the social world is one in which small children and those in charge of them are liable to find themselves at the mercy of these "vermin."

To the harshness of the social world in dealing with children is added the high risk of infant mortality from natural causes. Lawrence Stone, in his reconstruction of the real world of the seventeenth and eighteenth centuries, represents the death rate among infants as high enough to make it "folly to invest too much emotional capital in such ephemeral beings" (1977, 105). This may be an exaggeration, but behind it lies a truth. Novels and short stories of the period are set in a harsh world. While readers are seldom invited to approve or condone callousness, they are not allowed to ignore the reasons why some parents might wish their children away, or might reconcile themselves relatively easily to the disappearance or death of a child. When warmth and love break through, as they often do, there is always a danger that the novel will succumb, not merely to sentiment, but to sentimentality. In this atmosphere a touch of comic harshness can be redemptive. In the exemplary cases of Fielding and Richardson, especially, the reader often has cause to feel grateful when fine feeling fails to achieve undisputed mastery over the text.

We have already seen that in *Joseph Andrews* characters are judged, to a considerable extent, by the warmth of their feelings for their own offspring and for those of others. Not only does the plot, like that of a Roman comedy, lead up to the discovery of a long-lost child; in addition the pastoral paradise is represented as one which the presence of children helps to render complete. The chapter in which the Wilson household is described (Fielding 1970, 200–204) is idyllic in something close to the Bakhtinian sense: the parents' affection for their family is returned and rewarded. The children do housework, show themselves "dutiful and affectionate" to their elders, and grieve touchingly over the death of a favorite dog; and Wilson calls them "dearer Pledges" of the affection between himself and his wife than "can attend the closest male Alliance" (201). In an earlier chapter we noticed that such phrases could sound suspiciously formulaic; but the text of *Joseph Andrews,* unlike that of *Gulliver's Travels,* does not invite the inference that the speaker's protestations of affection for his family are insincere.

Parson Adams, the most attractive of all the characters, shares Wilson's affection for offspring. "I never scourged a Child of my own, unless as his School-master," he boasts, "and then have felt every Stroke on my own Posteriors" (202). Once again the utterance is affectionate, but in the references to scourging and to posteriors we detect a seepage from the world of comedy. The same suspicion surfaces when Fanny, Joseph's sweetheart, is kidnapped, and Adams well-meaningly but tactlessly mentions that if she had remained with Joseph the two might have married and had "many little Darlings, who would have been the Delight of [their] Youth, and the Comfort of [their] Age" (235). Since Joseph is tied to a bed-post, powerless to rescue the prospective mother of his as-yet unbegotten children, the remark takes on a comic flavor which effectively tempers the sentiment.

In a later chapter the parson hears that his own youngest son is drowned. When he receives the news he fails to summon the resignation that he recommended to Joseph on the loss of Fanny: instead he manifests "the bitterest agony" for the "little Prattler, the Darling and Comfort of [his] old Age," the "sweetest, best-temper'd Boy," who has been "snatched out of Life just at his Entrance into it" (278). Both Adams and his wife rhapsodize on the beauty and talent of their lost son, and are wild with delight when he is found to be alive after all. In this novel, strong emotions about the deaths of children are the mark, of a good person; but the joke at the expense of Adams, who fails to follow his own stoical precepts, again prevents the artistic balance of the novel from tipping too far in the direction of tenderness (cf. Donaldson 1973). Narrator, readers, and characters are still conscious that, since the death of a child is a relatively common event, the code of manliness requires the bereaved father to accept his loss with resignation, however difficult that code may be to follow. Even Adams lets slip the remark, "Had it been any other of my Children I could have born it with patience," and Mr. Wilson a little earlier says something similar about the loss of his eldest son (later identified as Joseph): "If he had died, I could have borne the Loss with Patience: But alas! Sir, he was stolen away from my Door by ... *Gipsies*" (200).

In *Joseph Andrews* the impulse to preserve a certain emotional distance between the child-figure on the one hand and the writer or reader on the other is displayed especially clearly in Fielding's account of his fictional hero. The history of Joseph's childhood extends to no more than one long paragraph (17–18), and the evocation of his youthful beauty and virtue is not so much rhapsodic as parodic. As an outdoor servant on a gentleman's estate Joseph is employed first as a crow-scarer, next as a whipper-in of hounds; but the sweetness of his voice disqualifies him for both tasks, for it "rather allured the Birds than terrified them" and the "Dogs preferr[ed] the Melody of his chiding to all the alluring Notes of the Huntsman." While willing to evoke the charms of childhood innocence, Fielding seems a little embarrassed by them: he has hardly finished referring to his hero as "little Joey" before he is hastening to describe Joseph's more manly pursuits, such as riding "the most spirited and vicious Horses to water." Heroic, as well as comic, connotations are used to keep sentimental ones at bay: the narrator and reader, as well as the characters, must—it seems—avoid investing too much emotional capital in a child-figure.

Elsewhere in *Joseph Andrews,* however, we encounter characters who seem in no danger of being embarrassed by excessive affection for children. One of the most important child-related themes that *Joseph Andrews* brings into play is the harshness of the social world, from the landed aristocrat at the top to the parish functionary near the bottom, in its treatment of poor families. Earlier fiction writers had, of course, portrayed minor parish officers as grasping, unsympathetic, and merciless, eager for any opportunity to harass pregnant women, vagrant children, and the poor in general; but in *Joseph Andrews* Fielding extends this criticism to the gentry and their underlings. Parson Adams's children, since their father is able (barely) to support them, are regarded by Lady Booby as nothing worse than a joke: she offers to divert her grand visitors with "one of the most ridiculous Sights they [have] ever seen, . . . an old foolish Parson, who, she said laughing, kept a Wife and six Brats on a Salary of about twenty Pounds a Year" (280). But with Joseph and Fanny the case is otherwise. Lady Booby refers slightingly to Joseph as a "Vagabond" who must not be allowed to settle in the village and "bring a Nest of Beggars into the Parish" (252).

Lady Booby's ulterior motive for refusing settlement to Joseph is jealousy: if she can't have him for herself, then at least she will strive to prevent Fanny from settling contentedly with him in her social superior's home village. But the pretext which the squire's widow gives for her action, that of restricting breeding among the poor, is plausible enough, as her toady, Lawyer Scout, can see: "Your Ladyship's ... Reason ... is a very good one, to prevent burdening us with the Poor, we have too many already; and I think we ought to have an Act to hang or transport half of them" (254). Against such inhuman notions Parson Adams can only offer the feeble pleas of nature, reason, humanity, and justice: "The Poor have little Share enough of this World already; it would be barbarous indeed to deny them the common Privileges, and innocent Enjoyments which Nature indulges to the animal Creation" (253). Here the emphasis is on the right of Joseph and Fanny to enjoy a full sexual life. The likely consequence, in the shape of numerous children, is admitted; but the conclusion, that lovemaking should be controlled in the interests of limiting population, is denied.

It is significant that Adams, so careful to restrain the pleasures of Joseph and Fanny before marriage, upholds their right to sexual enjoyment afterwards; and that where the consequence, procreation, is concerned, his attitude is close to that expressed almost a century before *Joseph Andrews* by Jeremy Taylor, who condemned the "huge folly and infidelity" of those who repined at having many children to support (Taylor 1875, 126). Adams's loving acceptance of a large brood, together with his tolerance of poor people enjoying sexual pleasure within marriage, sets him apart from the gentry: the latter are presented as frigid and life-denying, determined not to incur responsibility for superfluous infants born to inhabitants of their home parishes. This eagerness to avoid responsibility lay, as we have seen, well within the bounds of what was accepted in the value system of traditional ruthless comedy. But *Joseph Andrews*, which Fielding himself saw as initiating a new species of comic writing, systematically revises this system. The comedy of *Joseph Andrews* is humane comedy: one of its distinctive features is its readiness not only to celebrate fertility but to accept its logical consequences. While the problems and difficulties of parenthood are recognized—not the least of them being the hostility and frigidity of the social world—there remains a quiet certainty that providence will, eventually, come to the rescue. Fielding's novel radiates fondness for children and faith in the power of their innocence to procure their ultimate survival. At the same time there is enough vigor and rich coarseness in it to prevent it appearing sentimental. In other novels of the same era, including some by Fielding, the impulse to celebrate chil-

dren and childhood is less successfully reconciled with the need
to keep sentimentality at bay.

A powerful example of this is *Jonathan Wild,* first published
in 1743, a year later than *Joseph Andrews,* but almost certainly
written earlier, perhaps in 1740 (Battestin 1989, 281–82). Unlike *Joseph Andrews* it is a novel of unreconciled extremes. One
strand, which traces the career of the villain-hero Wild, is satirical, presenting its subject in a mock-heroic tone reminiscent of
Dryden or Gay. In the second strand, which follows the misfortunes of the generous and unsuspecting jeweller Heartfree, sentiment and pathos predominate. References to Heartfree's
"little Family" are frequent. When the jeweller is imprisoned
through the machinations of Wild, his elder daughter brings
tears to her mother's eyes by innocently asking where "dear
Papa" is, and then piles honey on cream by adding, "Don't cry,
Mamma; I am sure Papa would not stay abroad, if he could help
it" (Fielding 1932, 105). Later the same child, visiting her father
in gaol, asks: "O Papa, why did you not come home to poor
Mamma all this while; I thought you would not have left your
little Nanny so long" (126). Here the child is used rather too
transparently as an emblem of uncomprehending innocence in
a wicked world which sets snares for trusting people.

Lois Gibson is right to point out that the children of Heartfree
and his wife are invariably good, but wrong to add that this is
true of "all of the children in Fielding's novels": she herself
elsewhere cites passages from *Joseph Andrews* and *Amelia*
where the apparently spotless innocence of the child turns out
to be tainted with malice or self-interest, and it would be even
easier to prove the same point in reference to the young Tom
Jones, not to speak of his demonic brother Blifil (1975, 93,
108–9). The necessity for these balancing techniques becomes
especially obvious in cases where they are not used. It is difficult
to repress feelings of discomfort in reading the passages devoted
to the too-perfect and too-loving Heartfree family. The monologic quality of these passages is highlighted by the absence of
any convincingly realized narrator-figure to bring much-needed
distancing to the story. The theme of a predominantly cruel and
unfeeling world, made just tolerable by isolated occurrences of
love and goodness, is much less effectively conveyed in *Jonathan
Wild* than in *Joseph Andrews, Tom Jones,* or *Amelia.*

One of the foremost endeavors of the novel in the mid-
eighteenth century was to dissociate itself from the notion, implicit at times in Restoration comedy, that innocence and good-

ness were synonymous with weakness and folly. *Jonathan Wild* grapples unsuccessfully with the problem of innocence, the state of the kindly simpleton among knaves. Heartfree is vulnerable because he is trusting, but his confiding nature is part of what makes him likeable. Wild, the violator of trust, is by contrast an intolerable human being and also (since rogues notoriously betray one another) far from invulnerable.

In the pattern of associations set up by the narrative, trust is closely associated with childhood and with those who love children. Wild, it is implied, has become what he is partly because he has never had, or wished for, what by this date is coming to be considered a normal, loving childhood. In his youth he could not be terrified, but could be bribed; he quickly learned to bully and steal. His situation is like that of the young Colonel Jack. But Fielding, unlike Defoe, never credits his young criminal with a desire for anything better.

Where Wild never had a childhood, Heartfree remains childlike in some respects even after he has entered the adult world. His goodness, as well as his vulnerability, resemble a child's, and his empathy with his own wife and children is strong. He declines to place his "little Family" in the care of servants during the time of anxiety and confusion that follows his arrest for debt (2.8.102): in custody he dreams of

the Days of his Happiness and Prosperity, when the Provision they were making for the future Fortunes of their Children used to be one of the most agreeable Topics of Discourse, with which he and his Wife entertained themselves. (123)

So far, so good: the reader would rather identify with the loving, childlike, but vulnerable Heartfree than with the cunning, ruthless, relentlessly adult, and not invulnerable Wild. However, the creaminess of the descriptions of family partings and family distresses is excessive: Fielding's irony is only partly successful in bolstering the discourse against aberrant readings. Mrs. Heartfree, the narrator observes with heavy irony at the beginning of book 2, "was a mean-spirited, poor, domestic, low-bred Animal, who confined herself mostly to the Care of her Family" (68). Later, the heading to the ninth chapter of book 2 announces "a low Scene between Mrs. Heartfree and her Children," and the scene itself is followed by the words, "These are Circumstances which we should not, for the Amusement of six or seven Readers only, have inserted, had they not served to shew, that there are Weaknesses in vulgar Life, which are commonly called *Tenderness;* to which GREAT MINDS are so entirely Strangers, that they have not even an idea of them" (105). The irony here is directed, not at the Heartfree family, but at the contempt and lack of concern for children which make many people ridicule such close and loving relationships: each reader is appealed to as a member of a select group which will join the narrator in rejecting these supposedly dominant attitudes. The tone recalls that of Steele's rather smug *Guardian* essay (no. 150) in defense of domestic life. Writer and reader are invited to join a little band of initiates who feel concern for such things. The temptation to refuse the invitation—to reject the role of the model reader—is at times quite strong.

What is even more unsettling is that, in spite of Fielding's reliance on children as a source of the pathetic, there is little detailed observation of them in the book. The only example worth noting is a passage where Heartfree uses his elder daughter to make a point about the vanity and caprice of humankind:

> I have often noted my little Girl viewing, with eager Eyes, a jointed Baby [doll]; I have marked the Pains and Solicitations she hath used, till I have been prevailed on to indulge her with it. At her first obtaining it, what Joy hath sparkled in her Countenance! with what raptures hath she taken the Possession; but how little Satisfaction hath she found in it! (128)

Already the passage is beginning to turn toward a representation of the child as an epitome of human inconstancy:

> The Tinsel Ornaments which first caught her Eyes, produce no longer Pleasure; she endeavors to make it stand and walk in vain, and is constrained herself to supply it with Conversation. In a day's time it is thrown by and neglected, and some less costly Toy preferred to it. How like the Situation of this Child is that of every Man! (128)

What occurs here is not a failure of observation but a failure of imaginative identification. Following a tradition exemplified in Pope's "Behold the child, by Nature's eldest law, / Pleased with a rattle, tickled with a straw," Fielding uses the child as a vehicle for generalizations about human beings. But though the overt content of the passage is that everyone, child or adult, is guilty of caprice, it is the child who reaps the largest share of the writer's condescension.

Throughout *Jonathan Wild,* indeed, the little girls are used for moralizing, as incitements to sentimental feeling, as aids to differentiation between good and bad adults, or at best as emotional counters in the lives of their elders. Neither the narrator nor the other characters habitually envision them as independent beings who might exercise their own choices and live their own lives. When they visit their father in custody he hugs them with "the most passionate Fondness" and imprints "numberless Kisses on their little Lips" (125–26). There is something possessive and inward-turning about Heartfree's use of his children as consolations in time of trouble. At times the narrator seems willing to stand back and contemplate the unhealthy consequences: "The sight of his Children was like one of those alluring pleasures which Men in some Diseases indulge themselves often fatally in, which at once flatter and heighten their Malady" (182). (This is not the only occasion in the novel when the word "indulge" is used in such a context.) But the narrative is not always so alert to the tendency of the Heartfree family to turn in on itself.

The good angel who shakes Heartfree out of his melancholy is Friendly, the loyal apprentice, who notices that his master's "Agonies arise from the Thoughts of parting with [his] Children, and of leaving them in a distrest Condition." Friendly assures Heartfree, "I will employ my little Fortune ... in the Support of this your little Family"—we notice the use of the word "little" twice in three lines—"Your youngest daughter I will provide for, and as for my little Prattler, your eldest, as I never yet thought of any Woman for a Wife, I will receive her as such at your Hands; nor will I ever relinquish her for another" (182–83). Friendly's concern is touching. But there is something sinister about learning to think of someone as a wife who lives in the same house and who is young enough to be referred to as a "little prattler": it is this same kind of possessiveness that is ridiculed in comedies (such as Fielding's own *The Wedding Day* or Molière's *École des Femmes*) where men seek to marry girls young enough to be their daughters, or destine youthful wards to become their wives at the youngest age permitted by the law. In *Jonathan Wild* there is no suggestion that the little girl's feelings about the marriage are to be consulted. The omission is a striking one, since other eighteenth-century novels—not to speak of a succession of stage comedies stretching back to Plautus—display what amounts to an obsession with the question of individual choice in marriage.

At the end of the book we learn that Friendly married Heart-free's elder daughter when she reached the age of nineteen:

> As to the youngest, she never would listen to the Addresses of any Lover, . . . nor would give any other Reason . . . than that . . . no other Duty should interfere with that which she owed to the best of Fathers, nor prevent her from being the Nurse of his old Age.
> Thus *Heartfree,* his Wife, his two Daughters, his Son-in-Law, and his Grandchildren, of which he hath several, live all together in one House; and that with such Amity and Affection towards each other, that they are in the neighborhood called the *Family of Love.* (262–63)

In its closure, this final state of the Heartfree family marks a return to the state portrayed at the beginning of the book, where Mrs. Heartfree was commended because she "rarely went abroad, unless to return the Visits of a few plain Neighbours."

Yet there have been moments of restlessness in the middle sections of the novel, particularly over the condition of this maternal paragon whose "whole Soul was employed in reflecting on the Condition of her Husband and Children" (107). Mrs. Heartfree's slightly incongruous escape into the realm of adventure by land and sea, where she enjoys (in both senses of the word, it seems) miraculous escapes from drowning or ravishment, performs a necessary act of opening. This is the only sequence in *Jonathan Wild* that approaches the exuberance of the exploits of Parson Adams in *Joseph Andrews*. The passages in praise of home and motherhood, instead of conveying the idyllic feeling that pervades the earlier novel's account of the Wilson family, express an agoraphobia most uncharacteristic of Fielding, whose fictions normally move in a mainly outdoor world and declare their readiness to join the rough and tumble of life. To read *Jonathan Wild* is to be tempted to agree with Leo Bersani, who argues that a symbolic violation of family values, "a violent passage from one psychological and social order to another," confers new and needed prospects on parents and children (1984, 4). It is true, of course, that the Heartfrees' love and trust is set up as a counterweight to the treachery and inhumanity of the "great men" such as Wild, who are bound by no interpersonal ties. But as an alternative to their existence, that of the Heartfrees is unsatisfying. In particular the closing paragraphs, which describe their life after the death of Wild, read less like a celebration of family living as the foundation of good society than an admission that the ultimate goal of the affective family is that of cutting itself off from the world.

Yet one of the most expansively liberating evocations of infancy in eighteenth-century writing also came from Fielding's pen. This is the scene in the third chapter of *Tom Jones* where the infant Tom is discovered in Mr. Allworthy's bed, with the discussion between Allworthy and his housekeeper Deborah Wilkins over the baby's fate. Celebrated as it is, it must be analyzed and quoted at length.

Having summoned the housekeeper to his bedside, the Squire has to answer her question, "What's to be done?" He replies composedly that Deborah "must take care of the child that evening, and in the morning he will give Orders to provide it a Nurse." Deborah's response consists of an elaborated version of the censorious question, "Whose baby is that?"

> "Yes, Sir," says she, "and I hope your Worship will send out your Warrant to take up the Hussy its Mother ... Such wicked Sluts cannot be too severely punished. I'll warrant 'tis not her first, by her impudence in laying it to your Worship." (Fielding 1974, 1:40)

"Whose baby is that?" gives rise to the related question, "Whose will it be thought to be?" Deborah predicts (correctly, as it later transpires) that, since the child has been left in her master's bed, paternity will be ascribed to him, and indeed that the baby's mother left it there with that intention. She also infers that any woman with the resourcefulness and impudence to ascribe paternity to a rich and virtuous man must be a hardened case. Allworthy takes a different view:

> "In laying it to me, *Deborah*," answered Allworthy, "I can't think she hath any such Design. I suppose she hath only taken this Method to provide for her Child; and truly I am glad she hath not done worse." "I don't know what is worse," cries *Deborah*, "than for such wicked strumpets to lay their sins at honest men's doors." (1:40)

Deborah's reading of the scene belongs to the comic-satiric world of the old stage comedies or of Hogarth's painting "The Denunciation." From this viewpoint Allworthy must appear naive in his belief that the unknown mother, by laying the baby in his bed, was "only" intending to provide for her child, and Deborah will seem correspondingly worldly wise when she suggests that the squire will be taken to be the father. But here, for once, the worldly wise individual is not only successfully discredited but also made to look ridiculous; the reader's sympathies are with Allworthy, to whom the beauty and helplessness of the infant, and the need to ensure its survival, are of more moment than the task of finding and punishing the delinquent parents or ensuring that paternity is not ascribed to him.

This alignment with the accepting Allworthy against the rejecting Deborah is achieved partly by a reminder that the baby's life is at stake. Allworthy's comment that the mother might have "done worse" than lay the child in his bed alludes, however delicately, to the possibility that she might have smothered it or left it under a hedge to die. The insensitive Deborah cannot see that this would have been worse. "Why," she protests, "should your Worship provide for what the Parish is obliged to maintain?" She is adept at finding pseudomoral reasons for denying charity to foundlings:

> For my own Part, if it was an honest Man's Child indeed; but . . . it goes against me to touch these misbegotten Wretches, whom I don't look upon as my Fellow Creatures. Faugh, how it stinks! It doth not smell like a Christian. (1:40–41)

Having fueled her indignation, Deborah can easily bring herself to suggest that the baby should be left out in the rain:

> If I might be so bold to give my Advice, I would have it put in a Basket, and sent out and laid at the Church-Warden's Door. It is a good Night, only a little rainy and windy; and if it was well wrapped up, and put in a warm Basket, it is two to one but it lives till it is found in the Morning. But if it should not, we have discharged our Duty in taking proper care of it; and it is, perhaps, better for such Creatures to die in a state of Innocence, than to grow up and imitate their Mothers; for nothing better can be expected of them. (1:41)

The last comment, which represents the exposing of children (Locke's "most shameful action, and most unnatural murder") as a religious duty, would be horrifying if it came from a more consequential character or in a less ludicrous form of expression.

Still more potent in keeping horror at bay is the looming presence of Mr. Allworthy, in whom power and benevolence meet. The squire, his mind taken up with the infant, fails even to hear the housekeeper's speeches, so that he is not moved to check her with a rebuke:

There were some Strokes in [Deborah's] Speech which, perhaps, would have offended Mr. *Allworthy,* had he strictly attended to it; but he had now got one of his Fingers into the Infant's Hand, which by its gentle Pressure, seeming to implore his Assistance, had certainly out-pleaded the Eloquence of Mrs. *Deborah,* had it been ten times greater than it was. (1:41)

As we pass from Deborah's reaction to her master's, we move from the language of pragmatism and selfishness to the language of sentiment and sympathetic identification. There is still a hint, as in the old riotous comedy of *Three Hours After Marriage,* that a single man who likes babies, to the extent of taking on one begotten by someone else, must be something of a simpleton. But the rhetoric of the passage works to ensure that the reader will laugh more at Deborah than at Allworthy. The high-mindedness of the squire contrasts favorably with the pettiness of the housekeeper, who—incensed against the "wicked slut," its mother—is unable to respond to the charm and beauty of the baby.

Equally damaging to the reader's conception of Deborah is her ability to abandon her convictions at the drop of a pin in deference to those of her superiors. With Allworthy, she makes the mistake of embarking on a hostile speech without waiting to observe his reaction to the child. When it appears that her master does not share her opinions she quickly changes tack, taking the child in her arms "without any apparent Disgust at the Illegality of its Birth; and declaring it [is] a sweet little infant, walk[s] off with it to her own Chamber" (1:41). Later, when dealing with Allworthy's sister Bridget, Deborah is careful to wait to hear the other's reaction to the baby before offering her own opinion. When Bridget shows herself favorably disposed to the child, Deborah knows her cue: she begins "squeezing and kissing . . . crying out in a shrill voice, 'O the dear little Creature! . . . well, I vow, it is as fine a Boy as ever was seen!'" (1:46).

The most remarkable feature of the discovery scene in *Tom Jones* then, is Fielding's skill in reversing the pattern of sympathies of traditional comedy while retaining a strong comic and satiric bite, and resorting only for the briefest moment to the rival language of sentiment. In traditional comedy, the nearest the discourse comes to a sympathetic figuration of children is usually a brisk reference to a "chopping boy" lustily squalling. Fielding manages to retain the old briskness of tone, but he also risks an affectionate reference to the gentle pressure of the infant's hand on Mr. Allworthy's finger. In another context this might have sounded culpably sentimental; coming, as it does, immediately after Deborah's callous speech, it is tellingly effective.

So far, so simple. However, the schema in which good characters necessarily show affection for children and tolerance for the impulse to breed is not as conspicuous at the edge of the imaginative world of *Tom Jones* as it is near the center. Allworthy's discovery of the infant Tom takes place in the third chapter of book 1. In the tenth chapter of book 4 another birth is announced. This time the mother is Molly Seagrim, the gamekeeper's daughter, lover of the now-adult Tom Jones. Molly has been brought before Squire Allworthy, the local magistrate, for a breach of the peace. Allworthy, we hear from the lips of the complaisant Parson Supple, was

> inclined to have compounded Matters [with respect to the riot]; when, lo! on a sudden, the wench appeared ... to be, as it were at the Eve of bringing forth a Bastard. The Squire demanded of her who was the Father; but she pertinaciously refused to make any Response. So that he was about to make her Mittimus to *Bridewel,* when I departed. (1:188–89)

There are disturbing undercurrents here. One of the harshest manifestations of the "Whose baby is that?" response in early modern England was the law which required midwives to exploit the hurry, pain, and danger of childbirth to extort the name of the child's father from the frightened mother (Quaife 1979, 105). It is unsettling to find Mr. Allworthy, formerly champion of the "Let's bring it up" school of thought, suddenly obsessed with the question, "Whose baby is that?" (In the next chapter Fielding, himself a magistrate, hints that in his treatment of Molly the squire went beyond what the law strictly allowed.) Allworthy's harsh reaction to Molly is quite different from his tolerant, humane-comedy response to the unknown woman who sought privilege for her child by placing it in the squire's bed. Are we to infer that the difference lies in the fact that in Molly's case the birth is an open scandal while in the other case the woman responsible has had the wit and forethought to cover her tracks? If so, the rewards for brazen cunning and impudence are generous indeed, for the young Tom is brought up as a gentleman while Molly Seagrim's child is left on the parish.

The last detail is inferential, but that in itself is unusual. Novels, by this date, are expected to pursue many of those narrative threads which in stage plays could not be followed to the end: the subsequent fates of the characters, including children, are normally sketched in. When a baby is introduced into the narrative, readers want to be told what happens to it; at the very least they need to be assured that it has been taken away and fed. In comic novels and the newer comic dramas the seducer-figure, who would once have cracked cynical jokes about the deaths of illegitimate children from rickets, measles, or "overlaying" by nurses, is expected to express concern for their survival: even the young spark Nightingale, in an otherwise callous letter to his deserted mistress Nancy Miller in the third section of *Tom Jones* (2:763), promises financial assistance for the "unhappy Consequence" of their affair.

Over Molly Seagrim's baby, however, a silence hangs. We are not told whether, or how long, it survived, nor whether it was a boy or a girl. The narrative reveals no more than what Molly's sister tells Tom: "That the little Child, which he had hitherto so certainly concluded to be his own, might very probably have an equal Title at least, to claim *Barnes* [a brutal rustic] for its Father" (1:234). The form of words is evasive. It is far from definitively exculpating Jones, but it uses the mere hypothesis that Barnes was the child's father as a way of releasing Tom from an obligation and as a pretext for dropping the child itself from the story.

This seems strange, since the proposition that bastards deserve to be treated on their merits, not condemned out of hand for the baseness of their origins, is part of the book's *dianoia*. In the second chapter of book 2, for example, Mr. Allworthy has an argument with his brother-in-law Captain Blifil about the rights of illegitimate children. The captain, like Deborah Wilkins, professes to regard charity to bastards as irreligious. (More pertinently, he sees Tom as a potential rival for the Allworthy inheritance.) So he argues that Jones should be turned out of the house. Allworthy replies that the innocent foundling should not be punished for its parents' sin: that is why he, the squire, will "provide in the same Manner for this poor Infant, as if a legitimate Child had had the Fortune to have been found in the same Place" (1:80). It is obvious, however, that Allworthy—whether by the conventions of realistic or of romantic narrative—cannot behave in the same.generous manner to all local bastards. What, then, is so special about Tom? Clearly it is the fact that Allworthy found him in his own bed: he has come to associate him, covertly, with his own home and family. That becomes especially transparent when Deborah Wilkins, the housekeeper, claims to have established that Tom is the son of Partridge, a barber and schoolmaster living some distance away. This Fielding describes as "a Discovery, which in its Event threatned at least to prove more fatal to poor *Tommy,* than all the Reasonings of the Captain" (1:81). This seems to hint that Allworthy, having supposedly identified an outsider and inferior as Tom's father, might have sent him away after making an order for the supposed begetter to pay maintenance for him. Apparently it is solely the "extraordinary fondness" that the squire has by this time conceived for the baby that keeps Tom at Paradise Hall.

What we have here is a mixture of the old superstition that blood relationship, even when unknown, will give rise to spontaneous affection—Tom is in reality the son of Allworthy's sister Bridget—and the related romantic convention that birth and blood will reassert themselves in later life when fate restores the foundling to his "rightful" position. The converse of the same convention operates in the case of Molly Seagrim's bastard. Tom repeatedly shows concern for Molly herself, but neither he nor his creator shows the same interest in her baby, even before the helpful revelation that it is "very probably" unrelated to any of the people at the Hall. In this instance, then, the narrative implicitly condones the accident of birth by which some children are born to better fortunes than others, the very injustice that Fielding's narrator overtly satirizes at other times. When Allworthy sends Molly to the House of Correction, for example, the narrator observes sardonically that the "inferior Sort of People," including unmarried mothers, "rarely learn any other good Lesson" there except "the wide Distinction Fortune intends between those Persons who are to be corrected for their Faults, and those who are not" (1:192).

It may, of course, seem ungrateful to subject these inconsistencies to analysis. Much of the charm of *Tom Jones* consists in its exuberant claim to the best of both worlds. At times it dwells in a humane, responsible, compassionate manner on the plight of the baby whom parishes and individuals are competing to get rid of: at others, it adopts the devil-may-care comic attitude that the spawning of bastard children is to be expected from any young man of spirit. But while the contradiction is not as clamorous in *Tom Jones* as it is in *The History of the Human Heart,* a lesser-known novel which we shall consider in our next chapter, it is undeniably present and inescapably productive of unease.

In the world of Fielding's last novel, *Amelia* (1751), the operation of social sanctions is more rigorously examined. Here, stripped of the camouflage of romance conventions, the social codes are revealed as tending to the destruction of the family, which the narrative continues to present as the foundation of society. In high life the threats come from the duelling code, the code of military honor, the code of illicit love, and the gamblers' code. Captain Booth, father and husband, finds himself maneuvered into playing cards for stakes he cannot afford, fighting a duel in which if he is not killed he may suffer capital punishment for killing his adversary, keeping his commission in a regiment that is going on active service rather than exchanging it for one in a unit that is to stay in England, and violating his vows to his wife by accepting a love challenge from a beautiful and complaisant woman.

Early in his marriage Booth's duty as a soldier forces him to leave his wife during the final months of her first pregnancy, though he is fully alive to the "Danger and Agonies" of childbirth (Fielding 1983, 103). Later, though he knows his wife and children may suffer beggary if he loses his livelihood or life, he is repeatedly maneuvered into risking both. His concern for children and family is mocked by his social equals. "What, did you not even get drunk in the Time of your Wife's Delivery?" cries the shady Miss Matthews in astonishment, when she hears that Booth stayed home to tend Amelia after the birth of their second child. "Do you really," retorts Booth rather primly, "think it a proper Time of Mirth, when the Creature one loves to Distraction is undergoing the most racking Torments, as well as in the most imminent Danger?" (128). Another friend of the Booth family, Mrs. James, married to a member of Parliament, feels sufficiently coolly about children to assure Amelia that being childless is "the only Circumstance which makes Matrimony comfortable" (384). At Vauxhall Gardens two rakes try to steal kisses from Amelia, ignoring the presence of her children; their prank almost leads to a duel when Booth comes on the scene.

Low life, in the world of this novel, is hardly more hospitable to children and families than high life. A bailiff, describing one of his less-favored prisoners, adds: "He hath a Wife and seven Children.—Here was the whole Family here the other Day, all

howling together. I never saw such a beggarly Crew; I was almost ashamed to see them in my House" (315). At a barracks
an infantryman shakes and pinches Booth's small son Billy,
leaving a nasty bruise, when the child walks on the grass at
the parade ground. The officer on duty—who, ironically enough,
is himself scarcely out of his childhood, having received his commission by fifteen years of age—shows no sign of disapproval
when told of this "Inhumanity"; on the contrary, he declares
that the soldier has "done very well; for that idle Boys ought to
be corrected" (183). In prison, Booth encounters a little girl "sit-
ting by herself in a corner and crying bitterly": her stepfather,
a grenadier-guardsman, has had her imprisoned on the grounds
that she has put him in fear of his life or of "some bodily harm"
(33). In this fictional world, then, the reaction of many people
to children is one of resentment at their presence or at their
very existence: they are seen as trespassers on the living space
of adults, intruders in lives and routines which are not designed
to accommodate them.

In a world where barbarity and indifference toward children
are so widespread, fondness for them is represented by the narrative as a virtual guarantee of goodness. Some feel this fondness; a few feign it for their own ends. A motif from Mandeville
is silently borrowed when an unnamed nobleman who likes seducing married women gains their confidence by kindness to
their offspring. His first victim, Mrs. Bennet, chides herself
afterwards for her credulity in believing that "an Infant, not
three Months old, could be really the Object of Affection to any
besides a Parent; and more especially to a gay young Fellow"
(290). But Amelia, too, is taken in at first by the same deception;
and the fondness of adult males even for the children of others
is not made to seem totally implausible. The bluff but kindly
clergyman Doctor Harrison enjoys playing with Amelia's children, and at one stage agrees to help the family for the children's sake even though he has lost sympathy with their father
(502–3). Booth himself nurses an affection for his children that
goes far beyond the conventional. Amelia takes it for granted
that he can be left to look after them when her presence is
required elsewhere: on one such occasion he is found "lying
along on the Floor" with his "little Things crawling and playing
about him" (308). Elsewhere, when the little girl bursts into
tears and refuses to hold hands with Sergeant Atkinson, Booth
falls behind and walks with the children, letting Atkinson go
ahead with Amelia (183). The narrative often seems to be di-

rected toward the creation of a new ideal of the gentleman, of chivalry, and of gallantry, turning on the willingness of the man of valor to perform menial tasks for the family's sake.

Equally important, if not more so, is the ideal of the perfect, or almost perfect, woman. Maternal fondness, of course, is represented as characteristic of all good women; but Fielding, like Mandeville, is inclined to show it as a potential snare for its possessor. The noble lord who plays on it in his attempts to seduce married women shows his shrewdness thereby: each woman is predisposed to believe that her child must seem special, even to a stranger. Miss Matthews speaks with relief, somewhat in the old cavalier manner, of the death of her illegitimate baby (57); but she—like Mrs. Fitzpatrick in *Tom Jones,* who lets fall a rather similar comment (Fielding 1974, 2:597)—is a disreputable character, and in any case could comfort herself by the reflection that her child's prospects in life would have been poor if it had survived. Mrs. Bennet describes the death of her little son, her "poor dear *Charly,*" as the "most grievous Accident that ever befel" her (1983, 303), even though this child, too, would have had little to look forward to in life. Amelia leaves her little son in England when she goes to join Booth abroad—her sister, one of the heartless characters, writes resentfully, "Remember we have something of yours to keep" (121)—but on her return she is "so impatient to see the Child, which she [has] left behind" that the one she carries with her— the little girl she has borne while abroad—is "almost killed with the Fatigue of the Journey." When the Booths finally see their son, they make "Words and Meaning out of every Sound" uttered by the infant, who is almost ready to talk (141).

The language used in the book to refer to children is revealing. Already in earlier novels a pattern had begun to establish itself whereby evil characters used harsh epithets like "brat" while good ones used softer expressions. In *Amelia* the use of affectionate and even sugary language to describe children has become the rule among likeable characters, though there is still a hint of self-consciousness about it. The book is full of phrases like "My little growing Family," "these poor Babes," "those dear little Pledges of our Loves." But these soft phrases are saturated with apprehension as well as fondness: the parents are sadly aware that, if ruin or death overtakes them, their innocent offspring may be left to struggle with a "cruel hard unfeeling World" (162). Mrs. Bennet, speaking of her improvident first marriage, recalls,

I was now delivered of a Son, a Matter which should in Reality have increased our Concern; but on the contrary it gave us great Pleasure. ... The Day of a Christening is in all Families, I believe, a Day of Jubilee and Rejoicing; and yet, if we consider the Interest of that little Wretch, who is the Occasion, how very little Reason would the most sanguine Persons have for their Joy! (289)

Booth is a little more prescient about the cares of parenthood than the feckless Bennets: "Can I bear," he cries, "to think of entailing Beggary on the Posterity of my *Amelia?* On *our*—O Heavens! on *our* Children?" (74). But he marries, and starts a family, just the same.

Perhaps the most arresting feature of the treatment of children in this, Fielding's last novel, is that they begin to emerge as personalities. In Defoe's *Moll Flanders, Captain Singleton,* and *Colonel Jack,* and in Fielding's own *Tom Jones,* we are given the childish reflections of the protagonists; but other children appear only briefly, more as objects than as subjects. Their parents worry about them if they are ill or in danger, but the children themselves are seldom seen making choices or exercising initiative. However, in *Amelia* the children are made to express, from time to time, more independent feelings and judgments, almost as the child-figures in *Pamela* do: in their speeches the predictable requests for tarts and cheesecakes alternate with expressions of sympathy and love for their parents and of puzzlement at the ways of the adult world. When Amelia hesitates to accept an invitation to an oratorio because it will mean leaving them for the evening, the children selflessly urge her to go (187). When the noble lord comes to call, Booth's daughter runs in to announce that there is a "prodigious great Gentleman coming up Stairs" (202). When Mrs. Atkinson comes to tell Amelia that Atkinson is on his deathbed, the two elder Booth children share her distress (480). When Booth is out late and Amelia is putting her children to bed, a knock on the door makes the boy beg to stay up for a moment longer to see if his father has returned (490). Both children react sympathetically, too, when their parents are in trouble (315–16; 491), and are shocked when an adult tells a lie in order to entrap their father (316). At Vauxhall, when the rakes have harassed Amelia and she is hoping to prevent any fighting by keeping the incident from her husband, her little boy unwisely lets out what his mother is trying to conceal (397).

The result of all this detail is a markedly more successful

integration of children into the novel than Fielding had achieved in *Jonathan Wild,* another story of the struggles of a lovable family to survive in a hostile world. The false sentiment, the self-pity, the inward-turning of the earlier book have largely gone: the children behave with a natural mixture of waywardness and spontaneous affection. Sentimentality is kept in check by the book's clear recognition of how easily children can come to be regarded as a curse, a misery, a burden, or a nuisance, and also by occasional ironical apologies for the inclusion of matter which will be thought trivial or nauseating by some unsympathetic readers (142; 201). But there is also a sense of the joy, the happiness, the play that adults and children can enjoy together: this represents an important development of the child's fictional role.

Like *Amelia,* Richardson's *Sir Charles Grandison* (1753) presents the family, centered on a happily married couple, as the most promising field for the exercise of virtue and the attainment of happiness. Besides offering parenthood as a norm it also ventures interestingly, like the second part of *Pamela* before it, into the hitherto neglected territory of the emerging sensibility of the adolescent; and also into the relationships of the individual, at this transitional stage of life, with parents and parent-figures. However, the most notable child-scene in *Sir Charles Grandison,* as in so many other eighteenth-century plays and novels, centers on a baby. It is relayed to the reader by Charlotte, Sir Charles's married sister, who is fretting at the restrictions on her freedom caused by the birth of her first child. Like the passage describing the discovery of Tom Jones by Mr. Allworthy, Charlotte's narrative needs to be quoted at length:

> I bit my lip, and raved at the wretch to whom I attributed my durance: When, yesterday (after a *series* indeed of the most obliging and most grateful behaviour that a man ever expressed for a Present made him, which he holds invaluable) he entered my chamber; and surprised me, as I did him (for I intended that he should know nothing of the matter, nor that I would ever be so condescending); surprised me, as how? Ah, Harriet! In an act that confessed the mother, the *whole* mother!—Little Harriet at my breast; or at my neck, I believe I should say—should I not? (Richardson 1986, 402; cf. Kinkead-Weekes 1973, 390)

Sentimental literature, to which this passage surely belongs, regularly uses the language of transgression to describe good actions carried out by stealth: it seeks to make an enjoyable scandal out of goodness. An essential feature of such scenarios is that the secret shall be brought abruptly into the light of day, upon which the "guilty" party is overwhelmed with confusion at being discovered. In the scene from *Sir Charles Grandison* the "transgression" committed by Charlotte is that of suckling her own child. When caught in the act by her husband, she and her maids react somewhat as their equivalents in hard comedy might have done if the secret had been an act of fornication or adultery. And whereas Lady G's shadow role is that of the fallen woman, her husband's is that of the daring, encroaching rake: he is resourceful, nimble, ruthless, a violator of the privacy of a woman's body and of a scene intended exclusively for female eyes:

> The nurse, the nursery-maids, knowing that I would not for the world have been so caught by my nimble Lord (for he is in twenty places in a minute) were more affrighted than Diana's nymphs, when the goddess was surprised by Acteon; and each, instead of surrounding me in order to hide my blushes, was for running a different way, not so much as attempting to relieve me from the Brat.
> I was ready to let the little Leech drop from my arms—O wretch! screamed I—Begone!—begone! Whence the boldness of this intrusion? (402–3)

The game Richardson is playing is transparent enough. His aim is to present suckling as fulfilling rather than demeaning, the intimacy achieved when a husband watches his wife feeding her baby as healthful and life-giving. The social sanction against such things—like the secretive use of the word "neck" as a euphemism for "breast"—is exposed as one that was made to be violated:

> Never was man in a greater rapture. For Lady Gertrude had taught him to wish that a mother would *be* a mother. He threw himself at my feet, clasping me and the little varlet together in his arms. Brute! said I, will you smother my Harriet—I was half-ashamed of my tenderness—Dear-est, dear-est, dear-est Lady G.—shaking his head, between every *dear* and *est*, every muscle of his face working; how you transport me!—Never, never, never, saw I so delightful a sight! Let me, let me, let me (every emphatic word repeated three times at least) behold again the dear sight. (403)

The passage attempts a more decisive validation of breast-feeding than Richardson had given in *Pamela,* where the protagonist never succeeded in obtaining from her husband the longed-for permission to suckle her own babies. By this date, Richardson ventures to suggest, some men have been educated by their womenfolk to the point where they expect and desire a mother to "*be* a mother." Yet while he seems more confident by this time in his attempts to arouse an affective response, Richardson still feels the need to activate the comic response at the same time. Lord G's attempts to tear the handkerchief from his wife's breasts are implicitly likened to the encroachments of the seducer on the body of his victim in Restoration comedy:

> The wretch (trembling however) pulled aside my handkerchief. I try'd to scold, but was forced to press the little thing to me, to supply the place of the handkerchief—Do you think, I could not have killed him?—To be sure, I was not half angry enough. I knew not what I did, you may well think—for I bowed my face on the smiling infant, who crowed to the pressure of my lip. (403)

It is at this point that the baby comes into its own. We have seen in earlier chapters how Freud saw offspring as superfluous in encounters between lovers, and also how his insight seemed to have been anticipated by some early modern writers. But in the scene between Charlotte and her husband, Richardson boldly moves to transform the usual pattern. Charlotte's baby, though still at an age when it is capable of nothing more in the way of communication than smiles and crows, mediates between husband and wife, whose delight in the child stimulates their delight in each other. Whereas the handkerchief is simply a barrier, which the bold ravisher pulls aside—and Richardson undoubtedly means his readers to register the oddity of a wife and mother feeling shy of showing her breast to her husband— the baby, which Charlotte uses to "supply the place of the hand-kerchief," acts as a kind of conductor of electricity:

> Begone, Lord G. said I—See! see! how shall I hold the little Mar-mouset, if you devour first one of my hands, then the other?'
> He arose, took the little thing from me, kissed its forehead, its cheeks, its lips, its little pudsey hands, first one, then the other; gave it again to my arms; took it again; and again resigned it to me.
> Take away the pug, said I, to the attendants—Take it away, while any of it is left—They rescued the still smiling babe, and run away with it. (403)

The eventual removal of the baby comes just in time to help out its mother, who after months of coyness wants to surrender to her husband's love but still does not quite know how.

Charlotte's child plays, then, in this strange scene, a role that arises naturally out of the larger patterns of the book. At times it is referred to in the language of harsh comedy: it is "the Brat," "the little Leech," "the pug." At other moments it is described in the new register of tenderness: it is a "present," "the little thing," "the smiling infant," "the still smiling babe," a creature endowed with "little pudsey hands." The more dismissive phrases, adopted presumably to counteract the sugariness of the sentiment, make the passage, if anything, more rather than less embarrassing. But the blending of sweet and sour is, in its aim of setting up a character for Charlotte, successful enough.

At the beginning of the novel Charlotte has appeared as Richardson's version of the witty, marriage-shy wench, a favorite in stage comedy from *Much Ado About Nothing* onwards. But here, as so often, the novelist projects the lines of the comedy-plot into unaccustomed realms. He presents the witty wench's difficulty in giving herself—a difficulty experienced by Congreve's Millamant as well as by Shakespeare's Beatrice—as one that may survive marriage, the loss of virginity, and even the birth of a child. So the point of the suckling scene between Charlotte and her husband is that at this moment in their relationship there are still metaphoric as well as literal veils to be torn away. To some extent, we are to infer, Charlotte is still hankering after her virgin existence: she is wishing she could be with her brother and his new wife, a wish that her pregnancy and childbirth have frustrated. The blame for her confinement—in both senses of that word—is laid firmly on her husband, "the wretch to whom I attributed my durance." (It is noticeable that, for all the slighting expressions she applies to it, Charlotte never blames the equally guilty baby.) But in parentheses Charlotte is beginning to acknowledge the "obliging . . . behaviour" of Lord G., and the pleasure (so different from the reaction of Mr. B. in Pamela) that he takes in the child. Toward the end of the quoted passage she admits that she was not "half angry enough" at the intrusion of Lord G on the domestic scene. Her husband, for his part, takes no notice of her stern injunction, "Begone, Lord G!" A few lines later, instead of demanding that he leave her alone with the baby, Charlotte is asking for the child to be taken away so that she can be alone with the intruder.

The scene is, as we have noted, irredeemably sentimental. It lacks the spontaneity of the suckling scenes in Renaissance icons of charity; nor would it have commended itself to Bakhtin as an echo of the idyll. But to Richardson this might not have mattered greatly. He is aware that, in his time and for certain people, idyllic naturalness and spontaneity are not attained easily. The "naturalness" of breast-feeding, as of the mother's remaining uncovered in the presence of a man, is a sensation some mid-eighteenth-century women apparently have to work to attain.

In the novels that follow *Sir Charles Grandison*—works such as Frances Sheridan's *Memoirs of Miss Sidney Bidulph* (1761), Henry Brooke's *The Fool of Quality* (1761), and Sarah Scott's *A Description of Millenium Hall* (1762)—the tendency to show real warmth existing in the relations between children and adults grows steadily stronger. One of these novels,*The Fool of Quality,* deserves a closer look because of its closeness to the concerns of this chapter.

Brooke's novel is full of descriptions of hugging and kissing, and of words like "darling" addressed to children—by men as much as (if not more than) by women, and to boys as well as girls (Brooke 1979, 1:55, 4:64, 76; 5:176). But Brooke, like other novelists, shows considerable concern for aesthetic balance; and the quality he considers most effective in countering the threatened slide into sentimentality is a bluff heartiness. Two of the best scenes in an admittedly uneven novel are those where Harry, the younger son who has been left at nurse in the village with little notice taken of him by his parents, at last begins to be invited up to the great house. Harry resents having a fine hat put on his head, and skims it across a crowded room:

> The hat took the glasses and decanters in full career, smash go the glasses, abroad pours the wine on circling laces, Dresden aprons, silver'd silks, and rich brocades: female screams fill the parlour, the rout is equal to the uproar. (1:46)

Harry's next trick is to mount a large dog which is unaccustomed to being ridden:

> The dog grew outrageous, and rushing into a group of little misses and masters, the children of the visitants, he overthrew them like ninepins; thence proceeding, with equal rapidity, between the legs of Mrs. Dowdy, a very fat elderly lady .... (1:46)

There is an undercurrent of sexism in this scene: the chief victims are women who are either fat or over-dressed. On the positive side, however, Brooke shows a skill reminiscent of Hogarth in using dogs and children to bring a breath of needed anarchy to a fetid scene.

In Brooke's novel the contrast between Harry, the child of nature, and the spoilt and oversophisticated "small gentry" of the neighborhood is accentuated at the boy's second visit to his parents' home, where Harry shows so little of that competitiveness and acquisitiveness which have been instilled into the others that he is taken by them for an idiot. Brooke offers, in short, an early and potent example of the antithesis between the sturdy, good, but untutored child and the effete, cunning, oversophisticated weakling. While his elder brother is given an enervating and potentially corrupting upbringing at the great house, Harry romps with his genial uncle (who is living incognito in the village), and alternately fights with and befriends the local dogs, cocks, and children.

One question which *The Fool of Quality* might have been expected to shirk, but does not, is the danger of the emergence of illicit or psychologically disturbing sexual feelings and relations in a social milieu where not only fondness but also physical demonstrations of affection between children and adults are common. Despite his obvious pleasure in emotional and physical warmth, Brooke includes, in his long episodic tale, a number of incidents in which such warmth has embarrassing, threatening, or even disastrous consequences. The crudest is one involving Phoebe, a gentleman's daughter in her thirteenth year—"an age," as the girl herself observes later, "when the blood is in the tide of flow." (4:19). The tale is used partly to illustrate the Lockean precept that "there is nothing so pernicious to the breeding and morals of children as being permitted to keep the company of servants"; the villain is the butler, "a comely robust fellow, and one in whom [Phoebe's] father had placed great trust":

> One night, as we were playing Hide and Seek, this man watched the place where I sought to conceal myself, and, coming softly and suddenly to me, he caught me up in his arms, and, running with me to a distant apartment, he there ruined me. (4:20)

The seduced girl soon proves to be with child.

The reaction of Phoebe's father to this disaster is one which

Brooke shows to be cruel and loveless. The master summons the butler and informs him that he must marry the girl or risk being hanged for rape. Naturally the man chooses marriage: he and his new wife are dismissed with two hundred pounds and left to fend for themselves. Soon afterwards Phoebe's child dies in the womb and has to be surgically removed. "The remembrance of the pangs and miseries that I endured," the young woman recalls, "caused me to vow, within myself, that I would never more have any commerce with mankind." As a result of this decision her husband begins to show "great coldness and distance" toward her, and spends his time with low companions. After his execution for theft his wife is reduced to beggary, and avoids falling into a life of prostitution only "for fear of a second child-birth, which I dreaded more than I dreaded the torments of hell" (4:21–24). While Brooke does eventually steer the tale toward a reconciliation between the girl and her family, and to a marriage between her and a kindly clergyman who knew her in her youth and has heard the story of her ordeal, he shows no squeamishness in conveying the hideous consequences of the affair.

While the narrative tone of Phoebe's story encourages compassion for her, there are also suggestions that she was in some degree responsible for her own seduction: both on this and other occasions Brooke betrays his conviction that quite young girls are capable of feeling, as well as inspiring, sexual desire. Even the clergyman who eventually marries Phoebe is portrayed as having, when he first knew her, singled her out as his future wife:

> From your infancy, Miss Phoebe [he reminds her], you were the darling of my affections . . .
> Your brother, too, saw and approved my passion for you. What happiness did he propose in the union! We will be brothers, he cried. (4:32)

The Fool of Quality is set in the late seventeenth and early eighteenth centuries, when the law still permitted girls to be married at twelve years of age (Howard 1964, 1:357, 403n). In practice very few actually married so early. But knowledge of the state of the law may have had a considerable psychological effect on men, who perhaps saw no great objection to thinking of young girls as potential wives or sex-objects, and apparently considered them mature enough to give or withhold consent to sexual advances. In fiction—certainly in Brooke's novel—this conceptualization of the young female sometimes adds an extra dimension to the warm love which is shown to spring up, from time to time, between an older man and a girl.

Another of the incidental stories in *The Fool of Quality* concerns a child who falls in love with a genial uncle who seeks her friendship after the death of his first wife. She regards his second marriage, when it comes, as a desertion, and throughout her own first marriage remains unable to experience warm affection for her husband. The story of her frustrated love comes out when she meets her first sweetheart in later life and they begin to reminisce:

> In you, ...from your infancy, [the man recalls], ... I had centred all my sensations of fatherhood, brotherhood, all the affections and tender feelings that naturally arise from kindred and consanguinity. How have I been delighted with your infantine prattle! how have I exulted in your opening charms! On the death of my first wife you were my only consolation; and, in your innocent caresses and attractive endearments, I felt a sweetness of emotion that I never felt before. (2:277)

Here the language of consanguinity seems in danger of breaking down: the reader is likely to see the love of the man for the little girl as something more than that of fatherhood and brotherhood. The girl, once grown up and graced with the name of Lady Maitland, acknowledges, however, that her beloved uncle "knew the degree and kind of affection that was suitable between such relations" and kept himself "precisely within the limits." The difficulty was that she herself "knew no such distinctions. I was as a piece of virgin wax, warmed and willingly yielding to the first kindly impression. You made that impression, my cousin, you made it deep and entire." The man, who takes this confession with perfect seriousness and is, indeed, much perturbed by it, exclaims: "Gracious Heaven, ... is it possible that, at your years, you should actually conceive a passion for one who might almost have been your grandfather?" (2:278–79). It seems commendable in Brooke that, having raised the question of warm expressions of love between children and older people and shown, in general, a genial approval of it, he should also be prepared to expose its dangers.

In the course of this chapter we have seen various novelists contriving scenes and situations in which characters, and hopefully readers, experience sensations of fondness and compassion toward babies and children. In almost every instance the writer uses comedy to balance tenderness in the hope of preventing a surrender of the narrative to sentimentality and false feeling: an equally effective but less common method is to hint at the disturbing consequences of excessive love. While the attempt to achieve this balance is often successful, the attempt itself betrays uncertainty as to the right note to strike in scenes involving small children and babies. The growth and spread of concern and affection for children, so characteristic of eighteenth-century culture, did not, it seems, immediately bring with it free and unselfconscious forms of behavior toward them or writing about them. In the next chapter, which deals with the representation of the child as a thinking and speaking subject, the nature and extent of the inhibition is explored further.

8

The Child as Subject and Self

In Restoration and Augustan stage comedy the child is generally a baby. While this may be partly a matter of convenience—a baby can be represented on stage by a bundle of clouts—it also reflects comedy's inherent tendency to conceptualize human offspring as objects to be passed around. In other discourses, however, babies can be presented in strikingly different ways. They can, for example, be shown as constituting both the future of humanity (today's babies are the adults of twenty years hence) and its past (infancy is a state in which everyone has once been, but to which none of us can ever return). These ways of conceptualizing children lead logically to a series of questions about the growth and development of the human individual. When does its life begin? From what point in its existence should we begin to regard it as human—from the time of its conception, from the time of its birth, or from some earlier or later time? How does it feel to be a very small child? What are the child's or baby's thought processes like? If, as Descartes held, it is awareness of our own thinking that makes us confident of our own existence, can we fix an age or point of development at which a child achieves this awareness? Is there an essential core of self in each human being and, if so, how can we account for the amount of change in temperament and opinions that takes place in the course of many human lives? What is it that makes the experience of being a baby inaccessible to adults? How, and when, is the barrier between two phases of existence passed?

At the beginning of the early modern period, some of these questions were being posed and tentative answers being offered. Locke, for example, held that children in the womb "receive some few ideas, before they are born," including those of hunger and warmth (1961, 1:112–13). Elsewhere he suggested tentatively that "a foetus in the mother's womb differs not much from the state of a vegetable, but passes the greatest part of its time without perception or thought," since in the prenatal state "the eyes have no light and the ears. . . . are not very susceptible of sounds" (1:88). However, the conjecture that the child in the womb experienced sensations and ideas, however minimal, was a suggestive one, and Locke followed it up with equally significant hints as to the further development of the mind during infancy. "The thoughts of infants," he admitted, "are unknown to us," but from the words and actions that he observed in children he concluded that "there is certainly a time when children begin to think" (that is, to progress beyond the passive reception of ideas and sensations): "whether we can determine it or no. . . . the child certainly knows that the *nurse* that feeds it is neither the *cat* it plays with nor the *blackamoor* it is afraid of" (1:22–23). (Incidentally, it would be wrong to take this last comment as evidence of racism on Locke's part. Presumably, like most of his observations, it was based on experience: perhaps he had seen European children reacting with fear the first time they saw an African just as, in our own time, orphans from Vietnam have been known to show fear of white people when first brought to the West. In the early modern period the term "blackamoor," while sometimes used pejoratively, was also used neutrally to distinguish "white or tawnie Moores" from "Negros or blacke Moores."—see Jones 1965, 22–23.)

If philosophers and physicians exercised caution in their conjectures as to the sensations and thoughts of humans during the prenatal period and early infancy, writers of fiction took the periods before birth and immediately after it as opportunities for the exercise of imaginative freedom. First-person narrative of a baby's thoughts and experiences is encountered as early as 1691 (the year after the publication of Locke's *Essay Concerning Human Understanding*) in John Dunton's extravagant fiction *A Voyage Round the World* (Dunton 1691; cf. Salzman 1985, 299–307). Dunton alludes jokingly to the latest scientific theories about embryos, fetuses, and young babies, and embroiders them with exuberantly imagined detail. Early in the book the narrator announces,

[I] find my self in my *Mothers Belly,*—just Rambled *out of nothing,* or next to't, nothing like what I am now, into a little live thing, hardly as big as a Nit. Should I tell you, as the *virtuosi* do, that I was shaped at first like a Todpole, and that I remember very well, when my tail *Rambled off,* and a pair of little Legs sprung out in the room on't . . . this Infidel World wou'd hardly believe me. (29–30)

In the first moments after the birth, which took place in a carriage, the baby showed no signs of life, but the nurse revived him with brandy:

> I came *peeping into the World agen,* as brisk as a little Minew leaps up at a Fly in a *Summers Evening;* and soon fall a tugging at my Nurses brown Breasts, as hard as the *Country fellows do the Bell-ropes on a Holy-day.* (38)

What Dunton's fictional—but circumstantial—account emphasizes most strongly is the vigor and dynamism of childhood (though his evocation of the moment when the newborn child's life hangs in the balance also recalls its vulnerability.) But beside the empathic enjoyment of childish vigor there is an almost opposite quality which we will meet again later in Sterne's *Tristram Shandy* (a book which may owe something to Dunton; see Booth 1961, 237). The narrator, though supposedly recounting his own childhood experiences, does so with a detachment which makes them sound as if they happened to somebody else: he separates his older from his younger persona, allowing himself to laugh a little at the spectacle of the baby as a helpless plaything of fortune.

More confident than Dunton in exploiting the device of infant autobiography is Steele, who in the fifteenth number of the *Tatler* makes his own offer at description of birth and babyhood from the infant's point of view:

> The First Thing that ever struck my Senses, was a Noise over my Head of one shrieking; after which, methought I took a full Jump, and found myself in the Hands of a Sorceress [i.e. the midwife]. . . . The Witch, for no Manner of Reason or Provocation in the World, takes me and binds my Head as hard as possibly she could; then ties up both my Legs, and makes me swallow down an horrid Mixture. . . . I was carried to a Bed-Side, where a fine young Lady (my Mother I wot) had like to have hugg'd me to Death. (1987, 1:126)

Next he was given to a little girl who had been brought in to tend him, and who

> stuck a Pin in every Joint about me. I still cry'd: Upon which, she lays me on my Face in her Lap; and to quiet me, fell a nailing in all the Pins, by clapping me on the Back, and skreaming a Lullaby. . . . [Later he was entrusted to a wet-nurse who] was eternally romping with the Footmen, and downright starved me. (1:127)

At last a Fellow of the Royal Society who thought all babies should be given cold baths came to visit and soused the child "Head and Ears into a Pail of Water," where the infant "had the good Fortune to be drown'd, and so escap'd being lash'd into a Linguist 'till sixteen, running after Wenches 'till Twenty-five, and being married to an ill-natur'd Wife 'till sixty" (1:127–28).

For a writer, the chief disadvantage of imaginative identification with a baby is that of lapsing into sentimentality. But in Dunton and Steele's fictions the reader's feeling of pity for the baby is balanced by a feeling of complicity in a wide-ranging satire against adults, with their haphazard ways of raising children and their inability to comprehend babies' needs. The plight of the neonate, denied access to the linguistic code to which adult society owes its existence and thus prevented from protesting at the treatment it receives, is made into a kind of serious joke.

The atmosphere in Steele's piece is closer to that of Gay's *The What D'Ye Call It* (which belongs, incidentally, to the same year, 1715) than to that of the earlier "Restoration" comedies. It makes light, for example—or pretends to make light—of the child's suffering and even of its death, which is presented as a welcome release from the miseries of later life. But on balance it is strongly sympathetic to the infant: indeed, the device of letting the baby comment on the world in which it finds itself takes Steele's essay beyond the rather covert and tentative sympathy to be found in *The What D'Ye Call It*. The reader is certainly not encouraged, as to some extent the Restoration comedy audiences were, to feel indulgent toward carelessness or hostility to children on the part of adults, or even toward mere mishandling of babies. Indeed the device of letting fictional babies speak for themselves seems to have become almost a standard means of foregrounding the babies' plight and of encouraging people to think afresh about how they should be treated. When a medical writer at midcentury launched an attack on obstetric methods which he considered dangerous (*The Petition of the Unborn Babies*, 1751) he, like Dunton and Steele, satirized the objectionable procedures from the babies' imagined viewpoint (This, 1982).

In all these texts there is an implied admission that the idea of reconstructing what it feels like to be a baby is preposterous. But if it is preposterous it is also beguiling: it is an occasion for fantasy, an exuberant comic device. This is particularly refreshing in a period like that of the late seventeenth century and the first two decades of the eighteenth, when the fantasy element in mainstream prose fiction sometimes seems to be taking second place to documentary realism. (*Gulliver's Travels* is the miraculous exception.) Even in our own time, when fantasy and bizarre experiment have become the rule, interest can still be aroused by an extension of the same device, as when Carlos Fuentes in his novel *Christopher Unborn* (1989; cf. King 1989) casts as narrator an infant whose narrative issues from the womb and who does not enter the world until the last page.

Having encountered in early modern writing the bold device of using a baby as fictional narrator, we might expect novelists of the period to approach with confidence the apparently less challenging task of entering imaginatively into the experiences of older children. But in practice many of them, like their predecessors the comic dramatists, seem to feel more at ease with babies and toddlers than with children in the age groups from, say, seven to fifteen. It is remarkable that, despite the growing interest in childhood and education in the early eighteenth century, we learn little of this phase of the existence of Roxana, Robinson Crusoe, Pamela, Joseph Andrews, or Fanny Hill; while in *Tom Jones,* as Robert Pattison notes, "Fielding . . . is only too pleased to move, in two paragraphs, over the infancy of Tom Jones into the era of his budding reason and blooming sexuality; in fact, though the infant Jones [is] portrayed, Fielding speaks as if the reader could only really meet him not as a child, but as an adolescent" (1978, 43). In the passage which Pattison has in mind here, Fielding airily leaves his readers "a Space of twelve Years" on which to exercise their own imaginations and announces his intention to "bring forth our Heroe, at about fourteen Years of Age" (1974, 1:118).

Other novelists besides Fielding exercised the same option with as little apology. Eliza Haywood in *The Fortunate Foundlings* dismisses the twin orphans' childhood with the comment: "Nothing material happening during their infancy, I shall pass over those years in silence" (Haywood 1974, 5). James Ridley in *The History of James Lovegrove, Esq.* (1761) likewise decides to "pass over in Silence the Infancy" of his hero, and "hasten to that Part of Life wherein the Seeds of Virtue or Vice are first to be discovered" (Ridley 1974, 15). In both cases "infancy" seems to be used to cover a period up to the age of fourteen or fifteen. Ridley's remark seems to imply that nothing worth relating can happen before the middle teens: the seeds of virtue and vice may be germinating under the surface, but they are not yet "discovered" [sc. revealed].

The lack of any extended account of childhood and adolescence is especially hard to ignore in first-person narratives such as *Robinson Crusoe, Roxana,* or *Memoirs of a Woman of Pleasure (Fanny Hill)*. First-person narration is the method which brings novels closest to the related genre of confessional autobiography, one of whose implied rules is that everything, however trivial, which may relate to the character's spiritual development shall be revealed. Bunyan, in his autobiography *Grace Abounding to the Chief of Sinners,* felt the need to mention boyish exploits such as orchard-robbing: with what plausibility, then, could such things be omitted from longer and more circumstantial first-person narratives of the lives of fictional characters?

In avoiding extended narrations of childhood, the novelists do not seem to have been motivated by direct hostility or revulsion from children or the childhood state. Neither Haywood nor Ridley, for example, ignores childhood completely: the comments that are made, though tantalizingly brief, are indulgent and affectionate. Haywood mentions the pleasure taken by the twins' foster father (who is actually, though he does not know it, their real father) in their "childish prattle," and devotes a sentence or two to the steps he took to provide them with a suitable education. Ridley, too, emphasizes the parents' fondness for their child: one affecting scene in his novel shows a father laboring to convince his son, who is painfully conscious of his own ugliness, that a person not blessed with good looks can still lead a happy and useful life. Yet the details in question occupy no more than a page or two: that is all that these authors, in these novels, choose to devote to descriptions of childhood feelings and experience.

One reason for this paucity of evocation of the inner lives of children is the novelists' continued interest in the problems facing parents. The impulse to validate parental love and care, to discredit frigidity and rejection, and in general to explore the difficulties and ambivalences incident to parenthood, often results in an emphasis on the parents' reactions to the child rather than on the child's own feelings. But it is also possible to detect, especially in the nervous disclaimers of writers like Haywood and Ridley, a continuing diffidence about the nature of childhood and adolescence as distinctive states of being, and a consequent hesitancy in handling child-figures old enough to be portrayed as distinct personalities.

Why, though, did writers of fiction show so much more confidence with babies than with older children? Quite possibly it was the very implausibility of imagining a baby's thoughts—the very remoteness of its situation from everyday adult experience—that made the task easier. Nobody remembers much about what it was like to be a baby; besides, any evocation of what it might have been like must rely on language, a code which is unavailable to the very young. A baby, then, constitutes no threat. It is amusing to imagine a fictional baby turning on its parents or nurses and rebuking them for starving it, neglecting it, or sticking pins into it, for we know that no real baby will ever be able to do so. Older children, however, are more capable of registering, and resenting, not only cruelty and neglect but also well-meant child-rearing practices which they have come to resent. While many people in the early modern period seem to have been conditioned to suppress memories of childhood unhappiness or to consider it as a necessary stage of development—one thinks of the almost jovial tone in which Fielding describes the corporal punishments administered to Tom Jones—a few frankly recorded their unhappiness. John Aubrey's recollections of his seventeenth-century childhood, mentioned briefly in an earlier chapter, are especially scathing in their representations of the way adults behaved toward children. During a sojourn in the country in his teenage years, forced on him by the outbreak of the civil war, Aubrey conversed, he laments, "with none but servants and rustiques and soldiers quartred, to my great griefe, . . . for in those dayes fathers were not acquainted with their children. It was a most sad life to me" (1898, 38). And elsewhere,

> The Gentry and Citizens had little learning of any kind, and their way of breeding up their children was suitable to the rest: for wheras ones child should be ones nearest Friend, and the time of growing-up should be most indulged, they were as severe to their children as their schoolmaster; and their Schoolmasters, as masters of the House of Correction. The child perfectly loathed the sight of his parents, as the slave his Torturor." (Aubrey 1962, 25–26)

Aubrey's picture of parent-child relations, at least as regards neglecting children and leaving them to the conversation of servants, is echoed in fiction, almost a century later, in Shebbeare's novel *The Marriage Act* (1754), where the narrator observes that it is "the Custom of Country 'Squires to let their Children [pick up manners and conversation] amongst the Servants, and only keep Company themselves with the Hounds which lie snoring round the Fire in the Parlour" (1974, 2:108). Shebbeare, like many writers who sought to accelerate the shift toward companionate and affective family life, was probably alluding here to a pattern of behavior which was already outmoded in real society. But his comment does point to a lingering frigidity toward children in some quarters, with a consequent unwillingness to allow them full membership of the family group.

Aubrey's protest against the way children were treated in his youth may serve to remind us that incidents, utterances, and behavior whose significance a child fails to see at the time may be remembered and reinterpreted in later life. Eighteenth-century adults were becoming aware of this. "Philogamus," in his book on marriage and the family, offers a disturbing example:

> Sometimes the daughter is a pretended guardian to the mother, who thinks she is safe, if she carries her little daughter along with her, as a witness of her conversation; and imagines she can make signs and appointments before her, without her taking notice of it. But children are strange observers, and both remember and know what things meant when they come to greater maturity. (1985, 23)

This is a novelistic insight: it opens a promising scenario of intrigue. Why, then, does such material figure so seldom in the fiction of the period? It is perhaps understandable that a culture which was just coming to terms with childhood as a separate state, reaching an often guilty realization of its frequent failings in understanding of children, should turn its eyes away from some of the more threatening scenarios: the prevalence of such evasion would help to explain why so many novelists make only hesitant attempts to figure forth the child's state of existence from the child's own viewpoint. While there are many evocations of unsatisfactory methods of upbringing, there are few detailed, subjective accounts of the agonies and confusions of childhood such as we find, for example, in novels of the mid-nineteenth century.

An early and quite successful attempt to overcome inhibitions against describing the child's feelings about his family environment is Defoe's *The Family Instructor* (1715). This is not a first-person narrative: few of the novels considered in this chapter are so. But it can be said to consider the child as a subject in the less direct sense that it allows the child's own feelings to be inferred instead of confining itself to the adults' externalized perception of them.

The Family Instructor, though partly a conduct book, brings us close to the territory of the novel: it has a far more conspicuous and elaborate fictional frame than Rousseau's *Émile* almost half a century later. Moreover, the two authors' approaches to childhood are even more different than their techniques for describing it. Where Rousseau fears the corruption of the child by society, Defoe presents his hero—a boy of "about six years old" (1973, 1:5)—as the redeemer of the other members of his family, who cures his father, and later the others, of their social affectations and spiritual emptiness. The means of achieving this are the child's innocent goodness and his questions, humbly advanced but uncomfortably penetrating, about the world in which he is growing up. Needless to say this portrait belongs, not to the comic tradition which represents the child as a helpless victim or as a commodity of dubious value, but to the rival, devotional tradition of the child saint, moved by inner goodness to action which affects the lives of his elders. It is a cautionary tale in which the inadequacy of the education given to the child by its parents is revealed, and to a great extent remedied, by the child himself.

What Defoe contributes to the devotional tradition is a new element of realism in his portrayal not only of adult behavior in the contemporary social world but also of the child as a social being. In his introduction he boasts that his fictional youngster has "no questions put into his mouth but what are natural and rational. . . . Our little child asks very little of his father, but what a child at that age may be very capable of asking." Needless to say, neither this nor any other kind of realism is a virtue in itself: we have already felt, in our examination of Dunton and Steele's first-person narrations of early childhood experience, the lure of fantasy, realism's arch-rival. But an element of documentary realism can revitalize and defamiliarize a nonrealistic tradition such as that of the saint's life: it is just such combining of old modes and materials with new ones that gives the novel, as a genre, its vitality.

Defoe's innovative attempt at imaginative identification with a child, to the extent of placing it in a believable contemporary setting and giving it speeches suitable to a particular age, gives *The Family Instructor* a welcome freshness. Especially poignant is the passage where the little boy unconsciously reveals the hypocrisy of his elders by explaining that he thought church attendance was directed only toward display:

> Why, father, my mother has carried me to church a great many times, but I thought I was carried there only to show my new coat, and fine hat; I don't know what the man said when I went. (1:30)

When his father reproves him, telling him that he was not taken to church to show off his clothes, the child innocently remarks that he had gained the opposite impression:

> When it rained, and I could not wear my best clothes, my mother would not let me go out; or when the wind blowed the powder out of my hair, my mother would not let me go; and I heard you say, father, last Sunday, that you could not go to church, because the barber had not brought your new periwig home; and another Sunday, for want of a pair of gloves you stayed at home and played with me all Sunday long, or lay down on the couch to sleep. (1:30–31)

It is significant that the framing narrative of *The Family Instructor* is one in which the child, whose life and spiritual growth have been neglected by his parents, virtually forces himself upon their attention: they find that they can no longer avoid the attempt to enter imaginatively into his life and experience. This epiphany, as Joyce would call it, of childhood is one which the eighteenth century often seems about to achieve; but in a disappointing number of cases the inhibitions and embarrassment are imperfectly overcome. Even humor, which we have described as a saving grace of fictional portrayals of childhood at this period, sometimes seems to stand in the way of a satisfying realization of the child: writers find it hard to steer between the Scylla of bluff condescension and the Charybdis of sentimentality.

This is exemplified in the failure of Defoe's technique of rendering childhood experience to develop steadily in his later fiction; the childhood of Colonel Jack, for example, is compellingly narrated, but does not altogether live up to the promise of *The Family Instructor*. The story, as is usual in those works of Defoe which present themselves as "lives" or "histories" rather than as conduct books, is narrated in the first person by the principal figure. It begins with a vivid, though brief, account of Jack's childhood: he is born a bastard and soon becomes a thief. His parents, as we have seen, take the trouble to find him a wet-nurse: this woman, a sailor's wife, is made to sound commendably fond and careful of her family, which consists of one son of her own and two foster children. When she dies, however, all three are "turn'd loose to the World," and take to sleeping in "ash-holes" at the glass factories. "As to the Parish providing for us," Jack observes cryptically, "we did not trouble ourselves much about that" (Defoe 1965, 8). All three boys turn, predictably, to crime.

Defoe's evocation of the young Jack's inner life is at times impressive, especially in the well-known passage where the child hides some stolen money in a hollow tree, only to have it fall down too far for him to reach:

> As young as I was, I was now sensible what a Fool I was before, that I could not think of Ways to keep my Money, but I must come thus far to throw it into a Hole where I could not reach it; well, I thrust my Hand quite up to my Elbow, but no Bottom was to be found, or any End of the Hole or Cavity; I got a Stick off of the Tree and thrust it in a great Way, but all was one. (25)

The circumstantial detail concerning the recalcitrance of the world of things is soon enriched by a convincing description of the child's response to his problem:

> Then I cry'd, nay, I roar'd out, I was in such a passion, then I got down the Tree again, then up again, and thrust in my Hand again till I scratch'd my Arm and made it bleed, and cry'd all the while most violently: Then I began to think I had not so much as a half Penny of it left for a half Penny Roll, and I was a hungry, and then I cry'd again: Then I came away in dispair, crying, and roaring like a little Boy that had been whip'd, then I went back again to the Tree, and up the Tree again, and thus I did several Times. (25)

Soon afterwards Jack's despair turns to delight when he goes round to the back of the tree and finds another hole through which he recovers his treasure.

In this passage the characteristics attributed to childhood are simplicity, vulnerability, innocence, and a difficulty in coping with a refractory outer world. But the more positive traits are conveyed simultaneously with an evocation of what threatens them: Jack has, after all, resorted to theft—an illicit means of mastering the world—and has thus set in motion a process of engagement with, and corruption by, adult society. From a material point of view it is necessary for him to attain competence, efficiency, hard-headedness; but such qualities work to efface the natural goodness, the freshness, the fine fragility which mark his childhood state. However, *Colonel Jack*, like *The Family Instructor*, seems informed by faith in providence. Though Jack's growing efficiency in coming to terms with his environment is achieved through crime, not through legitimate business, his entry into the criminal fraternity will not lead him to the gallows. The implied reason for this immunity is that Jack never becomes thoroughly hardened to the ways of that adult world which he so longs to master: he always retains some of the naturalness and simplicity that characterized him as a boy.

Colonel Jack is permeated by what Ariès would call an "idea of the child"; but it is one that is less nostalgic and less thoroughgoing than Vaughan's or Traherne's. For Defoe, what is chiefly interesting about childhood is the question of whether its initial innocence will overcome, or be overcome by, the antithetical qualities so often encountered in adult life. Its survival will depend on something which it is hard not to call election or grace. For not all of Defoe's child characters are shown to possess innocence. Those who do possess it are protected by Providence in spite of their frequent backslidings; many, however, do not, and seem never to have had it. Colonel Jack, for example, is one of three foster brothers, all of whom bear the same name. The eldest, nicknamed Captain Jack, has nothing childish about him; he is

> sly, sullen, reserv'd, malicious, revengeful; and withal . . . brutish, bloody, and cruel in his Disposition . . . sharp as a Street bred Boy must be, but ignorant and unteachable from a Child . . . As if he was born a Thief, he would steal every thing that came near him, even as soon almost as he could Speak; and that, not from his Mother only, but from any Body else . . . He had no Taste or Sense of being honest, no, not, I say, to his Brother Rogues, which is what other Thieves make a point of Honour of. (6)

There is a quality of insistence, even hyperbole about this description: the Captain is as far from goodness or innocence as a boy could be.

The second brother, Major Jack, the bastard of an army officer, is "full of Jests and good Humour," with "a true Manly Courage" and "native Principles of Gallantry in him, without anything of the brutal or terrible Part that the Captain had." While the connotations of Captain Jack's character are those of the rogue, brute and barbarian, the low fellow who is born to be hanged, Major Jack is by temperament a fine gentleman, a little like

the rake of Restoration comedy: he is one who "in a Word, . . .
wanted nothing but Honesty to have made him an excellent
Man." Colonel Jack, by contrast, is the humblest of the three,
"a poor unhappy tractable Dog," who "set out into the World so
early, that when he began to do Evil he understood nothing of
the Wickedness of it, nor what he had to expect for it." First he
tries to live by roguery, like the Captain; next he tries to attain
the airs, courage, and *savoir-faire* of a gentleman, in unconscious imitation of the Major. By the end of his life he has attained what he needs of the skills of his foster brothers, while
casting off what is harmful in their natures. More importantly,
he has found his role in life as a husband, parent, and man of
substance. Yet he still retains some of his early humility, for
the dangers and indignities he has undergone have discouraged
complacency. In *Colonel Jack,* then, there is an embryonic doctrine of the child as father of the man, and of the importance of
keeping in touch with, or finally returning to, an authentic selfhood assumed to be conferred at birth.

With *Colonel Jack,* however, we are still a long way from
Wordsworth or Blake's lyrics, Dickens's novels, or (in some ways
a more pertinent comparison) Kipling's *Kim.* While the idea of
the child has considerable importance for the book as a whole,
the promising childhood sequences are relatively few and brief,
and the overall conception of Jack as a child remains oddly undeveloped. In the opening section of the novel we can often forget, for several paragraphs at a time, that Jack is still a boy:
much of the description of cheats and thefts could come equally
well from the biography of an adult rogue or from an adult
picaresque novel. *Colonel Jack* shares with *Moll Flanders* some
vivid evocations of how the orphaned child absorbs the lessons of
living in the world, including some amusing misunderstandings
about what constitutes that privileged state of adult gentility
which the shrewd child longs to reach. But in both cases the
account of childhood remains rudimentary. Defoe still seems
diffident about pursuing too relentlessly the still unfashionable
subject of childish hopes and fears.

His successors, for the most part, also fail to develop the newly
opened territory of distinctively childish or childlike feelings.
It is notable that, of the major novels of Fielding, Richardson,
and Smollett, only one, Smollett's *Roderick Random,* is both a
first-person narrative and one that contains an account of the
protagonist's childhood. (Fielding's only substantial first-person
narrative is *Shamela,* which parodies Richardson's use of the

form. Richardson's epistolary novels are written almost entirely in the first person; but all their main letter writers are adults, so that the new Richardsonian intimacy and self-revelation are never used to explore the inner life of a child.) In *Roderick Random* (1748), the exception to the rule, the narrator shows few signs of awareness that there may be anything special about childhood. Though some later parts of the tale border on the sentimental, there is nothing of that kind in the account of the young Roderick, and hardly any trace in him of childish tenderness or innocence. Instead the boy seems to leap straight from infancy to adulthood, in the manner described by Ariès as typical of the Middle Ages. As the son of a gentleman who has disobliged his father by marrying without permission, Rory is introduced at an early age to intrafamilial jealousies and jostling for favor. The more promise he shows in his early years, the more the "jealous enmity" of his cousins increases:

> Before I was six years of age, [they] had so effectually blockaded my grandfather, that I never saw him but by stealth; when I sometimes made up to his chair as he sat to view his labourers in the field; on which occasions, he would stroke my head, bid me be a good boy, and promise he would take care of me. (Smollett 1979, 5)

But head-stroking is the limit of the old man's affection. The only "child" he seems fond of is the eighteen-year-old offspring of a deceased eldest son, a "rascally sycophant" who "inherited his grandfather's antipathy to everything in distress" (7).

Distress is Roderick's portion in life; his account of his early years is full of the hard usage of the local schoolmaster, the neglect (verging on hostility) of his grandfather, the malice and scheming of his other relations, and a widespread victimization in the village community:

> I was often inhumanly scourged for crimes I did not commit, because having the character of a vagabond in the village, every piece of mischief whose author lay unknown, was charged upon me.—I have been found guilty of robbing orchards I never entered, of killing cats I never hurted, of stealing gingerbread I never touched, and of abusing old women I never saw. (6)

But the tone here is one of indignation rather than pathos: Roderick's recollections are the memoirs of a determined survivor, who seems even more inclined during his childhood than in his

adult years to regard tenderness and sentimentality as signs
of weakness.

The chief characteristic of childhood as represented in *Roderick Random* is not innocence or gentleness but helplessness:
"child" is simply the name for one of those categories of human
being who is at a disadvantage in the grim contest of existence.
If Locke expressed the opinion that children should be children,
that they should play and have playthings, Smollett's novel
serves to remind us that some individuals never have a childhood in that sense of the word. *Roderick Random* does not even
show the little boy weeping with misery, as Defoe's Colonel Jack
did before him and as Smollett's own Peregrine Pickle would
do later, much less trying to remember or imagine what his
dead mother and absent father may have been like.

There are advantages, of course, in Smollett's determined
avoidance of sentimentality, but it is surprising and perhaps
disconcerting to find so little in the way of attempts to figure
forth the specificity of childhood experience. To some extent, no
doubt, it is a characteristic of the picaresque mode that the
protagonist has no proper childhood because life does not allow
him one; and in the early chapters of *Roderick Random* the
protagonist qualifies as a picaresque hero by virtue of his tatter-
demalion existence and his assigned role as a rogue and outcast.
But in *Colonel Jack,* whose central character has even more of
the picaro about him, there are at least hints of what Jack might
have been like if he had had what by this date is coming to be
considered a "normal" childhood, whereas Roderick seems to be
filled from his earliest years with a cynical understanding of
the competitiveness of adult society. All that he shares with
other child heroes is a degree of naivety (which persists after
his childhood is over, and indeed causes him much trouble in
later life) and a tenacity, reminiscent of both Moll Flanders and
Colonel Jack, in clinging to his conception of himself as a displaced member of the gentry whose chief aim in life is to recover
his lost status.

It is evidently this last characteristic that makes Roderick
persevere in his studies at school, in spite of having every possible obstacle placed in his way by his teacher. He is kept going
by a fierce determination not to allow his natural talents to
be repressed:

Far from being subdued by [the schoolmaster's] infernal usage, my
indignation triumphed over that slavish awe which had hitherto

enforced my obedience; and the more my years and knowledge increased, the more I perceived the injustice and barbarity of his behaviour. (6)

This introduces a new consideration. Roderick's character and later development are apparently not determined in any crude or direct way by his education or environment. The narrative implies that treatment such as Roderick receives might have had a different effect on a different type of child. Another boy might have become slavish and learned to accept chastisement without complaint; but Roderick becomes proudly defiant, forming his own, fiercely negative valuation of his elders and their treatment of him. The flowering of his "uncommon genius" is not owing entirely to his own efforts: he is helped by an understanding junior teacher. But it is chiefly the power of the lifeforce in him that keeps him from succumbing to the cruelty and indifference of the world.

The childhood of Smollett's later hero Peregrine Pickle is dealt with more subtly than that of Roderick Random. As if to reassure readers that by this time he has come to share the new interest in the stages of childhood development, Smollett provides frequent updates on the age Peregrine has reached when particular incidents take place. Greater deference, too, is paid to the effects of education, since Perry is shown to flourish much more under some teachers than others, and the good and bad features of each educational method are described. By far the most successful educator is an usher at one of the three schools Perry attends, who

> had established an oeconomy, which though regular, was not at all severe, by enacting a body of laws suited to the age and comprehension of every individual; and each transgressor was fairly tried by his peers, and punished according to the verdict of the jury. No boy was scourged for want of apprehension, but a spirit of emulation was raised by well-timed praise and artful comparison. (Smollett 1964, 54)

As a system of education this is exceptional, whether in the fiction or the life of the time. But Smollett is careful not to spend too much time on this type of textbook description, however unusual its content: instead he proceeds to demonstrate the application of the janitor's principles to Peregrine's individual psychology. At this moment, though the first-person style of narrative has been avoided in this particular novel, the experience of being a schoolboy is conveyed with great plausibility. The tutor, we are told,

> began with Perry, according to his constant maxim, by examining the soil; that is, studying his temper, in order to consult the biass of his disposition . . . He found him in a state of sullen insensibility, which the child had gradually contracted in a long course of stupifying correction. (55)

Peregrine's state of blockish stupidity is attributed to his having been relentlessly flogged by a private tutor in the months before coming to the school. The new teacher's diagnosis is that the boy needs to have his natural feelings reawakened. The first step toward this end is to affect contempt for Peregrine's stubbornness and mulishness in the hope that "any seeds of sentiment" that remain will be stirred. (Here "sentiment" simply means "feeling" in the wide sense, as opposed to stupidity or blockishness: it does not carry the more specific meaning it acquires in the work of slightly later authors.) At first the mortification of being despised simply makes Peregrine miserable:

> The child lost all relish for diversion, loathed his food, grew pensive, solitary, and was frequently found weeping by himself. [But to his teacher] these symptoms plainly evinced the recovery of his feelings. (55)

The teacher concluded that the time had come to show more sympathy to the child: "His governor . . . by little and little altered his behaviour. . . . This produced a favourable change in the boy, whose eyes sparkled with satisfaction [when his master praised him]" (55).

This is one of the most notable instances in eighteenth-century fiction of an attempt to show a child being "educated" in the literal sense of being drawn out. There are parts of the program which a modern reader may feel inclined to reject: it sounds rather dangerous to subject a child who has already been psychologically damaged by flogging to a process which must begin with a further lowering of his self-esteem. But the approach is predominantly sympathetic. Moreover, it is psychologically oriented, directed to curing a malady which is not innate but induced, by tapping the springs of the boy's innate sociability and self-respect. However, this attempt at psychological insight into an individual child is an isolated one. While Smollett gives plenty of documentary description of life at different schools, it is only rarely that he attempts to explore a particular child's feelings about himself or his relationship with the world.

The most distinctive trait of the infant Perry is one which strengthens, rather than weakens, this conclusion, since it is that of a type-figure rather than a realistic or genuinely individualized character. What sets Peregrine apart from other children is "a certain oddity of disposition," chiefly manifested in practical jokes:

> It is reported of him, that before the first year of his infancy was elapsed, he used very often, immediately after being dressed, in the midst of the caresses which were bestowed upon him by his mother while she indulged herself in the contemplation of her own happiness, all of a sudden to alarm her with a fit of shrieks and cries, which continued with great violence till he was stripped to the skin with the utmost expedition by order of his affrighted parent, who thought his tender body was tortured by the misapplication of some unlucky pin. (52)

Smollett attributes to the child, even at this age, an awareness of his parents' fondness, and enough impudence to exploit it:

> When he had given them all this disturbance and unnecessary trouble, he would lie sprawling and laughing in their faces, as if he ridiculed the impertinence of their concern. (52)

Another roguish habit, equally implausibly attributed to Peregrine as a toddler, is to pull his nurse by the sleeve and wink broadly when she is helping herself from her bottle of "cordial waters" [sc. spirits].

These are clearly not realistic details. They belong to the tradition of the elvish foundling or changeling, the preternaturally sharp and teasing infant who intuitively knows how adults' lives are ordered and thus how best they may be disrupted. They link Smollett's Perry with Hogarth's child-figures, which Ronald Paulson tellingly couples with dogs in their capacity for "revealing something about adulthood without losing the animal, natural, instinctual truth they bring to it" (Paulson 1982, 73–74). More distantly, Smollett's portrayal of Perry as malicious trickster relates to the modern literary motif, explored by Reinhard Kuhn, of the demonic child (1982, 40–44). Yet even these ideas, more characteristic in some ways of folklore than of the novel, are not pursued. The early pages of *Pere-*

grine Pickle seem to promise a trickster-hero of the Till Eulenspiegel variety, a kind of goblin, a personification of mischief. But the later passage about the wise tutor Mr. Jennings hints at something quite different in Peregrine's character: an innate sensibility and nobility of soul which belongs to the psychological novel, not the picaresque trickster tale. Neither hint is very successfully or thoroughly developed, nor are the two satisfactorily balanced against one another. Smollett's handling of the child Peregrine suffers from a fatal uncertainty of tone and purpose.

More relentless and consistent than Smollett in his scrutiny of the child's emotional development is the unnamed author of *The History of the Human Heart* (1749). An unusually large proportion of this novel is devoted to the protagonist's infancy and childhood: the account, as usual, is strongly influenced by Locke. Like Locke, the narrator is convinced that babies in the womb already receive sensations; like Steele in the fifteenth *Tatler* essay, he is prepared to imagine what being a baby might be like (*History of the Human Heart* 1974, 18–21). His description of the birth and of the methods of feeding and upbringing in the weeks that follow is even more sharply focused than Steele's, which it strongly resembles:

> Young *Camillo* in an Hour or two grew very obstreporous, and resolved at all Events to get out of his Prison . . . At last, by a happy Tumble, he pitched Head foremost against the Portal of his Enclosure, Mother Midnight was on the Watch for such an Event, catched fast hold of him, and dragged him, now half spent with Fatigue, to this World of Care and Trouble. . . . He set up a piteous Cry, not that he was sorry he got out of the Dilemma, in which he had been plunged for some Hours before, but because he felt actual Pain, which was increased by the officious Tenderness of [the midwife], out of whose Hands he thought he could never be got. (22)

We are familiar with the device of entering, imaginatively, into the feelings of an unborn, or recently born, baby: on this occasion, however, the imaginative identification will be continued into later life to include fictional hypotheses about the older child's encounter with the world.

Another contrast with Steele is in the mildness of the satire now directed at the adults' attitudes to their infant charges. Any mistreatment of the child is due only to excessive kindness:

After the Admiration of his Parts and Features was over among the
Company, he was dressed and laid by his Mother, and fell into a
sound Sleep ... [When he awoke, his thirst] set little Master a
squalling; upon which the good Nurse in waiting, took him up and
suckled him from a Bottle; this afforded Pleasure equal to the Pain
he had before felt. . . . As for Hunger, it was some Days before he
knew anything of the matter, for the good People about him were
all so fond of the little Brat, that they were always a stuffing him.
(22–24)

In Camillo's later life his parents and instructors will meet difficulties in introducing him to the social world; but even these
will be due more to the inherent awkwardness of the transition
from childhood to adulthood than to any gross blunder in
upbringing.

The contradictions inherent in human existence are, indeed,
emphasized from the beginning of the book. Infancy and childbirth are made comical through their incongruities. The child
struggles to escape from the security of the womb, only to find
itself plunged into a "World of Care and Trouble." It is born into
a social world dominated by language and suffers constantly
from having no language at its command. Most of the humor,
of course, is at the expense of the adults rather than the child:
the baby at least knows what it wants whereas the older people,
well-meaning as they are, never fully understand its needs.
Even jokes directed against the child, as it were, are tolerant
rather than bitter: in the quoted passage, as in the whole first
part of the book, there is an implied assumption that though
infancy and childhood are comical they also are inherently pre-
cious and fascinating. The book's narrator, like the people he
portrays, has enough humility to interest himself in apparently
trivial matters such as bottle-feeding, teething, weaning, childish tantrums, orchard-robbing, and a special friendship with a
favorite sister. At one point he writes apologetically, "I believe
my Readers would have excused me if I had not dwelt so long
upon my Hero's Infant State," but he goes on to add another
"Adventure or two" just the same (29). Though inclined to gentle
mockery of his temperamental hero, he is free from lofty condescension toward the childishness of children.

The stage of Camillo's development that gets most attention
is that in which he learns about sex. The first intimation comes
when his favorite sister climbs a cherry tree and her brother,
"happening to look up," sees "something in his Sister's Make,
much different from his own, for hitherto he imagined the whole

Difference of her Sex consisted in the Dress" (30). Predictably he takes the cleavage for a wound, and puts innocent but comical questions about it to his Lockean tutor. For once the worthy man is nonplussed, and is "glad to change the Discourse, lest he should be obliged to come to an Explanation, which he chose to avoid" (32).

Sex instruction is a topic which Locke, too, "chose to avoid": a reading of *The History of the Human Heart* helps to explain why. As the fable unfolds, the child's awakening sexuality is seen undermining the whole Lockean educational system. A long footnote to the cherry tree incident explains the purport of this passage. The narrator is suggesting that man has no innate ideas about "the Art of generation" and that if a man could be kept "all his Life-time from seeing or hearing of Women" he would never acquire the knowledge (32n). It follows that "the utmost Care" should be taken "to keep Youth in Ignorance of this Matter, till their Reason is able to guide them in the Use and Subjection of it" (33n). But the procedure recommended in the footnote is precisely what the narrative shows to be impossible.

The hero, in true Lockean manner, is educated at home by a tutor instead of being sent to a public school. But he is not long kept in ignorance. He soon learns from the maids (one of whom "was so imprudent as to Jeer" (32) at his notion that his sister's vagina was a wound) that the female's cleft is "no Hurt, but a Mark which distinguishe[s] Girls from Boys" (33). A month or two afterwards—he is at this point "between eleven and twelve Years of Age"—Camillo goes to stay with a boy who has been to boarding school, and who promptly teaches him "the School-Boy's Vice" (37–38). Next a girl cousin "about twelve Years of Age" comes to live with the family on the death of her mother, a half sister of Camillo's own mother: she has "not been bred up with all the Strictness imaginable," is "much less reserved than Camillo's Sister" (38), has spent time at a boarding school, and has "there learned vicious Tricks" (40). But the inference that a more sheltered upbringing will protect children from such things does not seem to follow from the narrative: Camillo, after all, has been brought up in relative seclusion, and those who surround him have done their best to shelter him from sexual knowledge, but he finds sources of information on every side.

Camillo's friendship with his young cousin develops, predictably, into a tale of premature seduction. It is marked by radical

uncertainties of tone. The narrative unwinds in an ideal coun-
tryside, where sexual pleasure seems to come as naturally to
the children as riding on the haymakers' carts or romping
among the haycocks (39). The new cousin "naturally, and with
the most artless Innocence" lets the boy kiss her; he does so "a
thousand times, she returning his Caresses with all possible
Ardour" (39). (It's symptomatic of the narrator's uncertainty of
stance that his attitude to the girl should vary so sharply: one
moment she is characterized by "vicious tricks," the next by
"artless Innocence.") When Camillo begins to explore further,
his companion "after a little Struggle" lets him "survey the
secret Throne of mighty Love in all its Budding Bloom" (40).
(The narrator comments admiringly that "no shaggy Shrubs
had yet disfigured the sacred Vale"—40.) Two impulses seem,
at this point, to be struggling for possession of the narrative:
one would accept innocence as good in itself and worthy of preservation, while the other seems to locate its chief value in the
pleasurable process by which it is lost.

Which view, if either, does the book finally uphold? And what
constitutes a loss of innocence in its narrative terms? The adult
characters seem to think that unauthorized initiation into sex
constitutes a fall, but Camillo finds their attitude hard to comprehend and resists it as stoutly as he can. When the affair with
his cousin is discovered, after the two have achieved consumma-
tion (or something like it) for the first time, the boy expresses
surprise at being treated as if he has done wrong:

> I did not think it was so great a Crime to go to Bed to my Cousin,
> whom you all know I loved. . . . Mamma and Papa go every Night
> to Bed, and *Jacob* the coachman lies every Night with the Cook-
> maid, and yet no Harm follows; why should it then be a Crime for
> my Cousin and I to do the same? . . . Why may not we be married,
> and then it will be no Sin. (51–52)

Camillo then quotes the example of a girl as young as his cousin
who "was married but t'other Day." It is the child's clear-eyed
logic, irrefutable in the context-free realm of pastoral but inad-
missible in the complex social world. Especially poignant—and
comic—is the way in which Camillo innocently reveals that the
kitchen-maid and the coachman go to bed together every night:
it is a piece of information which he takes for granted, but it is
something that the master and mistress of the house—disap-

proving of servants' as well as children's extramarital loves—
are presumably not supposed to know.

Camillo receives no satisfactory answer to his innocent question as to what is wrong with what he and his cousin have done,
but he is left in no doubt that he should feel guilty about it. His
tutor tells him that he has

> been guilty of the most heinous Crime . . . and allowed himself to
> be carried away by the Instigation of a wicked Lust to defile himself,
> and Ruin his dear *Maria* for ever; that now he had made a Whore
> of her, she could neither be his Wife, nor fit for any other Gentle-
> man. (51)

This does not refute Camillo's plea of natural innocence: it simply rules his argument out of order. Camillo's claim has been
that natural law encourages what he has done and social law
allows it. (As we have seen, it is true that contemporary law
allowed girls to marry at twelve and boys at fourteen, though
few such marriages actually took place.) The retort Camillo
receives includes no explanation for the taboos it invokes, nor
is he told why he was not warned about them before he reached
an age where he might be in danger of infringing them.

It is here that the narrative begins, apparently involuntarily,
to expose the flaws in Locke's educational system. Locke admits
that, though humans have no innate ideas in the sense of intuitive knowledge, they do have innate urges and temperaments
(*"Temper,"* "particular Constitution of. . . . Mind," *"Predominant
Passions, and prevailing Inclinations"*), and that these must not
be too severely repressed (1968, 205–11). The problem he skirts
is that sex, which Rousseau was to identify as the most powerful
of urges (1969, 426), first becomes insistent at an age when,
according to Locke's other precepts, the human individual is too
young to take on the responsibilities of marriage or even, perhaps, to have the facts about sex and marriage fully explained
to him. Locke, we have seen, is inclined to blame parents for
marrying their heirs off too early. But what if the children
themselves wish to marry? How are they to control their sexual
longings during the interval between the onset of puberty and
the age when society deems them ready for wedlock? And how
is the need for control to be explained to them? Locke's implied
solution is some kind of induced latency period during which
the child is simply kept from learning about sex. (Rousseau was
to offer still more extreme recommendations, hinting that in

special circumstances a human being might be protected from full sexual knowledge until the age of sixteen or even twenty— 1969, 497, 503.) *The History of the Human Heart* suggests that when the period of ignorance and inexperience is cut short through the child's own initiative, as will probably happen, the only way for the preceptor to deal with the situation will be to make the child feel guilty, falling back on the un-Lockean doctrine of the depravity of natural desire.

Faced with a conflict between the promptings of desire and the demands of society, the Lockean tutor in *The History of the Human Heart* rules in favor of the latter. But this involves him in sophistry. He finds himself arguing that sex between young teenagers is bad in essence. Yet his comment that the "whored" Maria can neither be Camillo's wife nor be considered "fit for any other Gentleman" suggests that the young people's conduct has been imprudent rather than immoral. Their crime has been that of infringing, not a universal moral imperative, but a series of arbitrary social rules relating to marriage—rules which have never been explained to them and which are meant to come into operation at a later age than they have reached. The plight of the baby Camillo is thus repeated at puberty. As an infant he lived in a world controlled by the acquired codes of language, but could utter no more than inarticulate cries. Now he finds himself following innate and, to him, innocent impulses, only to come up against a carefully articulated set of prohibitory codes which he does not understand and whose existence he has barely suspected.

More confusing still to Camillo is the fact that his elders have, up to a point, encouraged the affection that has led to the supposed "crime." They have even used the bond between Camillo and Maria for "the Advancement of their Education"; for when the children did anything wrong they were told that they were making themselves unworthy of each other, and that "the only way *Camillo* could take to merit his Cousin *Maria* for a wife was to mind his Exercises" (41). For these adults, early teenage love is charming and good provided its ardor can be sublimated into extra attention to lessons: if it manifests itself more directly it is depraved and wrong.

To a modern reader there is something quaint about the novel's account of Camillo's initiation into the secrets of sexuality. Sexual innocence is something we associate with pastoral (there is an analogous sequence, which the author of *The History of the Human Heart* may have known, in Longus's *Daphnis and Chloe*—1956, 48, 50–51, 77–82) and any novel which makes extended use of it will place its plausibility at risk. (Some modern historians of childhood are convinced, though perhaps erroneously, that actual children of the seventeenth and eighteenth centuries took sexual knowledge and even experience for granted from an early age—see Hunt 1970.) However, *The History of the Human Heart* is not the only text of the period whose protagonist remains both ignorant and innocent of sex for many years and has to find out about it with little or no assistance from older people. The hero of Cleland's *Memoirs of a Coxcomb* (1751), who lives a sequestered existence on his aunt's estate and is brought up by a wise private tutor, is represented as having remained innocent until the age of eighteen, when his instructor left to take up another post. "I had not indeed waited till then," he explains,

> for the dawn of certain desires, and wishes: but besides their being only imperfect ones, and crudities of over-tender youth, my hours and opportunities had been all so confined either to my studies, exercises, boyish amusements, or my aunt's fondness for my being as little out of her sight as possible; that I had not the least room to encourage such ideas, or give them hope enough to live upon. Accordingly they generally died away of themselves, like a faint breeze that had just blown enough to ruffle the surface of my imagination, for a few instants, and flattened into a calm again. (Cleland 1974, 7)

The authors of *Memoirs of a Coxcomb* and *The History of the Human Heart* are fascinated not only by the possibility of a male child or adolescent coming late to sexual knowledge but also by the inevitability of his eventually acquiring it, even without adults' help. Cleland seems to take pleasure in contriving a first-person description of the healthy, uncorrupted innocent on the verge of an awakening:

> My blood now boiling in my veins, began to make me feel the ferment of desire. . . . And a robust, healthy constitution, manifest in the glow of a fresh complexion, and vigorous well-proportioned limbs, gave me those warnings of my ripening manhood, and its favorite destination, by which nature prevents instruction, and suggests the use of those things that most engage our attention, without putting us to the blush of asking silly questions. (6)

The hero of *The History of the Human Heart* is much younger when he begins to feel these desires than his counterpart in

Memoirs of a Coxcomb. Since he is not of an age to emancipate himself from the tutelage of adults, the inescapable result of the clash between his natural impulses and their cultural imperatives is a resort to hypocrisy. (It is the danger that Rousseau, in *Émile,* gloomily foresees from premature contact between the innocent child and corrupt society.) In *The History of the Human Heart* this can be seen developing even during the "innocent" stages of the affair between Camillo and Maria:

> They had both Dissimulation enough to conceal the vicious Emotions of their Passions, and the loose Freedoms they indulged themselves in, as often as they had any Opportunity: not from any Conception they had of the Nature or Crime of these Daliances, but because the one had been checked by his Tutor and Parents for attempting to treat his Sisters and the Maids with these kind of Freedoms, and the other had learned to dissemble all her Sentiments, that being the grand Principle on which the young Ladies depend in the present Generation. (41)

This undermines in advance Camillo's later plea that he doesn't know there is anything wrong in going to bed with his cousin, but it does little to lessen the responsibility of the adults for spoiling the children's innocence by encouraging "dissimulation." The children are respectively "checked" and taught to "dissemble" their feelings, but they are not told why they should be, at the same time, encouraged to love one another and forbidden to indulge their love. At the same time the narrative conveys to the reader that the adults are not altogether to blame: resolution of the conflict between sincerity and nature on the one hand and the demands of society on the other is more than they can be expected to achieve.

After the affair has been discovered and the lovers separated, Camillo, instead of learning to control his longings with the help of reason, continues to gratify them whenever he can: despite the vigilance of his Lockean tutor, Philotis, he has "some small Rencounters with the Maid-Servants," where he comes off "in better Condition than he did in the Green Room with *Maria.*" The narrator comments apologetically that "these [incidents] were so seldom, and conducted with such Secrecy, that they neither interrupted his Studies, nor came to be publick" (66).

Clearly this is a crux. The narrator's praise of purity and innocence, and his attempt to reconcile them with spontaneous desire, will continue after this point, but later developments will make it hard to maintain: the typical worldly attitude toward sex before marriage (the one we encounter in Restoration drama) will increasingly prevail. Lapses from chastity are now accepted as inevitable: they are even, perhaps, desirable because they help the growing youth to acquire sexual expertise. Provided they are kept secret and do not interrupt the boy's education they will do little harm. The adoption of this approach marks the abandonment of Locke's program of rational, unpolluted development from infancy through childhood and youth to marriage.

It is at this point in the narrative that the tutor, Philotis, dies. The narrator says that his death was responsible for "all the Errors of [Camillo's] After-Conduct" (66). "If that good Man had lived," the narrator observes, he would have conducted his pupil safely to manhood, instilling "Principles of Virtue" that would have kept Camillo's ruling passion in control. But the reader is likely to suspect that Philotis dies because he has become redundant: his educational philosophy has no answers to Camillo's most urgent questions.

Philotis is succeeded by Vilario, who hides an "amorous and rakish Disposition" under "the most sanctified Reserve" (67). Vilario is destined to become what the narrator calls the young man's "tutor in Iniquity." But in spite of this and other disapproving hints, the new mentor proves something of a relief after the old one. It soon becomes clear that without Vilario there would be nothing worth narrating in the second half of the book just as, without Maria, there would have been little in the first. Vilario is a hypocrite; but then earlier events have shown that hypocrisy in sexual matters cannot always be avoided. Besides, Vilario is not a very determined villain. He soon abandons his early attempts to gain a hold over his pupil by maneuvering him into a compromising situation with a prostitute, and begins helping Camillo out of scrapes rather than luring him into them. From this time onwards the narrative gradually turns into a kind of nondramatic version of *The Man of Mode*. Thus neither Locke's theory of education nor the rival one implicit in Restoration comedy is taken over entire; rather, the latter emerges as a needed complement to the former.

Locke, as we have seen, is committed to an idea of the child. He does not entertain the notion that children make a sudden leap from being babies to being adults: he sees the child as passing through many stages, each of which can turn out well or badly according to environment and influences. *Some Thoughts*

Concerning Education contains the germs of several ideas later developed by Rousseau. The child is a creature of nature and as such is mostly good: the task of his preceptor is to keep him in touch with nature as long as possible, delaying harmful contacts with culture as long as he can. The implied scene of the young man's education as Locke delineates it is the country estate; Locke would like to feel that in this environment the child need experience no conflict since he will roam the garden, like Adam before the creation of Eve, in the company of the firm, kindly tutor who stands in for God. But in *The History of the Human Heart* even this unpolluted environment is threatened with contamination by the seductive influences of servants, of misguided parents (in this case the boy's mother), and of other children who have been corrupted by going to boarding schools.

In his book on education, Locke suggests that natural impulses can be harnessed and controlled with the help of good educators and by the child's growing powers of reason. He advises that most of the questions children ask should be answered fully and truthfully; if they ask for knowledge which is forbidden to children they should be told frankly that they are too young to be given it, not fobbed off with old wives' tales (*Some Thoughts on Education,* 121.231). Presumably sexual knowledge falls into this category, but Locke makes no explicit statement to that effect. A speech of Amandus, Camillo's godfather, in *The History of the Human Heart,* looks like a systematic attempt to fill out Locke's sketchy teachings on the subject:

> It was a Principle of his, in the Education of Youth, to keep them as long as possible ignorant of the Difference of Sexes, at least till they arrived at an Age capable of putting it under the Government of Reason. . . . Appetite would never rise to any troublesome Height without the Helps of Conversation, and . . . Nature of itself would never find out the way, without the Help of Reason. And if we remained ignorant until Reason made the Discovery, the same Reason would then be strong enough to subject the Appetite to its Dictates. But he observed, that by the common Method of training up Children in much Company, they acquired the Appetite long before their Understanding could be of any use to them. (61–62)

This program, which sounds so reasonable, is precisely what the unfolding narrative shows to be impracticable. Thus *The History of the Human Heart,* which begins like a kind of paean to Locke's system of upbringing, ends by deconstructing it.

The History of the Human Heart has been dealt with at length because it offers the most thorough treatment in English fiction before Sterne of the processes and problems of growing up. While many another novel of the time can justifiably be called a bildungsroman, most concentrate on the construction of personality through formative experiences in later life: certainly no other is as relentless in its imaginative reconstruction of the transition from childhood to adulthood, from nature to culture. Needless to say, the book cannot be called realistic. Its childhood scenes have a strong pastoral and idyllic tinge, especially in their handling of the emergence of sexuality, which is narrated at what may seem excessive length. But if the chief characteristic of childhood is innocence, as novelists by this period are increasingly inclined to suggest, then it is surely not inappropriate to use sexual awakening as the vehicle for an enquiry as to whether adult knowledge is compatible with innocence, or whether it is necessary to lose one's "natural" goodness and simplicity in order to survive in the adult world. This more general question engages not only the author of *The History of the Human Heart* but also better-known writers: Fielding, Cleland, Rousseau.

Tom Jones has been considered in an earlier chapter, mainly in relation to its figuration of adults' responses to children. We shall now return to it briefly to analyze its representations of children's own behavior and feelings. Published in the same year (1749) as *The History of the Human Heart,* Fielding's novel shows something of the same impulse to narrate the growth of a sensibility and to do justice to the growing child's point of view. But unlike the author of the anonymous work, Fielding, as we have seen above, skips a large part of Tom's childhood and "bring[s] forth [his] hero at about fourteen years of age." This seems to be due in part to diffidence about the best means of handling childhood scenes, or even perhaps to lingering doubts about whether they should be included at all. In this as in other novels Fielding allows himself some tart references to the tendency of sophisticated or over-sophisticated readers to reject the minutiae of childhood as trivial or embarrassing. But there are also signs that he himself, willing as he is to present kindness to children in a favorable light, has inhibitions about entering imaginatively into the child's world.

The heading to the fourth chapter of book three prepares the reader for "a childish Incident, which perhaps requires an Apology." The incident in question proves to be a quarrel: Tom objects to being called a "beggarly bastard" by young Blifil. This

sounds promising, but in the event Fielding's account of the two
boys' feelings and behavior is much briefer than his outline of
their elders' subsequent argument about the rights and wrongs
of the dispute. The eighth chapter of the same book has a similar
heading, promising the reader "A childish Incident, in which,
however, is seen a good-natur'd Disposition in Tom Jones." This
time Tom sells a favorite horse in order to buy food for the
dismissed gamekeeper George Seagrim and his family. Here
Fielding, in the speech where Tom excuses himself for selling
the present given him by his foster father, for once allows himself to exploit the child and his unfeigned feelings of compassion
and sensitivity for the purpose of creating pathos, not only in
relation to the "naked and starving" Seagrims but even in relation to the pony:

> Could the little Horse you gave me speak [Tom tells his protector
> Squire Allworthy], I am sure he could tell you how fond I was of
> your Present: for I had more Pleasure in feeding him, than in riding
> him. Indeed, Sir, it went to my Heart to part with him. (Fielding
> 1974, 1:143)

However, Fielding seems afraid that in this paragraph he may
have ventured too far into sentimentality: in the rest of the
short chapter he is careful to include some gusty sentences
about the corporal punishment prepared for Tom if he will not
tell what he did with the money for the horse, and some manly
undertakings from Tom himself about taking a cudgel to his
tutor as soon as he is old enough to do so.

This hesitancy is understandable. In any detailed evocation
of childhood, problems of tone and register are liable to arise
and will prove by no means easy to solve. Part of the difficulty
lies in evolving a satisfactory idiolect for the child-figure. Fielding's novel clearly requires a form of speech for Tom to express
his tender feelings that will avoid excesses of sentiment but will
still be sufficiently distant from that of his hypocritical brother
Blifil. But nothing of the kind emerges: in the chapters dealing
with the shared childhood of the two boys, the good youth expressing sincere sentiment or compassion and the hypocritical
rogue who feigns a sensitivity that is alien to his nature use
registers which are basically the same. The only strategy Fielding can find for distinguishing the two is to interlard Tom's
compassionate and affectionate speeches with hearty references
to flogging and fighting. Thus in *Tom Jones,* as in Smollett's

Peregrine Pickle of two years later, the apparent contradiction between the child's tender feelings and his aggressive or self-assertive impulses is never resolved. When an attempt is made to prevent representations of the child's speech and descriptions of his feelings from sounding sentimental, the idiolect is represented as bluff and blustery, to the extent that the child begins to sound like an adult. But whenever a more resolute attempt is made to render the specificity of children's speech and responses to the world, the discourse becomes sentimental. The closest that Fielding can come to achieving a satisfying compromise is to mingle the two registers, somewhat incongruously, in the speech of the same individual.

By the fourth book Tom and his sweetheart Sophia have grown into young adults, but the third chapter recalls a time when a "very young" Tom gave Sophia a pet bird. "Very young" proves to be a relative term, for in the next sentence it is revealed that Sophia was already "about thirteen," which would make Tom a little older. But some of the language attributed in these chapters to boys in their early teens seems more appropriate to a younger age. Blifil, in particular, is made to use juvenile expressions like "wicked fib" and "nasty hawk." And it is significant that, of the relatively few glimpses of childhood which are afforded in this novel, several betray a curious indecision about the ages and states of mind of the children involved. Again it appears as if Fielding senses and deplores the embarrassment felt by many readers at the idea of entering into a young child's mind, without being quite able to overcome the inhibition himself. Thus, though *Tom Jones* gives more heed than many novels of the time to the details of children's lives— the pet bird and the favorite pony; the lessons and the whippings; the climbing of trees and the falls into streams; the deference or defiance to tutors and other authority figures—it still pays relatively little attention to the inwardness of childhood. Readers are offered much clearer, and more intimate, glimpses into the mind of the adult Tom than into the mind of Tom as a child. And in the accounts of Tom and Blifil's childhood years, attention is often diverted from the children's own feelings to reactions of adults to their behavior.

In all this *Tom Jones* is representative of its time. In eighteenth-century novels, a strong impulse is felt to come to terms with the phenomenon of the child and to represent children as helpless and tender beings who deserve (but often fail to receive) the love, care, and attention of adults. But there is still a marked tendency to avoid extended portrayals of the inwardness of childhood, a topic fraught with difficulty and embarrassment.

9

Issue and its Connotations

Contrary to the assertion of Peter Coveney quoted at the beginning of this book (Coveney 1957, ix), the child became an important and continuous theme of English fiction well before the last decades of the eighteenth century, though its chief function is often to serve as a focus for discussions of the feelings of adults for children rather than to permit an exploration of children's feelings about themselves. What, though, of Coveney's accompanying assertion that in the period following the French Revolution the child-figure acquired a new significance and became an image of the "isolation, alienation, doubt and intellectual conflict" endured by the Romantic artist? Another writer, Tony Tanner, seems to disagree, detecting in the novel from Rousseau onwards a steady rise in the prestige of the life of art, accompanied by an increasing "negativity" in the presentation of children. Tanner is "tempted to say that the emergence of the artist-as-hero is coincident with a sense of the family-as-ruin" (1979, 97–98).

The two analyses are not as incompatible as they may seem. Whether as subjects or symbols, the child and the artist may indeed fulfill parallel functions: both may be set in opposition to the ordered adult society to which neither properly belongs. Seen from another perspective, however, the child can pose a threat to the life of art, as it can to other modes of freedom. The same artist who feels an affinity with children as fellow human beings may resist the idea of parenthood, fearing that it may impede his (and even more her) artistic development. Besides, there are important distinctions (and rivalries) between the children of the flesh and the children of the spirit: in our own century the poet and novelist Stevie Smith noted wryly that a poet, unlike a mother, doesn't have a poem on her hands for twenty years (Barbera & McBrien 1985, 65). More than a hundred years before the rise of the novel, Shakespeare began a sonnet sequence by urging a young man to perpetuate himself by marrying and begetting children, only to reverse his argument in later phases of the sequence by proclaiming that the best means for the youth to achieve immortality was through the poet's undying verse.

These ideas had their counterparts, of course, in the seventeenth and eighteenth centuries. In Restoration drama the exuberant young man and woman—notionally types of artist, whose works of art are their own own swashbuckling, freewheeling lives (Birdsall 1970)—openly express what Tanner would call their sense of "the family as ruin." Indeed it is strange that Tanner, in his discussion of adultery and the artistic temperament as major preoccupations of the novel, should ignore their much earlier emergence in drama. He represents the early novel as a discourse which, after a brief period of innocence, stumbles unknowingly yet inevitably on the new and compelling theme of adultery; but he forgets that the early novelists, when they set up family life as an ideal, did so from a vantage point not of innocence but of awareness. The processes of fiction in the eighteenth century involve not only the construction of the family as ideal but also the subversion of the value system of Restoration comedy, based as it was on an assertion of freedom and nonconformity very like that of the artist.

In early novels the quasi-artistic freedom of the young, occupationless urban bachelor or spinster, a commonplace of earlier stage comedy, is exposed as inauthentic, while the life of the artist, when mentioned at all, is seldom presented as a worthwhile or rewarding alternative. On the contrary, the artist is more likely to be shown as dogged by poverty, misery, madness, failure, and frustration; and these hazards are not, at this period, considered to be worth the risk. The poet Melopoyn in *Roderick Random* attracts sympathy, but also mockery: he is still embarrassingly close to those ridiculous pseudocreators, the scribblers of Pope's *Dunciad*. A few creative artists of the period, including Pope himself, venture to present themselves as profoundly dedicated to their work; but more often such dedication is regarded as an unnatural obsession, and even Pope can be found referring to poetry as in some degree a substitute for a longed-for but unattained domestic happiness:

> The Muse but served to ease some Friend, not Wife,
> To help me through this long Disease, my Life.

(1963, 602)

While this couplet hints at the choice mentioned by Tanner—family *or* art—it does not foreshadow the later judgment that art is to be preferred. Nor is it easy to find such judgments made or implied within the discourse of the early novel and related drama. Moll Flanders expends far more words brooding on the fates of her children and on her relationships with them than she does in reflecting on the survival and dissemination of her narrative. Even Tristram Shandy seems to regard his endlessly proliferating tale as a poor compensation for his lack of bodily potency and fertility. A modern writer (Folkenflik 1982, 91–108), seeking to trace the motif of the artist as hero in the eighteenth century, is hard-pressed for examples in the first half of the century and is forced to lean rather heavily on the bard in Gray's poem of that name, which dates from 1757. This relatively low valuation of art and the artistic life helps to explain the fact that in the early eighteenth century the figure of the artist was not yet linked connotatively with that innocent, unspoiled being, the child.

The metaphoric link which does establish itself is with the work of art rather than with the artist (cf. Castle 1979, 193–208). Even so early, and so apparently unsophisticated, a fiction as Richard Head's *The English Rogue* (1665) deploys the metaphor in quite a complex form, using it to claim for the work the characteristics most desired for bodily offspring, namely freshness, legitimacy, and vigor:

A generous resolution commanded me to scorn a Lithuanian humour or custom, to admit of *adjutores tori,* helpers in a marriage bed, there to engender little better than a spurious issue. [My book] is a legitimate offspring, I'll assure ye, begot by one singly and solely. (1928, 2)

Almost a century later Henry Fielding, in the preface he wrote for his sister Sarah's novel *David Simple,* complained that the Muses had "behaved to [him] like the most infamous Harlots," having laid "many a spurious, as well as deformed, Production" at his door. In all of these, Fielding complained, his "good Friends the Critics" had, "in their profound Discernment," discovered "some Resemblance of the Parent," until he had found himself held responsible for "half the Scurrility, Bawdy, Treason and Blasphemy" which the previous few years had produced (1973, 3–4). After the publication of *Tom Jones* a detractor adopted the same metaphor, derisively visualizing the

new book being "mid-wived into the World" by Fielding's patron
Lyttleton (1974, 1:xlvi). Later still Fielding himself wrote of his
last novel, *Amelia*, "I declare I am the Father of this poor Girl.
... Of all my Offspring she is my favourite Child. ... I do not
think my Child is entirely free from Faults. I know nothing
human that is so; but surely she doth not deserve the Rancour
with which she hath been treated by the Public" (1983, lix; cf.
Barnett 1989).

In many of these instances the book is implicitly associated
with spurious, ill-omened, or illicit births. This complex of ideas
harks back to *Mac Flecknoe* and *The Dunciad*, where the imagery of childhood coalesces with that of the theater and
writing:

> Near these [brothels] a Nursery erects its head,
> Where Queens are form'd, and future Hero's bred;
> Where unfledg'd Actors learn to laugh and cry,
> Where infant Punks their tender Voices try,
> And little Maximins the Gods defy.
>
> (Dryden 1969, 188)

The word "Nursery," used to denote a training house for actors,
leads Dryden to a whole series of metaphors suggestive of childhood, which were echoed by Pope in the *Dunciad* in lines like
"How hints, like spawn, scarce quick in embryo lie" and "How
new-born nonsense first is taught to cry" (1963, 723). The fact
that these are metaphors, not primarily descriptions of children,
childhood, or conception, only sharpens the point that the negative connotations of human reproduction were still conspicuously available to writers, since the tenor of the metaphor
relates to the murky world of failed literary and theatrical
endeavor.

When the analogy between book and child did take on more
positive connotations it worked to exalt biological reproduction
over literary production. In *Three Hours After Marriage* the
spinster intellectual Phoebe Clinket causes a sensation when
she refers unthinkingly to her child: the allusion seems to solve
the main mystery of the play, the parenthood of the baby which
has been left at Dr. Fossile's house. There is a strong sense of
anticlimax when Phoebe turns out to have been referring not
to an actual baby but only to her latest literary composition
(1:258–59). Her airy allusion to it as a "child," made without
the least consciousness that others might misunderstand her,

shows an obsession with writing, and a distancing from the life of nature, which the play represents as ridiculous.

Something of the same lack of self-awareness lies behind the assumption of the real-life Lord Chesterfield that his son will enjoy being likened to a work of art. Hearing that a fashionable tailor has just finished an outfit for the young man, the Earl comments:

> The natural partiality of every author for his own works makes me very glad to hear that Mr. Harte has thought this last edition of mine worth so fine a binding.

Later in the same passage Chesterfield expresses the hope that the "edition" will not be esteemed for its outside alone, but will be "opened and read," and that "the best judges" will find "connection, consistency, solidity, and spirit" in it (Stanhope 1959, 26–27). In the novel such imagery is rare, except in prefaces, and while these will often refer, lovingly or ruefully, to the novels they introduce as the authors' intellectual offspring, the assumption almost always is that the comparison is flattering to the book, not to the child.

Surprisingly, one of the rare appearances in the eighteenth-century novel of the idea that the products of the mind deserve priority over biological offspring occurs in the work of Richardson, the most notoriously domestic novelist of all. In *Clarissa* the reforming rake Belford, the friend of Lovelace, is sufficiently impressed with the heroine's spirituality to wish that she may never have to bear or care for offspring:

> She is in my eye all mind: and were she to meet with a man all mind likewise, why should the charming qualities she is mistress of be endangered? Why should such an angel be plunged so low as into the vulgar offices of domestic life? Were she mine, I should hardly wish to see her a mother, unless there were a kind of moral certainty that minds like hers could be propagated. For why, in short, should not the work of bodies be left to mere bodies? (Richardson 1932, 2:243–44)

In a letter to his admirer Lady Bradshaigh, Richardson decries this suggestion, ruling that Belford here shows "too high Notions of [Clarissa's] Excellencies." At the same time he concedes that parenthood is full of dangers: "the Perils of Child birth," the "manifold Hazards of the Infantile State," the possibility that children of an unreliable father may inherit his bad quali-

ties, and the fact that even good parents "are not sure they shall
have good children" (Richardson 1964, 107). Clearly there were
moments when even Richardson, the eulogist of family life, felt
a yearning for the life of the spirit. In modern writing this
feeling has become almost commonplace: Julia Kristeva, for example, quotes a Dostoyevsky character as asking why, once the
aim of mystical insight is achieved, it should be necessary for
procreation to continue (Kristeva 1980, 26).

To read this feeling back into the eighteenth-century novel
is, however, misguided: utterances like those of Belford in *Clarissa* are remarkably rare. There is little to justify W. Austin
Flanders's assertion that "in most novels the family is portrayed
as, at best, a necessary evil" (1984, 116). It is true, as Flanders
notes (126 ff.), that most protagonists of eighteenth-century novels are bastards or outsiders. However, what these figures are
shown to resent is not the family as such but the cruel fate
which excludes or expels them from it. While grateful to foster
parents, surrogate parents, and teachers for protection or sustenance in a hostile world, these problematic individuals feel the
lack or loss of their legitimate parents, or their rejection by
them, acutely; and they are anxious to give their own children
an unproblematic upbringing in a nuclear family rather than
leave them to the mercy of those aleatory processes hinted at
in Restoration comedy. The closing paragraphs of *Tom Jones*
(which in this is typical of many other novels) glow with satisfaction, not nausea, at the idea of the proliferation and perpetuation of the family:

> Sophia hath already produced two fine Children, a Boy and a Girl,
> of whom the old Gentleman [their grandfather] is so fond, that he
> spends much of his Time in the Nursery, where he declares the
> tattling of his little Grand-Daughter, who is above a Year and a half
> old, is sweeter Music than the finest Cry of Dogs in England. (Field-
> ing 1974, 2:981)

This does not mean that the early novelists ignore the problem implicit in Restoration comedy; namely, the threat posed
by the new generation to the freedom and selfhood of the old.
In their writings there are still, as we have seen, some negative
figurations of children and of parenthood, and plenty of recalci-
trant adult characters to put the case against "brats" and "little
bastards." But the more likeable figures are shown aspiring to
a prosperous domestic life in which family members love and

respect one another. They enjoy making friends of children, playing with the younger ones, and interesting themselves in the development of the elder.

This tendency gathers momentum as the 1740s are left behind. We have seen that one of the few positive characteristics of Captain Booth in *Amelia* (1751) is his willingness to play with his children and to look after them when his wife is elsewhere. In the novels which follow there is an increasing emphasis on the need for men as well as women to bestow attention and affection on children—younger sons as well as heirs, girls as well as boys, ugly children as well as beautiful ones, other people's children as well as one's own, poor children as well as rich. In Brooke's *The Fool of Quality* (1766–70), an earl and his family incur disapproval for lavishing all their attention on the eldest son while keeping the younger at nurse in the village, hardly noticing him until he is five years old. In Ridley's *The History of James Lovegrove*, a mother's preference for the more beautiful of her two children is punished with the child's death: having taken "the Care of him entirely to herself" she wakes one morning to find that she has "overlaid" him. The end result is an increased care for the "little infirm twin" who is left, and an awakening to the "Vanity and Impropriety of [the parents'] former Desires," which included a wish that Providence might "kindly take [the sicklier infant] off [their] hands . . . [that] he should be graciously relieved of this troublesome World. (1974, 11–14).

Frances Sheridan's *The Memoirs of Miss Sidney Bidulph* (1761) has even Mr. Arnold, who later goes to the bad, showing fondness for his infant daughters: in a letter to a friend his wife gently chides him for preferring the elder, Dolly, to the recently born Cecilia, but records with pleasure that "he spends most of the time he is at home in the nursery" (1987, 109). Earlier in the same novel Faulkland, a vivacious young gentleman, is found at breakfast

> with two pretty children on his knee, to one of whom he had given some cake; and the elder of the two, a boy of about five years old, he was gravely lecturing, though with great gentleness, for having told a lye. (26)

When asked whether he normally allows these children in the house, Faulkland replies that he has done so on this occasion out of sympathy for their parent, his coachman, whom he admiringly describes as "a very affectionate husband and father," devastated by the recent death of his wife in giving birth to their third child. This latter passage is not a mere piece of incidental description: it is an early indicator of the way we are to respond to Faulkland during the ensuing action. Though his character sometimes appears to Sidney and her mother as that of a callous seducer like Richardson's Lovelace, he is really a man of feeling and sympathy, who will emerge as the undisputed hero of the book.

Tom Jones, too, wins sympathy when, instead of revenging himself on other children for the insecurity of his own childhood (as a Restoration rake might have done), he goes out of his way to comfort and protect the children of his landlady Mrs. Miller and those of the reluctant highwayman Enderson (Fielding 1974, 2:680–82). This move on the part of the novelist is a significant one. We have seen that the early eighteenth-century novel generally falls short of its apparent intention of developing a positive and sophisticated figuration of the child. But the attempt to resolve the conflict of feelings which may surround children is made, albeit hesitantly, and was to be taken further by later novelists. In *Jane Eyre* and *Great Expectations* (to name only the best-known examples) characters who once spoke to readers from a child's viewpoint, justly resenting the way adults treated them, grow up to pity and remedy the loneliness and neglect that other people's children suffer. To Pip in *Great Expectations* many failings are attributed, but hostility and resentment toward the young are not among them. On the contrary, the memory of his own unhappy childhood makes Pip anxious for the welfare of the children he encounters in adult life. He is concerned for the young Pockets, left by a neglectful mother to the care of slothful servants; and he later becomes a second father to young Pip, the child who in other circumstances might have been his own. In *Jane Eyre*, likewise, the protagonist is resentful of the way she was treated in her early years. But instead of treating children harshly once she grows to adulthood, as she might have felt inclined to do, she makes a career as a teacher and governess, and learns to win the confidence of her charges.

All this reveals that Tanner, in describing the assimilation into the novel of a concept of "the family as ruin," and suggesting that an atmosphere of "negativity" was beginning to surround the child, was following one strand of development of the novel while neglecting others equally important. Tanner

himself, in a valuable book on Jane Austen, notes without ran-
cor that "'marriageableness' is indeed the key to existence as
she knew it," and that the "good marriage" is in her eyes "indispensable for the renewal of society" (Tanner 1986, 10). This is
equally true of her predecessors, and in this the novelists were
at one with their contemporaries. According to the historian
Randolph Trumbach, the marital tie was the strongest of all
ties between family members in the eighteenth century: people
in general (at least those in reasonably prosperous circumstances) simply "liked matrimony" (1978, 34, 51).

The literary representation of children and family life remained problematic, of course. There were, as we have seen,
numerous inhibitions that lay in the way of real inwardness in
the portrayal of children. But while the child's own experience
becomes central only on rare occasions, there are a myriad small
instances of the evocation of parents' observations, feelings,
wishes, longings, of, with, and for their children: feelings for
the young, as projected in fiction, become steadily more benign.
And this change occurred in concert with a similar, contempora-
neous movement in the culture at large. The derogatory comic
and satiric connotations which attached to the child linger long-
est in those passages from poems and prefaces where malformed
or spurious offspring are used as a metaphor for bad books.

That the child did not play a still larger part in fiction may
be attributed in large measure to the sheer difficulty of devising
literary means of representing domestic happiness in a positive
light. The nature of the impediment is perhaps best explained
by means of a comparison with painting. The art historian John
Barrell, writing of the difference between two versions of
Gainsborough's *The Harvest Wagon,* notes that in the later
painting

> the two clowns fighting over the bottle have been removed. . . . The
> women in the cart are no longer the neat but slightly dishevelled
> and unattached wenches of the comic tradition: they are more re-
> laxed, less alert, and they are the mothers of children. The new
> Pastoral is . . . essentially domestic: it celebrates no longer the imag-
> ined vitality of the rural community, but the imagined peace of a
> properly conducted family life. (1980, 69)

The process Barrell describes in pastoral painting is one which,
as we have seen, had been anticipated in the transition from
Restoration comedy to the early novel. The novel, unlike painting, is able—and urgently needs—to show comic and idyllic

scenes alternately or even simultaneously: the two modes of painting described by Barrell correspond closely to the alternating modes of Moll Flanders or Roxana's fictional existence. Indeed Defoe's novels, written forty to forty-five years before Gainsborough painted the earlier version of *The Harvest Wagon,* are organized around the very antitheses that Barrell describes. Yet in the novel the value judgement which is offered is the opposite of Barrell's: the novelists, like the painter, come to prefer idyll to comedy, and regularly allow it to prevail.

It is true, of course, that rhapsodies on domestic peace can become tiresome. Tanner devotes some playful pages to the awfulness of the family paradise delineated in Rousseau's *La Nouvelle Héloïse* (1979, 143–65): he could have undertaken, with equal success, a similar critique of the second part of *Pamela.* However, this is due less to an underlying sense of "the family as ruin" on Rousseau or Richardson's part than to their failure to grasp a truth well known to their contemporaries: namely, that while the domestic idyll may be experientially satisfying, it is resistant to narrative treatment, except when suitably enlivened by comedy, satire, or periods of adversity. When Defoe made Moll Flanders pass over her interludes of domestic peace in a few lines while invariably recalling them with nostalgia, he set a precedent which Rousseau and Richardson would have done well to follow. Ironically, the few passages in which the second part of *Pamela* comes alive are those which raise the specter of the desecration or destruction of the family: it is the threat to family cohesiveness which allows the value of that cohesiveness to be shown.

To deduce a critique of marriage and domesticity, as Tanner seems inclined to do, from the failure of narrative figurations of the domestic idyll is, therefore, to make a naive assimilation of narrative to existence. It is precisely at this point that the two most stubbornly refuse to correspond. Fielding, in his character of all-controlling narrator, makes the point with skill and delicacy:

> Most Histories, as well as Comedies end [with marriage]; the Historian and the Poet both concluding they have done enough for their Hero when they have married him; or intimating rather, that the rest of his Life must be a dull Calm of Happiness, very delightful indeed to pass through, but somewhat insipid to relate. And Matrimony in general must, I believe, without any Dispute, be allowed to be this State of tranquil Felicity, including so little variety that,

like *Salisbury Plain,* it affords only one Prospect, a very pleasant one it must be confessed, but the same. (1932, 149)

In *Amelia,* Captain Booth encounters the same problem when he offers the sophisticated, urbanized Miss Matthews a narrative of his life as a married man in the country. "The whole," he recalls, "was one continued Series of Love, Health, and Tranquillity. Our Lives resembled a calm Sea." Miss Matthews observes snidely that this is "the dullest of all Ideas." But she makes no new point. Booth was aware, before he began, that his narrative was likely to bore his listener; for, as he says, "The greatest Happiness is incapable of Description" (Fielding 1983, 146–47). Patricia Spacks, in a discussion of Charlotte Lennox's *The Female Quixote,* advances a related idea to the one broached by Miss Matthews when she notes that "good women don't *have* adventures," whereas a life (or a fiction) without adventure is difficult to endure (1990, 15). But it is romance, the preferred reading of Cervantes and Lennox's protagonists, that makes adventure seem desirable. The novel (which often goes out of its way to distance itself from romance) concentrates more on the type of adventure to be found in the real world, a type which is unpleasant enough to lend allure to the tranquillity which awaits the characters at the end of the book.

In most eighteenth-century novels this quiet life is deliberately drawn in the sketchiest possible way. This is to be expected: the appropriate artistic medium for the expression of the ideal of untroubled family life is not the dynamic mode of the novel or stage comedy but the relatively static and atmospheric mode of the idyll, the periodical essay, or the pastoral painting. John Barrell makes an elementary error in chiding Gainsborough for moving away from the "comic tradition" toward images of parenthood and "properly conducted family life." While painting can, of course, narrate, and can achieve comic effects, it is also capable—to a degree that many other art forms are not—of mastering a synchrony, of calling forth lyric or rhapsodic (as opposed to comic) feelings. Criticism of a painter for figuring forth an imaginary rural peace where the female figures are the mothers of children is not only unnecessarily puritanical: it is misguided in its attempt to deprive painting of a territory which is peculiarly its own. The novelist who wishes to evoke such serenity does best to confine it to a single descriptive chapter, approaching the condition of a painting. Fielding's brief figurations of familial happiness in *Joseph Andrews* and *Amelia* work much more powerfully than their lengthier equivalents in *La Nouvelle Héloïse* or the second part of *Pamela*.

Barrell is, of course, on much firmer ground in his evocation of comedy. Jokes against children and the family, or against usually staid family members taking a holiday from the restraints that the family imposes, are exhilarating: they are even, perhaps, a necessary balancing element in any fiction which aspires to a satisfying representation of marital or familial relations. Even a novel as deeply penetrated with the imagery of fecundity and ideal marriage as D. H. Lawrence's *The Rainbow* can impishly present its protagonist Ursula as "all for the ultimate. . . . Always in revolt against babies and muddled domesticity." "Multiplying and replenishing the earth bored her," the narrator remarks, "Altogether it seemed merely a vulgar and stock-raising sort of business. . . . In her soul she mocked at this multiplication, every cow becoming two cows, every turnip ten turnips" (Lawrence 1977, 275). Eighteenth-century novelists, too, are not above allowing characters to make points at the expense of procreation. And there are times when, by their failure to fulfill their apparent promise of a fully internalized and predominantly positive vision of childhood, these early novelists seem to share some of the reservations of earlier and later writers about children and the family. Overall, however, early modern novels work to repudiate the notion of the family as ruin—so wittily and devastatingly formulated in Restoration comedy—and to deny that self-fulfillment for the parent is incompatible with the needs of the child. Like Steele in *Spectator* 263 (1 January 1712) they pursue the Lockean project of establishing a cultural ambience in which tensions between generations can be minimized, and in which the obligations of parents to children are as sharply etched as those of the child to its elders.

Modern interpreters of eighteenth-century fiction mostly succumb to the temptation to read their own low estimates of the nuclear family back into early modern texts. W. Austin Flanders, for example, makes play with the fact that in eighteenth-century law the bastard, who figures so largely in the novels, was *filius nullius*, nobody's son: Flanders takes this as proof of the rigidity and callousness of the patriarchal nuclear family (1984, 130). In practice, as the historian Randolph Trumbach shows,

> neither the law, nor certainly their fathers, acted entirely on this principle. . . . The law required fathers to support such children. . . .

Fathers. ... brought home their bastards, gave them the family name, arranged advantageous marriages for them, and left them with inheritances. But they could do these things only with the sufferance of their legitimate families. (1978, 161–62)

The tolerance and flexibility that Trumbach finds in the society likewise prevails in the novels, at least among the characters whom readers are invited to admire. In *Tom Jones* the hero is still just as indubitably a bastard at the end of the book, after his real parentage has been discovered, as he was at the beginning; but that does not prevent Squire Allworthy from making Tom his heir. Both social and fictional parents and parent-figures testify to a growing cultural set toward love and acceptance of children as human beings with a life of their own, not merely as links in a social chain or as potential perpetuators of names and fortunes.

We must not, of course, make the mistake of idealizing the typical eighteenth-century family (insofar as there was such a thing), or of exaggerating the idyllic element in the representation of family life and family feelings in the novels. It may well be true, for example, that "as romantic love loosened the knees of the aristocracy, it tightened the hold of patriarchy on the wives and children whom it sang" (Trumbach 1978, 76–77; cf. Perry 1991) There are, as we have seen, times when the writers of fiction betray their fear of this possibility, as also of other possible shifts in the balance of power. One of the few generalizations that can be safely made about the family as such is that it is a polity, a power structure. (One modern writer [Spacks 1982, 57] notes that "Clarissa, who ... believes that all the world was originally one family—and ironically ignores the possibilities for conflict implicit in that metaphor—would prefer to avoid power struggles but finds herself precipitated into them.") The possibility of change always, of course, brings with it the possibility of conflict. The novelists show awareness of this, as earlier chapters of this book have shown, and their sensitivity may have something to do with their failure to achieve greater inwardness in their portrayal of the potentially encroaching child-figure. But it is misleading to suggest that, while the overt ideology behind the novel was one which exalted the family, unconscious (and more authentic) wishes to break loose from and repudiate the family were always welling up to negate the overt message. Awareness of the possibility of failure—of, to use Tanner's phrase, "the family as ruin"—is for the most part

conscious and overt. The novelists incorporate the traditional
jests and critiques, inherited from Restoration drama and traditional culture, but it is never in these that the energies of the
novels lie. The antifamilial outlook is repeatedly linked with
cold reason and frigidity. While the notion of the family as a
little kingdom is common in the middle years of the century,
few writers of any kind—and certainly few novelists—present
this kingdom as one riven by discontent, much less threatened
with civil war. Predominantly, the family is made to appear as
a refuge from strife, not as a cause, or locus, of strife.

"From its start," writes Frederick Karl, "the English novel
has represented an adversary culture. Although it seemed to
bow to the tastes and needs of the new bourgeoisie, it also stood
for new and often dangerous ideas" (1975, 5). This suggestion,
while useful, must be treated with caution: in its exaggeration
it is reminiscent of the symmetrical but opposite notion that
Restoration comedy ultimately accepts the ideal of marriage
(Hume 1977, 2). There can be no doubt that both pro-and anti-
familial attitudes are present in both Restoration comedy and
the early novel, and that their coexistence gives rise to some of
the most creative tensions in both literary modes. But to compare the two bodies of work is to restore a sense of proportion.
In Restoration comedy criticisms of marriage and parenthood
are more frequent and more cogent, and are assigned to characters with whom there is more temptation to identify. They are
still present in novels and are frequently made to seem amusing; but instead of being uttered by glamorous or likeable figures they are mostly assigned to fops, trollops, sadists, or boors.
It is true that there is in the eighteenth-century novel a tension
between the longing for tranquillity and settlement on the one
hand and the desire to encounter the turbulent and dangerous
world on the other. But it is misguided to accord to the second
of these impulses an absolute privilege over the first—to dis-
count or erase, for example, all Moll Flanders's declarations of
love for her children, all her expressions of disgust for incestuous unions, or all her praises of marriage at the expense of other
forms of male-female relationship.

It is prudent, too, to recall that an ideology based on the affective nuclear family can be, and in eighteenth-century novels
frequently is, presented as being in itself an "adversary position
to accepted values" (cf. Mount 1982). The typical eighteenth-
century fictional protagonist is engaged in a search for a prosperous, stable, and above all emotionally satisfying family life

in a world which is shown to be markedly inhospitable to such things. It is often noticed that the heroes and villains of eighteenth-century novels are at one in their scorn for politics and their studied avoidance of involvement in political life (see, e.g., Spacks 1982, 57). In a culture which boasted of the superiority of its own political system but in practice showed contempt and distrust for politicians and politics, it was inevitable that the family should become a powerful signifier of a longed-for private existence, called into being to redress the balance of the world of public affairs. The novelists, in giving their support to this idea, were fond of implying that they and their readers made up an enlightened but embattled minority for whom such values were paramount.

To explore representations of parents and children in early eighteenth-century English writing is, then, to re-open some of the most important territories in the cultural geography of the time. But to do so is not to undertake a merely thematic study. Our investigation is, as much as anything, an analysis of the child as signifier, seeking to re-activate the creative and imaginative connotations of children at a relatively remote period of time. And while the child as signifier in the early novel still sometimes carries overtones of nervousness and even fear, the dominant impression is far from the negative one projected by Restoration comedy. It is, rather, that of the child as an emblem of hope, freshness, vigor, spontaneity, and new life.

Bibliography

Addison, Joseph, et. al. 1965. *The Spectator*. Edited by Donald F. Bond. 5 vols. Oxford: Clarendon Press.

Adultery and the Decline of Marriage: Three Tracts. 1984. New York and London: Garland. (In the series *Marriage, Sex and the Family in England 1660–1800*. Edited by Randolph Trumbach.)

The Adventures of a Kidnapped Orphan. 1974. London, 1747. Facs. reprint, New York: Garland.

[Allestree, Robert?]. 1977. *The Whole Duty of Man, Laid down in a Plain Way for the Use of the Meanest Reader*. London, 1659. Reel 650 of *Early English Books, 1641–1700*. Ann Arbor, Mich.: University Microfilms.

Ariès, Philippe. 1973. *Centuries of Childhood*. Translated by Robert Baldick. London: Jonathan Cape.

Ashcraft, Richard. 1987. *Revolutionary Politics and Locke's Two Treatises of Government*. Princeton: Princeton University Press.

Astell, Mary. 1986. *The First English Feminist: Reflections Upon Marriage and other Writings by Mary Astell*. Edited by Bridget Hill. Aldershot: Gower/ Temple Smith.

Aubrey, John. 1898. *Brief Lives, Chiefly of Contemporaries*. Edited by Andrew Clark. Oxford: Clarendon Press.

———. 1962. *Aubrey's Brief Lives*. Edited by Oliver Lawson Dick. Harmondsworth: Penguin.

Austen, Jane. 1970. *Mansfield Park*. Edited by John Lucas and James Kinsley. London: Oxford University Press.

Bage, Robert. 1979. *Hermsprong or, Man As He Is Not*. Originally published in 3 vols. London, 1796. Facs. reprint, New York and London: Garland.

Bakhtin, Mikhail. 1981. *The Dialogic Imagination: Four Essays*. Translated by Caryl Emerson and Michael Holquist. Austin: University of Texas Press.

Barbera, Jack, and William McBrien. 1985. *Stevie: A Biography of Stevie Smith*. London: Heinemann.

Barnett, Carol H. 1989. "The 'Children of the Brain' and 'All-Devouring' Time: Swift on Books." *College Language Association Journal* 32: 494–512.

Barrell, John. 1980. *The Dark Side of the Landscape: The Rural Poor in English Painting 1730–1840*. Cambridge: Cambridge University Press.

Bataille, Georges. 1979. *L'Érotisme*. Paris: Éditions de Minuit.

Battestin, Martin, with Ruthe R. Battestin. 1989. *Henry Fielding: A Life*. London: Routledge.

Behn, Aphra. 1967. *The Works of Aphra Behn*. Edited by Montague Summers. 6 vols. 1915. Reprint, New York: Phaeton Press.

[Behn, Aphra?] 1933. *The Ten Pleasures of Marriage and the Second Part, The Confession of the New Married Couple.* New York: Godwin. (The attribution to Aphra Behn is no longer accepted.)

Bell, Ian A. 1991. *Literature and Crime in Augustan England.* London: Routledge.

Bersani, Leo. 1984. *A Future for Astyanax: Character and Desire in Literature.* New York: Columbia University Press.

Birdsall, Virginia O. 1970. *Wild Civility: The English Comic Spirit on the Restoration Stage.* Bloomington: Indiana University Press.

Booth, George, Earl of Warrington. 1985. *Considerations upon the Institution of Marriage.* London, 1739. Reprint, New York: Garland. In one volume with Philogamus [pseud.]. *The Present State of Matrimony.* In the series *Marriage, Sex and the Family in England 1660–1800.*

Booth, Wayne C. 1961. *The Rhetoric of Fiction.* Chicago: University of Chicago Press.

Boucé, Paul-Gabriel, ed. 1982. *Sexuality in Eighteenth-Century Britain.* Manchester and Totowa, N.J.: Manchester University Press and Barnes & Noble.

Braudy, Leo. 1974. "Penetration and Impenetrability in *Clarissa.*" In *New Approaches to Eighteenth-Century Literature: Selected Papers of the English Institute,* ed. Philip Harth. New York: Columbia University Press.

Brinkley, Alan. 1989. "Mythic but Useful." *The Times Literary Supplement* (10–16 November): 1246.

Brooke, Henry. 1979. *The Fool of Quality.* 5 vols. London, 1766–70. Reprint, New York: Garland.

Brooks, Douglas. 1969. "*Moll Flanders:* An Interpretation." *Essays in Criticism* 19: 46–59.

Brown, Laura. 1987. *English Dramatic Form, 1660–1760: An Essay in Generic History.* New Haven: Yale University Press.

Brown, Norman O. 1970. *Life Against Death: The Psychoanalytical Meaning of History.* Middletown, Conn.: Wesleyan University Press.

Brown, Tom (trans.) 1704. *Marriage Ceremonies, as now Used in all Parts of the World, . . . Written Originally in Italian, by Seignior Gaya . . . Put into Modern English by Mr. Tom Brown.* London.

Bunyan, John. 1928. *Grace Abounding and The Life and Death of Mr. Badman.* Edited by G. B. Harrison. London: Dent.

Burney, Francis. 1972. *Evelina, or, A Young Lady's Entrance into the World.* 1958. Reprint, with introduction by Lewis Gibbs. London: Dent.

———. *Camilla, or a Picture of Youth.* Edited by E. A. and L. D. Bloom. London: Oxford University Press.

Castle, Terry J. 1979. "Lab'ring Bards: Birth Topoi and English Poetics, 1660–1820." *Journal of English and Germanic Philology* 78: 193–208.

———. 1984. Lovelace's Dream. *Studies in Eighteenth-Century Culture.* 13: 29–42.

Centlivre, Susannah. 1968. *The Dramatic Works of the Celebrated Mrs. Centlivre, with a New Account of her Life.* 3 vols. London, 1872. Reprint, New York: AMS Press.

Cleland, John. 1974. *Memoirs of a Coxcomb.* London, 1751. Facs. reprint, New York: Garland.

Collins, R. G. 1979. "The Hidden Bastard: a Question of Illegitimacy in Smollett's *Peregrine Pickle*." *Publications of the Modern Language Association of America* 94: 91–105.

Congreve, William. 1925. *Comedies of William Congreve*. Edited by Bonamy Dobrée. London: Oxford University Press.

Connely, Willard. 1937. *Sir Richard Steele*. London: Jonathan Cape.

Coveney, Peter. 1957. *Poor Monkey: The Child in Literature*. London: Rockliff.

Crawford, Patricia. 1990. "The Construction and Experience of Maternity in Seventeenth-Century England." In Fildes, *Women as Mothers in Preindustrial England,* 3–38.

Crowne, John. 1967. *The Dramatic Works of John Crowne*. 4 vols. Edinburgh, 1874. Reprint, New York: Blom.

Davis, Lennard J. 1983. *Factual Fictions: the Origins of the English Novel*. New York: Columbia University Press.

Day, Geoffrey. 1987. *From Fiction to the Novel*. London: Routledge & Kegan Paul.

De Beauvoir, Simone. 1972. *The Second Sex*. Translated and edited by H. M. Parshley. London: Jonathan Cape.

Defoe, Daniel. 1964. *Roxana: The Fortunate Mistress*. Edited by Jane Jack. London: Oxford University Press.

———. 1965. *The History . . . of Colonel Jacque*. Edited by Samuel Holt Monk. London: Oxford University Press.

———. 1967. *Conjugal Lewdness; or, Matrimonial Whoredom. A Treatise Concerning the Use and Abuse of the Marriage Bed.* London, 1727. Facs. reprint. with introduction by Maximillian E. Novak. Gainesville, Fla.: Scholars' Facsimiles and Reprints.

———. 1972. *The Life Adventures and Pyracies, of the Famous Captain Singleton* London, 1720. Facs. reprint. New York: Garland.

———. 1973. *The Family Instructor*. Vols. 15 and 16 of *The Novels and Miscellaneous Works of Daniel Defoe*. Oxford, 1841. Reprint, New York: AMS Press.

———. 1976. *The Fortunes and Misfortunes of the Famous Moll Flanders*. Edited by G. A. Starr. London and Oxford.

de La Fayette, Marie. 1957. *La Princesse de Clèves*. Paris: Grund.

deMause, Lloyd, ed. 1976. *The History of Childhood*. London: Souvenir Press.

de Waal, Franz. 1983. *Chimpanzee Politics: Power and Sex among Apes*. London: Unwin.

Dewhurst, Kenneth. 1954. "Locke's Midwifery Notes." *Lancet* 4: 490–91.

Dinnerstein, Dorothy. 1987. *The Rocking of the Cradle, and the Ruling of the World*. London: Women's Press. New York: Harper & Row, 1976, as *The Mermaid and the Minotaur*.

Donaldson, Ian. 1973. "Cato in Tears: Stoical Guises of the Man of Feeling." In *Studies in the Eighteenth Century* 2, edited by R. F. Brissenden, 377–95. Canberra: Australian National University Press.

Doody, Margaret. 1974. *A Natural Passion: A Study of the Novels of Samuel Richardson*. Oxford: Clarendon Press.

———. 1988. *Francis Burney: The Life in the Works*. Cambridge: Cambridge University Press.

Dryden, John. 1969. *Selected Poetry and Prose of John Dryden.* Edited by Earl Miner. New York and Toronto: Random House.

[Dunton, John] 1691. *A Voyage Round the World.* London [1691]). Reel 300, item 2 in *Early English Books 1641–1700.* Ann Arbor, Mich.: University Microfilms.

Durfey, Thomas. 1967. *The Campaigners.* London, 1698. In Wells, *Three Centuries of Drama.*

Erickson, Robert A. 1986. *Mother Midnight: Birth, Sex and Fate in Eighteenth-Century Fiction.* New York: AMS Press.

Faludi, Susan. 1992. *Backlash: The Undeclared War against Women.* London: Vintage.

Farquhar, George. 1988. *The Works of George Farquhar.* Edited by Shirley Strum Kenny. 2 vols. Oxford: Clarendon Press.

Fielding, Henry. 1932. *The Life of Jonathan Wild.* London: Oxford University Press. A list of changes made in the 1754 edition is given in an appendix.

———. 1970. *Joseph Andrews and Shamela.* Edited by Douglas Brooks. Oxford: Oxford University Press.

———. 1974. *The History of Tom Jones, a Foundling.* Edited by Martin C. Battestin. 2 vols. Oxford: Clarendon Press.

———. 1983. *Amelia.* Edited by Martin C. Battestin. Oxford: Clarendon Press.

———. 1988a. *The Covent-Garden Journal; and, A Plan of the Universal Register-Office.* Edited by Bertrand A. Goldgar. Oxford: Clarendon Press.

———. 1988b. *An Enquiry into the Causes of the Late Increase of Robbers and Related Writings.* Edited by Malvin R. Zirker. Oxford: Clarendon Press.

Fielding, Sarah. 1968. *The Governess, or, Little Female Academy.* Edited by Jill E. Grey. London: Oxford University Press.

———. 1973. *The Adventures of David Simple.* Edited by Malcolm Kelsall. London: Oxford University Press.

Fildes, Valerie. 1986. *Breasts, Bottles, and Babies.* Edinburgh: Edinburgh University Press.

———. 1988. *Wet Nursing: A History from Antiquity to the Present.* Oxford: Blackwell.

———, ed. 1990. *Women as Mothers in Pre-industrial England: Essays in Memory of Dorothy McLaren.* London and New York: Routledge.

Filmer, Robert. 1949. *Patriarcha.* In *Patriarcha and Other Political Works.* Edited by Peter Laslett. Oxford: Blackwell.

Flanders, W. Austin. 1984. *Structures of Experience: History, Society and Personal Life in the Eighteenth-Century British Novel.* Columbia: University of South Carolina Press.

Fletcher, Edward G. 1934. "Defoe and the Theatre." *Philological Quarterly* 13: 382–89.

Fliegelman, Jay. 1982. *Prodigals and Pilgrims: The American Revolution against Patriarchal Authority, 1750–1800.* Cambridge: Cambridge University Press.

Folkenflik, Robert. 1982. "The Artist as Hero in the Eighteenth Century." *Yearbook of English Studies* 12: 91–108.

Freud, Sigmund. 1959. "Family Romances." In vol. 9 of *Complete Psychological*

Works, translated by James Strachey. London: Hogarth Press and the Institute of Psychoanalysis.

————. 1961. *Civilization and Its Discontents.* In vol. 21 of *Complete Psychological Works.*

Frye, Northrop. 1971. *The Critical Path: An Essay on the Social Context of Literary Criticism.* Bloomington: Indiana University Press.

Fuentes, Carlos. 1989. *Christopher Unborn.* Translated by Alfred MacAdam and the author. London: André Deutsch.

Gay, John. 1983. *Dramatic Works.* 2 vols. Edited by John Fuller. Oxford.

Gibbon, Edward. 1971. *Gibbon's Autobiography.* Edited by M. M. Reese. London: Routledge & Kegan Paul.

Gibson, Lois R. 1975. *Attitudes Towards Childhood in Eighteenth-Century British Fiction.* Ph.D. diss., University of Pittsburgh.

Gillis, John R. 1985. *For Better, For Worse: British Marriages, 1600 to the Present.* New York and Oxford: Oxford University Press.

Girard, René. 1965. *Deceit, Desire and the Novel: Self and Other in Literary Structure.* Baltimore: Johns Hopkins University Press.

Goldsmith, Oliver. 1966. *Collected Works.* Edited by Arthur Friedman. 5 vols. Oxford: Clarendon Press.

Harris, Jocelyn. 1979. "Learning and Genius in *Sir Charles Grandison.*" In *Studies in the Eighteenth Century* 4, edited by R. F. Brissenden and J. C. Eade, 176–80. Canberra: Australian National University Press.

Haywood, Eliza. 1974. *The Fortunate Foundlings.* 1744. Reprint, New York: Garland.

Head, Richard. 1928. *The English Rogue, Described in the Life of Meriton Latroon.* New York: Dodd/Mead.

Hill, Bridget. 1989. *Women, Work, and Sexual Politics in Eighteenth-Century England.* Oxford: Blackwell.

The History of the Human Heart, Or, The Adventures of a Young Gentleman. 1974. London, 1749. Facs. reprint, New York: Garland.

Howard, G. E. 1964. *A History of Matrimonial Institutions, Chiefly in England and the United States.* 3 vols. 1904. Reprint, New York: Humanities Press.

Howard, James. 1967. *All Mistaken.* London, 1672. In Wells, *Three Centuries of Drama.*

Howard, Jean E. 1986. "The New Historicism in Renaissance Studies." *English Literary Renaissance* 16: 13–43.

Hughes, Mary Joe. 1984. "Child-Rearing and Social Expectation in Eighteenth-Century England: The Case of the Colliers of Hastings." *Studies in Eighteenth-Century Culture* 13: 79–100.

Hume, Robert D. 1962. "Dryden, James Howard, and the date of *All Mistaken.*" *Philological Quarterly* 51: 422–29.

————. 1970. "The Conclusion of Defoe's *Roxana:* Fiasco or Tour de Force?" *Eighteenth Century Studies* 3: 475–90.

————. 1977a. *The Development of English Drama in the Late Seventeenth Century.* Oxford: Clarendon Press.

————. 1977b. "Marital Discord in English Comedy from Dryden to Fielding." *Modern Philology* 74: 248–72. Reprinted in Hume's *The Rakish Stage.*

———. 1983. *The Rakish Stage*. Carbondale: Southern Illinois University Press.

———. 1992. "Texts within Contexts: Notes Towards a Historical Method." *Philological Quarterly* 71: 69–99.

Hunt, David. 1970. *Parents and Children in History: The Psychology of Family Life in Early Modern France*. New York: Basic Books.

Irigaray, Luce. 1985. *This Sex Which Is Not One*. Translated by Catherine Porter with Carolyn Burke. Ithaca: Cornell University Press.

Jones, Eldred. 1965. *Othello's Countrymen: The African in English Renaissance Drama*. London: Oxford University Press.

Karl, Frederick R. 1975. *A Reader's Guide to the Development of the English Novel in the Eighteenth Century*. London: Thames and Hudson. First published 1974 as *The Adversary Literature: The English Novel in the Eighteenth Century: A Study in Genre*. New York: Farrar, Straus & Giroux.

[Keith, Alexander] 1753. *Observations on the Act for Preventing Clandestine Marriages*. London.

Kerber, Linda K. 1980. *Women of the Republic: Intellect and Ideology in Revolutionary America*. Chapel Hill: University of North Carolina Press.

King, John. 1989. "The Carnival at the End of the World." *The Times Literary Supplement* 1386.

Kinkead-Weekes, Mark. 1973. *Samuel Richardson: Dramatic Novelist*. London: Methuen.

Konigsberg, Ira. 1968. *Samuel Richardson and the Dramatic Novel*. Lexington: University Press of Kentucky.

Kristeva, Julia. 1974. *La Révolution du Langage Poétique*. Paris: Éditions du Seuil.

———. 1980. *Pouvoirs d'Horreur: Essai sur l'Abjection*. Paris: Éditions du Seuil.

Kuhn, Reinhard. 1982. *Corruption in Paradise: The Child in Western Literature*. Hanover, N.H.: University Press of New England for Brown University Press.

Langer, Susanne K. 1953. *Feeling and Form: A Theory of Art Developed from "Philosophy in a New Key."* New York: Scribner.

Laslett, Peter. 1968. *The World We Have Lost*. London: Methuen.

———. 1976. The Wrong Way Through the Telescope. *British Journal of Sociology* 27: 319–42.

———. 1977. *Family Life and Illicit Love in Earlier Generations*. Cambridge: Cambridge University Press.

———. 1983. *The World We Have Lost Further Explored*. London: Methuen.

Lawrence, D. H. 1949. *The Rainbow*. Harmondsworth: Penguin.

Leavis, F. R. 1963. *New Bearings in English Poetry: A Study of the Contemporary Situation*. Harmondsworth: Penguin.

Lerenbaum, Miriam. 1977. "Moll Flanders: 'A Woman on her own Account.'" In *The Authority of Experience: Essays in Feminist Criticism*, edited by Arlyn Diamond and L. R. Edwards, 101–17. Amherst: University of Massachusetts Press.

Lévi-Strauss, Claude. 1984. *Tristes Tropiques*. Translated by J. and D. Weightman. Harmondsworth: Penguin.

Lillie, Charles, ed. 1725. *Original and Genuine Letters Sent to the Tatler and Spectator.* London.

Locke, John. 1961. *An Essay Concerning Human Understanding.* Edited by John W. Yolton. 2 vols. London: Dent.

———. 1967. *Two Treatises of Government.* Edited by Peter Laslett. Cambridge: Cambridge University Press.

———. 1968. *The Educational Writings of John Locke.* Edited by James L. Axtell. Cambridge: Cambridge University Press.

Longus. 1956. *Daphnis and Chloe.* Translated by Paul Turner. Harmondsworth: Penguin.

Malcolmson, R. W. 1977. "Infanticide in the Eighteenth Century." In *Crime in England 1550–1800,* edited by J. S. Cockburn, 187–209. London: Methuen.

Malekin, P. and D. E. L. Crane. 1972. The Later Seventeenth Century. In *The Year's Work in English Studies* 51: 241–61.

Mandeville, Bernard. 1975. *The Virgin Unmasked.* London, 1709. Facs. reprint, New York: Scholars' Facsimiles and Reprints.

Manley, Mary Delarivière. 1971. *The Novels of Mary Delarivière Manley.* Edited by Patricia Koster. 2 vols. Gainesville, Fla.: Scholars' Facsimiles and Reprints.

Marcus, Leah S. 1978. *Childhood and Cultural Despair: A Theme and Variations in Seventeenth-Century Literature.* Pittsburgh: University of Pittsburgh Press.

Marriage Promoted. In a Discourse of its Ancient and Modern Practice. 1984. London, 1690. Facs. reprint. In *Adultery and the Decline of Marriage,* edited by Randolph Trumbach.

Marshall, Dorothy. 1969. *The English Poor in the Eighteenth Century.* London: Routledge & Kegan Paul.

McClure, Ruth. 1981. *Coram's Children.* New Haven: Yale University Press.

McGraw, Patricia M. 1986. *Ideas About Children in Eighteenth-Century British Fiction.* Ph.D. diss., University of Connecticut.

McKeon, Michael. 1987. *The Origins of the English Novel.* Baltimore: Johns Hopkins University Press, 1987.

McLaren, Angus. 1984. *Reproductive Rituals: The Perception of Fertility in England from the Sixteenth Century to the Nineteenth Century.* London: Methuen.

Memoirs of a Coquet, or the History of Miss Harriot Airy. 1974. London, 1765. Reprint, New York: Garland.

Middleton, Thomas. 1969. *A Chaste Maid in Cheapside.* Edited by R. B. Parker London: Methuen.

———. 1975. *Women Beware Women.* Edited by J. R. Mulryne. London: Methuen.

Miller, Nancy K. 1980. *The Heroine's Text: Readings in the French and English Novel 1722–1782.* New York: Columbia University Press.

Montrose, Louis. 1986. "The Elizabethan Subject and the Spenserian Text." In *Literary Theory/Renaissance Texts,* edited by Patricia Parker and David Quint. Baltimore: Johns Hopkins University Press.

Mount, Ferdinand. 1982. *The Subversive Family.* London: Jonathan Cape.

Nelson, T. G. A. 1990. *Comedy: The Theory of Comedy in Literature, Drama, and Cinema.* Oxford: Oxford University Press.

———. 1992. "Incest in the Early Novel and Related Genres." *Studies in the Eighteenth Century* 8. Special number of *Eighteenth-Century Life* 16: 127–62.

Novak, Maximillian E. 1963. *Defoe and the Nature of Man.* London: Oxford University Press.

———. 1964. "Defoe's Theory of Fiction." *Studies in Philology* 61: 650–68.

Parfitt, George. 1972. "The Case Against Congreve." In *William Congreve,* edited by Brian Morris, 23–38. London: Benn.

Pattison, Robert. 1978. *The Child Figure in English Literature.* Athens: University of Georgia Press.

Paulson, Ronald. 1971. *Hogarth: His Life, Art, and Times.* 2 vols. New Haven: Yale University Press.

———. 1979. *Popular and Polite Art in the Age of Hogarth and Fielding.* South Bend, Ind.: Indiana University Press.

———. 1982. *Book and Painting. Shakespeare, Milton and the Bible: Literary Texts and the Emergence of English Painting.* Knoxville: University of Tennessee Press.

Perry, Ruth. 1982. "The Veil of Chastity: Mary Astell's Feminism." In *Sexuality in Eighteenth-Century Britain,* edited by Boucé, 141–58.

———. 1986. *The Celebrated Mary Astell: An Early English Feminist.* Chicago: University of Chicago Press.

———. 1991. "Colonizing the Breast: Sexuality and Maternity in Eighteenth-Century England." *Journal of the History of Sexuality* 2: 204–34.

Philogamus [pseud.]. 1985. *The Present State of Matrimony, or, The Real Causes of Conjugal Infidelity and Unhappy Marriages.* London, 1739. In one volume with Booth, *Considerations upon the Institution of Marriage.* Facs. reprint, New York: Garland.

Pickering, Samuel F., Jr. 1981. *John Locke and Children's Books in Eighteenth-Century England.* Knoxville: University of Tennessee Press.

———. 1993. *Moral Instruction and Fiction for Children, 1749–1820.* Athens and London: University of Georgia Press.

[Pix, Mary] 1967. *The Different Widows.* London, 1703. In *Three Centuries of Drama,* edited by Wells.

Pollock, Linda. 1983. *Forgotten Children: Parent-Child Relations from 1500 to 1900.* Cambridge: Cambridge University Press.

———. 1987. *Lasting Relationships: Parents and Children Over Three Centuries.* Hanover, N.H.: University Press of New England.

Polwhele, Elizabeth. 1967. *The Frolics: or, the Lawyer Cheated.* Edited by Judith Milhous and Robert D. Hume. Ithaca: Cornell University Press.

Pope, Alexander. 1963. *The Poems of Alexander Pope. A One-Volume Edition of the Twickenham Text.* Edited by John Butt. London: Methuen.

Quaife, G. R. 1979. *Wanton Wenches and Wayward Wives: Peasants and Illicit Sex in Seventeenth-Century England.* London: Croom Helm.

Richardson, Samuel. 1741–42. *Pamela, or, Virtue Rewarded, in a Series of Letters from a Beautiful Young Damsel to her Parents.* 4 vols. London. Microfilm supplied by the Bodleian Library.

———. 1932. *Clarissa.* Edited by John Butt. 4 vols. London: Dent. (References, except where otherwise stated, are to this text, based on the third edition of 1751.) Many passages added in the third edition are pertinent to my theme, and I am unimpressed by recent attempts to confer privileged status on the first edition.

———. 1964. *Selected Letters of Samuel Richardson.* Edited by John Carroll. Oxford: Clarendon Press.

———. 1974. *Pamela, or Virtue Rewarded. The Revised Text of 1801.* 4 vols. Facs. reprint, New York: Garland Press. References, except where otherwise stated, are to this edition.

———. 1985. *Clarissa, or the History of a Young Lady.* Edited by Angus Ross. Harmondsworth: Penguin. Based on the first eighteenth-century edition.

———. 1986. *Sir Charles Grandison.* Edited by Jocelyn Harris. Oxford: Oxford University Press. I have used the one-volume paperback edition.

Ridley, James. 1974. *The History of James Lovegrove, Esq.* London, 1761. Facs. reprint, New York: Garland.

Rodgers, Betsy. 1949. *Cloak of Charity: Studies in Eighteenth-Century Philanthropy.* London: Methuen.

Rosenblum, Michael. 1975. "Smollett as Conservative Satirist." *Journal of English Literary History (ELH)* 42: 556–79.

Rothstein, Eric. 1967. *Restoration Tragedy: Form and the Process of Change.* Madison: University of Wisconsin Press.

Rousseau, Jean-Jacques. 1969. *Émile, ou de l'Éducation.* In *Oeuvres Complètes de Jean-Jacques Rousseau,* edited by Charles Wirz, 4 vols. Paris: Gallimard.

Salzman, Paul. 1985. *English Prose Fiction 1558–1700: A Critical History.* Oxford: Clarendon Press.

Schaller, George B. 1991. "The Gorilla and the Guerillas." *The Times Literary Supplement,* 21 June, 5.

Scott, Sarah. 1974. *A Description of Millenium Hall.* London, 1762. Reprint, New York: Garland.

Scouten, Arthur H., and Robert D. Hume. 1980. "'Restoration' Comedy and Its Audiences, 1660–1776." *Yearbook of English Studies* 10: 45–69.

Shahar, Shulamith. 1990. *Childhood in the Middle Ages.* London: Routledge.

Shebbeare, John. 1974. *The Marriage Act. A Novel.* 2 vols. London, 1754. Reprint in one volume. New York: Garland.

Sheridan, Frances. 1987. *Memoirs of Miss Sidney Bidulph, Extracted from her Own Journal, and Now First Published.* Edited by Sue Townsend. London, 1761. Reprint, London: Pandora. The modern edition does not include the sequel.

Shinagel, Michael. 1969. "The Maternal Theme in *Moll Flanders:* Craft and Character." *Cornell Library Journal* 7: 3–23.

Sloane, William. 1955. *Children's Books in England and America in the Seventeenth Century.* New York: King's Crown Press, Columbia University.

Smallwood, Angela. 1989. *Fielding and the Woman Question.* Hemel Hempstead: Harvester.

Smith, Norah. 1978. "Sexual Mores in the Eighteenth Century: Robert Wallace's *Of Venery.*" *Journal of the History of Ideas* 39: 419–33.

Smollett, Tobias. 1969. *The Adventures of Peregrine Pickle*. Edited by James L. Clifford. London: Oxford University Press.

———. 1979. *The Adventures of Roderick Random*. Edited by Paul-Gabriel Boucé. Oxford: Oxford University Press.

Spacks, Patricia Meyer. 1982. *Desire and Truth: Functions of Plot in Eighteenth-Century Novels*. Chicago: University of Chicago Press.

———. 1990. "Always at Variance: Politics of Eighteenth-Century Adolescence." In *A Distant Prospect: Eighteenth-Century Views of Childhood*, Patricia Meyer Spacks and W. B. Carnochan. Los Angeles: William Andrews Clark Memorial Library.

Stanhope, Philip, Earl of Chesterfield. 1959. *Letters to His Son and Others*. Edited by R. K Root. London: Dent.

Staves, Susan. 1979. *Players' Sceptres: Fictions of Authority in the Restoration*. Lincoln: University of Nebraska Press.

———. 1990. *Married Women's Separate Property in England, 1660–1833*. Cambridge, Mass., and London: Harvard University Press.

Steele, Richard. 1971. *The Plays of Richard Steele*. Edited by Shirley Strum Kenny. Oxford: Clarendon Press.

———. *The Tatler*. 1987. Edited by Donald F. Bond. Oxford: Clarendon Press.

——— et al. 1982. *The Guardian*. Edited by John Calhoun Stephens. Lexington: University Press of Kentucky.

Sterne, Laurence. 1967. *The Life and Opinions of Tristram Shandy, Gentleman*. Edited by Graham Petrie with an introduction by Christopher Ricks. Harmondsworth: Penguin.

Stone, Lawrence. 1965. *The Crisis of the Aristocracy, 1558–1641*. Oxford: Clarendon Press.

———. 1977. *The Family, Sex and Marriage in England 1500–1800*. London: Weidenfeld & Nicolson.

———. 1990. *Road to Divorce: England 1530–1987*. Oxford: Oxford University Press.

Summerfield, Geoffrey. 1984. *Fantasy and Reason: Children's Literature in the Eighteenth Century*. Athens: The University of Georgia Press.

Swift, Jonathan. 1948. *Irish Tracts and Sermons*. Edited by Herbert Davis. Oxford: Blackwell.

———. 1955. *Irish Tracts 1728–1733*. Edited by Herbert Davis. Oxford: Blackwell.

———. 1965. *Gulliver's Travels*. Edited by Herbert Davis. Oxford: Blackwell.

Tanner, Tony. 1979. *Adultery in the Novel: Contract and Transgression*. Baltimore: Johns Hopkins University Press.

———. 1986. *Jane Austen*. Basingstoke: Macmillan.

Taylor, James Stephen. 1979. "Philanthropy and Empire: Jonas Hanway and the Infant Poor of London." *Eighteenth-Century Studies* 12: 285–306.

Taylor, Jeremy. 1875. *The Rule and Exercises of Holy Living and of Holy Dying*. Oxford: James Parker.

This, Bernard, ed. 1982. *La Requête des Enfants à Naître*. Paris: Éditions du Seuil.

Traugott, John. 1984. "The Yahoo in the Doll's House: *Gulliver's Travels* the Children's Classic." *Yearbook of English Studies* 14: 127–50.

Trumbach, Randolph. 1978. *The Rise of the Egalitarian Family.* New York: Academic Press.

Vanbrugh, Sir John. 1967. *The Complete Works of Sir John Vanbrugh.* Edited by B. Dobrée and G. Webb. 4 vols. 1927–8. Reprint, New York: AMS Press.

Van Ghent, Dorothy. 1959. *The English Novel: Form and Function.* New York: Rinehart.

Vichert, Gordon S. 1975. "Bernard Mandeville's *The Virgin Unmask'd.*" In *Mandeville Studies: New Explorations in the Art and Thought of Dr. Bernard Mandeville (1670–1733)*, edited by Irwin Primer, 1–10. The Hague: Martinus Nijhoff.

Voltaire, F. M. A. 1966. *Candide, or Optimism.* Translated by Robert M. Adams. New York: Norton.

Walton, Izaak. 1906. *The Life of George Herbert.* In *The Complete Angler and Lives.* London: Macmillan.

[Ward, Ned] 1954. *The London Spy.* Part 2, 3rd ed. London, 1704 Reproduced on reel 1 of *English Literary Periodical* series. Ann Arbor, Mich.: University Microfilms.

Watt, Ian. 1957. *The Rise of the Novel: Studies in Defoe, Richardson and Fielding.* London: Chatto & Windus.

Wells, Henry W., ed. 1967. *Three Centuries of Drama.* New York: Readex Microprint, 1967. Early editions of plays reproduced photographically on microcards.

Wilson, Adrian. 1993. "The Perils of Early Modern Procreation: Childbirth with or without Fear?" *British Journal for Eighteenth-Century Studies* 16: 1–19.

Wrightson, Keith. 1975. "Infanticide in Early Seventeenth-Century England." *Local Population Studies* 15: 10–21.

Wrigley, E. A. 1966. "Family Limitation in Pre-Industrial England." *Economic History Review.* 2d ser, 19: 82–109.

Yolton, John W. 1985. *Locke: An Introduction.* Oxford: Blackwell.

Young, Wayland. 1969. *Eros Denied.* London: Weidenfeld & Nicolson.

Index

Abortion, 18, 73–74, 81–82
Addison, Joseph, 83, 101; *The Guardian,* 80, 81–82; *The Spectator,* 42, 66–68, 78, 79
Adolescence, 28, 86, 93, 115, 186–88, 194–96, 205–7, 210–16, 218
Adultery, 72, 182; novel of, 13, 222; spurious issue of, 38–40
Adventures of a Kidnapped Orphan, 70
Alexander, William, 39
American Indians, 18, 72, 73
Amnesia, in relation to childhood, 17
Anglicans, 17
Animals, 19, 99, 107, 134, 162, *185–86,* 191–92, 197, 207, 219, 220, 232
Arbuthnot, John: *Three Hours After Marriage,* 55
Ariès, Philippe, 15, 16, 20–21, 28, 87, 201, 203
Aristocracy, 22–23, 38, 39, 73, 75, 88, 110, 114, 119–20, 126, 133, 145, 164–65, 177, 178, 180, 185–88, 227, 229
Artificial feeding: of children, 19, 56, 209
Artists, 221–25
Ascham, Roger, 86
Ashcraft, Richard, 94
Astell, Mary, 130
Aubrey, John, 29, 196, 197
Austen, Jane, 229; *Emma,* 14; *Mansfield Park,* 128.

Baby talk. *See* Language
Bage, Robert: *Hermsprong,* 88
Bakhtin, Mikhail, 13–14, 42, 71, 76, 162, 185
Barbera, Jack, 221
Barnett, Carol H., 224
Barrell, John, 229–31
Barrie, J. M., 87

Bastardy, 30–34, 38, 39, 45–47, 51, 57, 60, 63, 66–69, 77, 79–84, 92, 96, 104–5, 108, 110, 123–24, 145–47, 158, 171–177, 199, 201, 218, 226, 229, 232–33
Bataille, Georges, 43–44
Battestin, Martin, 79, 166
Beauvoir, Simone de, 43, 80
Behn, Aphra: "The Black Lady," 68, 160–61
Bersani, Leo, 170
Bettelheim, Bruno, 98
Birdsall, Virginia O., 36, 222
Birth control, 20, 37, 41, 73–74, 81, 133, 147
Blake, William, 202; "Holy Thursday" poems, 81
Book, compared with child, 221–25, 229
Booth. George, earl of Warrington, 110; *Considerations on Marriage,* 109–10, 130, 133
Bottle feeding. *See* Artificial feeding
Boucé, P.-G., 79
Braudy, Leo, 126
Breast-feeding, 19, 52, 76, 77, 96, 102, 106, 110, 113–15, 122, 124, 132, 135, 150, 181–85
Brinkley, Alan, 21
Brome, Richard: *The Antipodes,* 36
Bronte, Charlotte: *Jane Eyre,* 228
Brooke, Henry: *The Fool of Quality,* 41, 185–88, 227
Brooks, Douglas, 138
Brown, Laura, 25
Brown, Norman O., 43–44, 150
Brown, Tom: *Marriage Ceremonies,* 74, 130
Bunyan, John, 70; *A Book for Boys and Girls,* 35; *Grace Abounding to the Chief of Sinners,* 23, 195; *The*

Life and Death of Mr. Badman, 32, 66, 69
Burney, Frances: *Camilla,* 27; *Evelina,* 112–13

Cannibalism, 71–73, 143
Castle, Terry J., 123, 223
Centlivre, Susannah: *A Bold Stroke for a Wife,* 48
Cervantes Saavedra, Miguel de, 231
Charity schools, 30, 64, 81
Chesterfield. *See* Stanhope
Childbirth, 32, 36, 40, 69, 80, 115, 135, 174, 177, 187, 193, 208, 225
Children's literature, 34–35, 86, 97–100
Chodorov, Nancy, 18
Clarke, Edward, 94
Clarke, Mrs. Edward, 94–95
Class, 14, 21, 22–23, 30–31, 60–61, 70, 73, 75, 77, 88, 90, 104–5, 110, 114, 119–20, 145–46, 164–65, 174–76, 177, 202, 204
Cleland, John, 218; *Memoirs of a Coxcomb,* 214–15; *Memoirs of a Woman of Pleasure (Fanny Hill),* 194, 195
Collins, R. G., 158
Colostrum, 19
Comedy, 15, 22, 25–26, 27, 30, 33–34, 36–65, 66, 68, 78, 82, 85, 88, 101, 103, 104–5, 112, 114, 118, 119–21, 127, 134, 137, 138, 140, 143–44, 151, 160, 190, 193, 201, 209, 229–30, 231, 232, 234, 235; balanced against sentiment, 160–89
Congreve, William, 54; *The Double Dealer,* 36–37, 41; *Love for Love,* 51–54, 115; *The Old Bachelor,* 38, 39; *The Way of the World,* 35, 39–40, 41, 42, 184
Connely, Willard, 77
Contraception. *See* Birth control
Cooper, Anthony Ashley, third earl of Shaftesbury, 85
Coram, Thomas, 31
Corporal punishment. *See* Education: severity in
Coveney, Peter, 13, 14, 20, 24–25, 81, 221
Crane, D. E. L., 36
Crawford, Patricia, 130

Crowne, John: *The Country Wit,* 45
Cumberland, Duke of, 22

Davis, Lennard J., 22
Defoe, Daniel, 25–26, 77, 230; *Captain Singleton,* 70, 180; *Colonel Jack,* 70, 81, 96, 104–5, 137, 167, 180, 199–202, 204; *Conjugal Lewdness,* 73–74; *The Family Instructor,* 26, 78, 110, 197–99, 201; *Moll Flanders,* 25–27, 45, 68, 77, 96, 129, 137–42, 150–51, 152, 159, 161, 180, 202, 204, 223, 230, 234; *The Review,* 78; *Robinson Crusoe,* 105, 194, 195; *Roxana,* 27, 96, 129, 137, 142–51, 152, 159, 161–62, 194, 195
de la Vega, Garcilaso, 72
Deloney, Thomas: *Jack of Newbury,* 38
deMause, Lloyd, 15, 16, 18, 34, 50
Descartes, 190
de Waal, Franz, 19
Dickens, Charles, 202; *Great Expectations,* 228; *Hard Times,* 98
Dinnerstein, Dorothy, 129
Doody, Margaret, 27, 114
Dostoyevsky, Fyodor, 226; *The Brothers Karamazov,* 14
Dunton, John: *A Voyage Round the World,* 191–93
Durfey, Thomas, 79; *The Campaigners,* 55, 64, 78
Dryden, John, 166; *The Indian Emperor, or, The Conquest of Mexico,* 22; "Mac Flecknoe," 224; *The Spanish Fryar,* 26

École des filles, 134
Education, 62, 85–100, 105, 109–10, 128, 130–33, 153–59, 163, 196, 197, 204–7, 208–18; expense of, 37; freedom in, 15, 16, 34; severity in, 15, 16, 87–88, 156, 193, 196, 203, 204–5, 206, 219, 220; sex education, 209–18; theories of, 19, 21, 34
Eliot, George: *Middlemarch,* 14
Erickson, Robert A., 45
Etherege, George: *The Man of Mode,* 36, 78, 216

Fairy tales, 98, 140. *See also* Fantasy, Folklore

Family Romance, 38–39

Fantasy, 61, 68, 93, 98, 123–24, 191–94, 196, 208

Farquhar, George, 79, 83; *Love and a Bottle*, 45–46, 48; *The Recruiting Officer*, 26, 58–61, 79, 112

Fathers, 66; attempts to prolong authority, 29, 53–54, 88, 93; caring, 22–23, 56, 57, 74, 82, 87, 90–94, 106, 109–10, 119, 121, 122–23, 127–28, 159, 167–70, 178–81, 181–84, 195, 227; compared to monarchs, 29, 159, 234; deaths of, looked forward to by children, 88–89; neglectful or rejecting, 22–23, 27, 28, 33, 37, 53–54, 55–56, 60, 64, 67–69, 71, 72, 74, 86, 87, 88, 90–94, 101–28, 131–32, 159, 186–87, 196, 227; tamed by paternity and marriage, 41, 115, 116, 124–25

Fielding, Henry, 22, 25, 79, 101, 110, 202–3, 218, 223; *Amelia*, 27, 96, 109, 110, 127, 159, 166, 177–81, 224, 231; *The Covent Garden Journal*, 79–80; *Enquiry into the Late Increase of Robbers*, 80; *Jonathan Wild*, 166–70, 181, 230–31; *Joseph Andrews*, 119–21, 151–52, 162–66, 170, 194, 231; *Shamela*, 202; *Tom Jones*, 27, 30, 31, 57, 80, 101, 158, 166, 171–77, 179, 180, 181, 194, 195, 218–20, 223, 226, 228, 233; *The Wedding Day*, 169

Fielding, Sarah: *Adventures of David Simple*, 89–90, 223; *The Governess*, 97

Fildes, Valerie, 19, 31, 52, 82

Filmer, Robert, 29, 54, 72–73, 94, 130

Flanders, W. Austin, 25, 105, 226, 232

Fletcher, Edward G., 26, 78

Fliegelman, Jay, 92, 94

Folkenflik, Robert, 223

Folklore, 140, 207–8. *See also* Fairy tales

Foundling hospitals, 31, 81–82, 112

Foundlings. *See* Bastardy

Freud, Sigmund, 43–44, 150; *Civilization and Its Discontents*, 42–43, 104; "Family Romances," 38

Frye, Northrop, 43

Fuentes, Carlos: *Christopher Unborn*, 194

Gainsborough, Thomas: "The Harvest Wagon," 229–31

Gay, John, 83, 166; *The Beggar's Opera*, 58, 63; *Three Hours After Marriage*, 55–57, 173; *The What D'Ye Call It*, 61–64, 79, 193

Gaya, Louis de, 74, 130

Gentleman's Magazine, 75

Gentry, 14, 23, 38, 61, 73, 88, 90, 104–5, 114, 119–20, 164–65, 174–76, 177, 185–86, 196, 203, 204, 227, 229

Gibbon, Edward, 29; *Autobiography*, 18, 30

Gibson, Lois R., 15, 69, 85, 166

Girard, René, 149

Girl children: special needs, 94–97, 109, 127–28, 169, 186–88

Goldsmith, Oliver: *The Vicar of Wakefield*, 57

Gray, Thomas: "The Bard," 223; "Eton College" Ode, 18

Harris, Jocelyn, 77

Hansel and Gretel, 140

Hay, Douglas, 20

Haywood, Eliza: *The Fortunate Foundlings*, 109, 128, 194, 195

Head, Richard: *The English Rogue*, 24, 223

Hegel, G. W. F., 43

Herbert, George, 30

History, modern readings of, 15, 20; monolithic, 15; objectivity in, 21; relation to literature, 21; relativity and, 14, 17, 19

History of the Human Heart, 177, 208–18

Hobbes, Thomas, 130

Hogarth, William, 68, 186, 207; "The Christening," 22; "The Denunciation," 32; "The Conquest of Mexico," 22

Howard, G. E., 79, 187

Howard, James: *All Mistaken*, 46–47, 48, 58, 67, 79

Howard, Jean E., 15, 17, 21

Hume, Robert D., 34, 46, 148

Hunt, David, 214

Idyll, 13, 76, 142, 151, 159, 185, 218, 229–31
Individual, 14, 20, 67
Infanticide, 18, 19, 33–34, 51, 66, 68, 72–73, 81–82, 172
Infant mortality, 19, 31, 48, 51, 77, 111, 115, 131, 138, 139, 146, 162–63, 175, 187, 193, 225, 227

Jesuit order, 20
Joyce, James, 199

Karl, Frederick, 234
Keith, Alexander, 79
Kerber, Linda K., 96, 130
Kidnapping, 69–70
King, J., 194
Kinkead-Weekes, Mark, 181
Kipling, Rudyard: *Kim*, 202
Konigsberg, Ira, 26
Kristeva, Julia, 43, 116, 141, 226
Kuhn, Reinhard, 17, 25, 207

La Fayette, Marie de: *La Princesse de Clèves;* 38
Langer, Susanne, 160
Language, used to, by, or about children, 35; baby talk, 47, 55, 89, 91, 166, 220; circumlocution, 39, 65, 181; harsh and disparaging usages, 41–42, 47–48, 51, 55, 67, 74, 77, 79, 87, 102, 106–8, 114, 115, 125, 134, 136, 143–44, 164, 172, 179, 182–84, 226; tender usages (often hypocritical), 23, 57, 58–59, 62, 74, 76, 107–8, 109, 111, 114, 118, 122–23, 134, 136, 139, 141, 143–44, 146, 162–63, 166, 173–74, 178, 179, 183–84
Laslett, Peter, 19, 24, 34, 39
Lawrence, D. H.: *The Rainbow*, 232
Lazarillo de Tormes, 14
Leavis, F. R., 132
Lennox, Charlotte: *The Female Quixote,* 231
Lerenbaum, Miriam, 137, 140
Lévi-Strauss, Claude, 18
Lillie, Charles, 33
Locke, John, 18, 28, 29, 53–54, 57, 85, 116, 130, 131–32, 154, 156, 186, 204, 208, 209–10, 212, 213, 215, 216, 232; *Essay Concerning Human*

Understanding, 190–91; *Some Thoughts Concerning Education,* 85–97, 130, 154–55, 210, 212, 216–17; *Two Treatises of Government,* 44, 54, 72–73
Longus: *Daphnis and Chloe,* 14, 213–14
Luther, Martin, 23
Lyttleton, George, 224

McBrien, William, 221
McClure, Ruth, 31, 69, 112, 140
McGraw, Patricia M., 15, 129
McKeon, Michael, 105
Magistrates, 55–56, 60–65, 174
Malcolmson, R. W., 33
Malekin, P., 36
Mandeville, Bernard, 106, 178, 179; *The Virgin Unmasked,* 101–4, 112, 127, 134–37
Manley, Mary Delarivière, 134: *The New Atalantis,* 28
Marcus, Leah, 14, 17, 25, 29, 110
Marriage Act of 1753, 79
Marriage, failure of, 13, 230
Marriage Promoted, 73
Marshall, Dorothy, 20, 32, 56
Masham, Damaris Cudworth, Lady, 95
Masturbation, 210
Memoirs of a Coquet, 41
Menopause, 140
Middle Ages, 16, 17, 28, 203
Middleton, Thomas: *Women Beware Women,* 46; *A Chaste Maid in Cheapside,* 45
Midwives, 32, 69, 139, 192, 193, 208
Miller, Nancy K., 137, 140, 151
Milton, John: *Paradise Lost,* 108
Montaigne, Michel de, 86
Montrose, Louis, 19, 20
Mothers, 17, 43, 67–68, 109–10; caring, 19, 22, 24, 41, 74, 75–76, 77, 82, 87, 90–91, 106, 129–30, 134–36, 138, 139, 144, 149, 156, 170, 179, 181–84, 208–9, 227; neglectful or rejecting, 13, 18, 27, 40–42, 74, 76, 77, 81, 87, 91, 104–5, 128, 129–59, 227, 228, 232; possessive or dominating, 129, 155–56; saddled with responsibility, 119–20, 122, 131–33, 143; tamed by motherhood,

40, 116, 122, 133, 159, 184; vulnerability of, 135–36
Mount, Ferdinand, 234

Nietzsche, Friedrich, 49
Nobility. *See* Aristocracy
Novak, Maximillian E., 26, 142

Overlaying. *See* Infant Mortality

Paedophilia, 186–87
Painting, 22, 42, 68, 124, 229–31
Parish: authorities 24, 31–32, 62, 67–68, 71, 83, 160–62; obligation to provide for destitute children, 45, 52, 55, 61, 64, 143–44, 174, 176, 200
Passing the baby, 30–32, 38, 44–46, 49, 55–56, 68, 104, 118, 137–39, 142, 143–44, 145, 150, 161, 176, 190
Patriarchy. *See* Fathers
Pattison, Robert, 85, 194
Paulson, Ronald, 22, 92–93, 207
Periodical essay, 50, 78–79, 83, 85, 101, 160, 231
Perry, Ruth, 62, 76, 79, 122, 131
Petition of the Unborn Babies, The, 193
Philogamus: *The Present State of Matrimony,* 130, 132, 153, 197
Picaro, 24, 58, 70, 137, 143, 150, 200–202, 204
Pickering, Samuel F., 86, 97
Pix, Mary: *The Different Widows,* 41
Plautus, 112; *Poenulus,* 57
Play, 34, 86, 87, 92, 100, 102, 178, 207–8, 220, 227
Pollock, Linda, 16–17, 19, 110
Polwhele, Elizabeth: *The Frolics,* 47–48
Poor families. *See* Working classes
Pope, Alexander: "Epistle to Doctor Arbuthnot," 222; *The Dunciad,* 222, 224; *Essay on Man,* 168; *Three Hours After Marriage,* 55, 224
Pregnancy, 24, 30, 32, 34, 36, 39–42, 61–62, 65, 67–68, 85–86, 113, 122, 134–35, 141, 144, 152, 153, 155, 157, 160–61, 177
Prenatal state, 80, 190–92, 194, 208–09

Present State of Matrimony. See Philogamus
Puberty. *See* Adolescence; Education
Puritans, 17, 23

Quaife, G. R., 32, 33

Raising. *See* Education
Realism, 14, 15, 21–22, 33, 62, 68–70, 114, 135, 175, 194, 198, 201, 205–7, 218
Recruiting. *See* War
Register. *See* Language
Richardson, Samuel, 25–26, 77, 110, 142, 162, 202–3, 225–26; *Clarissa,* 26–27, 30, 35, 40–41, 87, 96, 121–27, 159, 225, 228, 233; *Pamela,* 26, 27, 96, 108, 110–119, 159, 180, 181, 182, 194, 230, 232; *Sir Charles Grandison,* 65, 96–97, 181–85
Ridley, James: *The History of James Lovegrove,* 194, 195, 227
Rodgers, Betsy, 64
Rogue. *See* Picaro
Rosenblum, Michael, 159
Rothstein, Eric, 42
Rousseau, Jean-Jacques, 35, 87, 96, 218, 221; *Émile,* 49, 89, 198, 212–13, 215, 217; *La Nouvelle Héloise,* 230, 232

Salzman, Paul, 38, 191
Schaller, George B., 19
Scott, Sarah: *A Description of Millenium Hall,* 128, 185
Sentiment, 28, 160–89, 204, 206
Servants, 88, 99, 133, 144–45, 186–87, 196, 211–12, 215, 217, 227–28
Shaftesbury, third earl of. *See* Cooper
Shahar, Shulamith, 16
Shakespeare, William, 142; *King Lear,* 127; *Much Ado About Nothing,* 184; *Sonnets,* 221; *The Winter's Tale,* 84
Shaw, George Bernard, 49, 120
Shebbeare, John: *The Marriage Act,* 196–97
Sheridan, Frances: *Memoirs of Miss Sidney Bidulph,* 185, 227–28
Shinagel, Michael, 137
Sloane, William, 35

Smith, Norah, 39
Smith, Stevie, 221
Smollett, Tobias, 127, 202; *Peregrine Pickle*, 87, 91, 152–59, 204, 205–8, 220; *Roderick Random*, 68, 202–5, 222
Sophocles, 112
Spacks, Patricia M., 25, 231, 233, 235
Spenser, Edmund: *The Faerie Queene*, 42
Spoon feeding. *See* Artificial feeding
Stanhope, Philip Dormer, fourth earl of Chesterfield, 92–94, 225
Staves, Susan, 54, 130, 152
Steele, Richard, 77, 83, 96, 101; *The Guardian*, 75–76, 78, 168; *The Spectator*, 53, 78, 96, 232; *The Tatler*, 78, 192–93, 208; *The Tender Husband*, 41
Sterne, Laurence, 35, 218; *Tristram Shandy*, 38, 44, 91–92, 133, 192, 223
Stone, Lawrence, 17, 19, 21, 22, 29, 30, 32, 33, 34, 53, 58, 59, 87, 110, 114, 120, 162
Subjectivity, 28
Suckling. *See* Breast-feeding, Wet-nursing
Summerfield, Geoffrey, 97
Swaddling, 19, 86, 116, 153, 192
Swift, Jonathan, 30–31; *Gulliver's Travels*, 30, 44, 91, 105–8, 163, 194; *Modest Proposal*, 31, 71–72, 73; *Sermons*, 30.

Tanner, Tony, 13, 14, 221, 228–30
Tatler, The, 67–69, 71, 72, 73
Taylor, James Stephen, 33
Taylor, Jeremy: *Holy Living*, 37, 57
Ten Pleasures of Marriage, 37, 118

This, Bernard, 193
Thompson, E. P., 20
Tolstoy, Lev: *The Brothers Karamazov*, 14
Toys. *See* Play
Trading classes, 14, 30–31, 37, 70, 75, 110, 147, 196
Tragedy, 42, 140, 142, 148
Traherne, Thomas, 201
Trumbach, Randolph, 229, 232–33

Upbringing. *See* Education

Vanbrugh, John: *The Provoked Wife*, 38
Van Ghent, Dorothy, 77, 141
Vaughan, Henry, 201
Vichert, Gordon S., 134
Voltaire, F. M. A.: *Candide*, 38

War, 58–61, 62–63, 79–81, 119–20
Ward, Ned: *The London Spy*, 83
Walton, Izaak, 30
Warrington, earl of. *See* Booth
Watt, Ian, 14, 105
Wet-nurses, 19, 33, 52, 55, 68, 76, 77–78, 114, 139, 140, 143, 145, 161, 199, 227
Whole Duty of Man, The, 88
Whore's Rhetoric, The, 134
Wordsworth, William, 202
Working classes, 23–24, 60, 63–64, 74–75, 119–20, 139, 146, 164–65, 174–78, 219, 227
Wrightson, Keith, 33
Wrigley, E. A., 58, 74
Wycherley, William, 126; *The Country Wife*, 36, 78

Young, Wayland, 30